THE
ARMCHAIR
ACTIVIST

THE
ARMCHAIR
ACTIVIST

Simple Yet Powerful Ways to Fight the Radical Right

Felice N. Schwartz
and
Suzanne K. Levine

RIVERHEAD BOOKS
NEW YORK

Riverhead Books
Published by The Berkley Publishing Group
200 Madison Avenue
New York, New York 10016

Copyright © 1996 by The Estate of Felice N. Schwartz
Book design by Irving Perkins Associates
Jacket design and photography by Judith Kazdym Leeds

First Riverhead edition: August 1996

The Putnam Berkley World Wide Web site address is http://www.berkley.com

Library of Congress Cataloging-in-Publication Data

Schwartz, Felice N., and Levine, Suzanne K.
    The armchair activist : simple yet powerful ways to fight the radical right /
Felice N. Schwartz and Suzanne K. Levine.
       p.   cm.
    Includes index.
    ISBN 1-57322-549-5
    1. United States—Social policy—1993-   2. Conservatism—United States.
3. Lobbying—United States.   I. Title.
HN59.2.S35   1996
361.1'0973—dc20

96-10218
CIP

Printed in the United States of America

10 9 8 7 6 5 4 3 2 1

For Kate, Emily, Alexander,
Eli and Daniel;
and for Andy

Acknowledgments

This book was a group effort. We especially thank Sasha Abramsky, Jennifer Keiser, and Andy Zimmerman—not only for their excellent research, but for their insight, commitment and friendship.

We are also grateful to the following for their generous assistance: Jean Zimmerman, Gil Reavill, Ken Toole, Chip Berlet, Skipp Porteous, Barbara Simon, Meg Riley, Kathy Kilmer, Judy Gueron, Richard Stratton, Steve Thompson, Lill Erickson, Marc Mauer, Laurence Hooper, Laura Benedict, Herbert Kouts, Dean Allen, Marcella Rosen, Christine Beshar, Barbara McDermott, and, of course, Genese.

Contents

THE ARMCHAIR ACTIVIST

Introduction:
Sleepers Awake

An ideological shift of seismic proportions is rumbling through American society. It is still unclear just how intense the shock will be, but there's no doubt which way the ground is shifting—to the right.

The radical right, a loose coalition of movements that threaten democratic ideals, is shaking the foundations upon which this country was built.

The warning signs have gone unnoticed by many Americans. Indeed, seen as isolated instances, the activities of radical right-wingers might not seem alarming. But in the aggregate, they are moving even previously apolitical observers to respond to this challenge to our way of life.

This book has three purposes. First, we'll give you an overview of significant antidemocratic movements, their interconnections and their growing influence. Second, we'll explore in depth the divisive issues the right is using to catapult itself into power. And third, we'll offer practical and effective suggestions for action to those who recognize that the upheavals we are seeing today might eventually lead to cataclysm.

Imagine a modern-day Rip Van Winkle, awakened in the mid-1990s after a decades-long snooze. Naturally, he wants to catch up on the state of the world. He picks up the morning newspaper, where he reads about the bombing of a government building in Oklahoma City, resulting in the death of dozens of men, women, and children. The alleged bomber is a young man linked to a newly emergent movement of armed militias.

He turns the page and reads that legislation permitting discrimination against homosexual men and women has been passed in nearly thirty cities in the last few years—and that gay-bashing is the fastest-growing hate-crime category. A photo of an anti–gay rights demonstrator runs with this article. She holds up a sign that says, "Thank God for AIDS."

Shaking his head, he tosses the paper aside. He flips through his mail (now mountainous after his long years of sleep) and is hit by another blast from the right. There's a letter from a parent concerned about some newly elected school board members who are attempting to impose their religious views on the whole student body. The board members are attempting to get the book of Genesis taught alongside the theory of evolution as part of the high school science curriculum. They are also seeking to ban classroom dress-up parties at Halloween because, they say, the holiday celebrates the occult. The letter warns that though these measures violate the separation of church and state, they may just pass if enough parents don't speak up.

Venturing out into the wide world, our observer drives by some teenagers who are in the process of spray-painting racist graffiti in six-foot-tall letters on a highway trestle. As he rounds the corner, he sees a group of anti-abortion activists harassing women as they enter a health clinic.

Driving along, he scans the car radio dial and pauses at a talk station. Rage-radio icon Rush Limbaugh questions whether the grievances of minorities in America should be addressed: "They [African Americans] are 12 percent of the population. Who the hell cares?"[1] The next show is hosted by Bob Grant, who chats cordially with neo-Nazi leader Tom Metzger, head of White Aryan Resistance.[2] On both of these shows, angry callers rant about a range of issues—including welfare, immigration, crime, and the environment.

As Rip reacquaints himself with his hometown, he strikes up a casual conversation with someone he used to know. Rip's friend anxiously spouts conspiracy theories that he's absorbed from the Internet. He's afraid that the United Nations is orchestrating a takeover of the United States by foreign troops, and points to recent gun control legislation as proof that there is a plot afoot by the federal government to disarm all citizens in an effort to aid this takeover.

Increasingly uneasy about the new political atmosphere, Rip returns home. Watching the news that evening, he learns that Congress is trying to roll back environmental regulations, with some members suggesting that America open up its pristine wilderness areas, such as the Alaska National Wildlife Refuge, to industrial development. One U.S. representative, Helen Chenoweth of Idaho, suggests that the Endangered Species Act is part of a plan to create a "New World Order," the same conspiracy Rip's friend warned him about.

Our hero switches channels, settling in to watch televangelist Pat Robertson peddle his theocratic vision of America. Robertson tells his congregation that only Christians (as he narrowly defines them) are fit to be elected to office—and predicts that in his lifetime he will see Robertson-style Christians take control of all the social and political institutions in the United States.

Click! Off goes the TV, and Rip Van Winkle lets out a huge sigh. He lies in bed and wonders what is happening to America—his America. Has it become a nation rife with disunity, inflamed prejudice, and conspiracist hysteria? He considers taking another nice, long nap. . . .

Sleeper awake!

The adventures of our friend Rip are not so improbable. All of the events described are based on fact—and too many of us are sleeping right through them.

Perhaps if these incidents hadn't occurred all in one day, Rip could have dismissed them. But he cannot shake the feeling that they are somehow interrelated. His real awakening will come when he realizes there is a single thread that stitches its way through the whole cloth.

In the 1990s, the radical right has been successful in appealing to a mass audience and shifting the parameters of public debate over key issues. It is bolstered by a national infrastructure of well-funded organizations, such as media ministries, political action committees, think tanks, legal foundations, and lobbying groups. Right-wing ideology is spread through every form of communications imaginable: TV, radio, books, magazines, newspapers, direct mail, computerized bulletin boards, the Internet, phone trees, fax networks, and more. The talk-radio craze, with Rush Limbaugh at the helm, has dispersed right-wing ideas to millions in the form of entertainment.

Jean Hardisty, executive director of Political Research Associates, a research center that monitors the U.S. political right, is one of many political scientists who views this resurgence of the right not as a passing phase, but instead as a fundamental realignment in American politics. Ideas once considered part of the fringe are increasingly seeping into the mainstream. For the majority of Americans who disagree with these ideas, the time to speak up is now. "As the McCarthy period showed," says Hardisty, "if you let a right-wing movement go long enough without serious challenge, it can become a real threat and cause real damage."[3]

THE ARMCHAIR ACTIVIST

As the right-wing resurgence gains momentum, more and more citizens are becoming uneasy about where it is headed—and uncertain about what they can do to counter it. If you are one of the silent majority who feels that the radical right is leading our country in a dangerous direction, but feels powerless to effect change, then this book is for you.

The Armchair Activist is addressed to people who sense a degradation in our national political dialogue and want to help reestablish a democratic debate among responsible conservative, moderate and progressive voices. Complex problems demand solutions based on accurate information. Though we may not all agree on what the solutions are, a discourse swamped in scapegoating, demagoguery, name-calling, and lies will get us less than nowhere.

All those who value equality, diversity, and a healthy democratic system are potential Armchair Activists. Whether we are male or female; black, brown, or white; religious, agnostic or atheist; Republican, Democrat, or independent; gay or straight; rural, urban or suburban—the radical right agenda ultimately affects us all.

This guide is designed for those who might want to dip a toe in the waters of activism, rather than jump in headfirst. Even if you've never considered yourself an activist, even if you're wary of getting involved, we'll give you quick, easy steps that can make a difference. Our basic premise is that every act of individual intervention has an impact—and that simple ones can often be the most powerful.

The radical right, though a small minority of the population, has a disproportionate influence because it makes its voice heard so effectively. This passivity of the majority creates a political vacuum that is too often filled by well-organized right-wing forces.

We see this time and again when ultraconservative groups deluge a congressperson's office with letters, giving the message that many active constituents feel strongly about a piece of legislation. For example, the Christian Coalition printed thirty million postcards protesting President Clinton's health plan, which were then distributed to sixty thousand churches around the country. The cards were addressed to House and Senate leaders—individuals only had to sign them and drop them in the mailbox.

Fortunately, this type of mailing has only a limited impact. As a spokesperson for one senator stated, "The receipt of five thousand postcards or form letters is noted, but it is also noted that they were prepared by a special interest political group. Individual letters are handled with much greater respect."

Every act of civic responsibility counts. Those well-argued letters you and other Armchair Activists write to your legislators can be a significant counterweight to the mass mailings of the radical right. There is so much that you can do to let your opinion be heard: voting; composing a letter to the editor of your local paper; sending out a neighborhood alert; calling in a rebuttal to bigotry on right-wing radio; holding politicians accountable for their slogans and advertising; educating coworkers on an issue; organizing your friends on campus. Starting now, you can take just one action a week. We hope that, once you acquire a taste for activism, you'll want to take it further and further as time goes on.

The Achilles heel of right-wing movements is that they offer little positive vision for the future. They are characterized by a negative outlook that holds that things are only going to get worse. Most people would instinctively rather look forward to a future filled with hope, not fear.

Together, we can give a voice back to the vast majority of Americans who believe in positive change. Now is the time for you to translate outrage into action. It's time to transform yourself from a couch potato into an Armchair Activist!

PART I
Aerial View of the Radical Right

1

Extremism Goes Mainstream

By the words "radical right," we mean repressive political movements in the United States that threaten democracy and pluralism. Some of the views that characterize the people who make up these movements are truly "radical," advocating extreme change by coercive measures. Other ideas are reactionary in that they promote turning back the clock of history at a rapid rate. And some of their opinions simply support the status quo.

The spectrum of the radical right runs from the moral crusaders of the religious right (such as Pat Robertson, founder of the Christian Coalition) and their secular counterparts known as the New Right (such as Paul Weyrich and the Heritage Foundation), to the more marginal white supremacist and paramilitary groups of the far right (such as the militias, the Ku Klux Klan and Aryan Nations). Among these diverse movements, which are discussed in detail in the following three chapters, there are important differences, though there does exist ideological and membership overlap. Overall, the radical right is largely linked by its ideas about power: who should have it and how to exercise it.

In the 1990s, right-wingers have made a tactical decision to spread their ideology to a more mainstream audience by concealing the full range of their beliefs. Militia organizers, for example, use patriotic language and issues such as taxes and the right to bear arms to recruit new supporters, yet many of their ideas have white supremacist roots. The religious right, which seeks to inject religion into government, has tried to appear more acceptable by strengthening its ties with the Republican party, focusing on economic as well as social issues, reaching out to minority communities, and deliberately softening its fiery rhetoric.

Individuals attracted to the "moderate" fronts of these movements risk becoming entangled in the more fanatical ideas at their core. Unfortunately, the factions of what has been termed the anti-democratic right are striking a sympathetic chord with broader parts of the population. The genuine anger, fear, and alienation felt by many people in America today are emotions which have been exploited by radical right leaders to gain support.

As a result, right-wing ideas, often backed up by half-truths and skewed arguments, are increasingly influencing the entire political culture. Positions once considered "extreme" are now complacently accepted as part of mainstream political dialogue. For many current members of Congress to advocate the abolition of the federal food stamps program would have been unthinkable a decade ago, but today the debate is centered on not whether it should be cut, but by how much. The suggestion to bring back chain gangs, a punishment banned as inhumane for over forty years, would have been scorned by respectable policymakers in the recent past, but today we can see shackled convicts laboring along the roads in Alabama, Florida, and Arizona. As the political center shifts rightward, we are also witnessing the dismantling of affirmative action programs, the revoking of environmental protections, the passing of discriminatory "English only" and anti–gay rights measures, and the restricting of access to abortion services.

Radical right groups risk schism by trying to simultaneously appeal to their hardcore supporters and a mainstream audience. Therefore, exposing the two-faced nature of these groups is a central activist strategy. A clear understanding of the following themes will help you identify and reveal right-wing extremism in the political process:

- **Ethnic and cultural homogeneity.** The radical right resists diversity and is striving to transform the United States from a thriving multicultural society into a homogeneous one. This goal is at the heart of right-wing campaigns against multicultural education, free expression, immigration, and gay rights. The far right is working toward a racially pure white nation, while the religious right ultimately seeks to build a theocratic state led by and for Christians. The imposition of one group's blueprint on our society jeopardizes everyone's freedom.

"We intend to purge this entire land area of Every non-White person, gene, idea and influence."

—Louis Beam, Aryan Nations
spokesperson[1]

"I want you to just let a wave of intolerance wash over you. . . . Yes, hate is good. . . . Our goal is a Christian nation. We have a biblical duty, we are called by God, to conquer this country. We don't want equal time. We don't want pluralism."

—Randall Terry, founder of
Operation Rescue[2]

"[The only endangered species is the] *white Anglo-Saxon male.*"

—Representative Helen
Chenoweth (R-ID)[3]

- **Reversing social change.** There is a backlash against the gains achieved by the liberation movements of the 1960s— including the civil rights, women's rights, gay rights, and environmental movements. The traditionalist ideology of the radical right is supportive of class, race, and gender hierarchies, as well as the unlimited dominion of humankind over nature.

"The feminist agenda is not about equal rights for women. It is about a socialist, anti-family political movement that encourages women to leave their husbands, kill their children, practice witchcraft, destroy capitalism and become lesbians."

—Pat Robertson, founder of the
Christian Coalition[4]

"The so-called 'anti-gay' agenda of religious conservatives is geared toward nothing more than preserving people's freedom to decide for themselves how to respond to gays. . . . [I]f a person believes homosexu-

ality is normal, he is free to act accordingly. But if he believes that it is immoral or unhealthy and doesn't want his children exposed to it, he cannot be forced to rent his spare bedroom to a practicing homosexual couple."

> —House Majority Leader DICK
> ARMEY[5]

- **Redefining "Christianity."** Appropriating the term "Christian" as their own, the religious right has made it into a political code word signifying individuals who agree with their political point of view. Many groups in the far right have twisted the idea of Christianity further, adopting an explicitly racist theology called Identity Christianity.

"Our culture is superior to other cultures, superior because our religion is Christianity."

> —PAT BUCHANAN, at the 1992
> Republican National
> Convention[6]

"We had lost the fight for the preservation of the white race until God himself intervened in earthly affairs with AIDS to rescue and preserve the white race that he had created. . . . I praise God all the time for AIDS."

> —J. B. STONER, white supremacist
> leader, to the 1994 Aryan
> Nations Congress

- **Redefining "family."** Referring to itself as the seemingly innocuous "pro-family" movement, the religious right has turned the concept of family into an ideology. "Family" has become a code word for opposition to abortion, feminism, gay rights, single motherhood, and premarital sex. In fact, all opponents of the religious right are condemned by its leaders as "anti-family," implying that all who don't fit their mold are second-class citizens. A "return to family values" has become the battle cry of those who want the government to legislate morality.

- **Claiming victimhood.** A finely tuned rhetoric of persecution has been developed by the radical right to malign anyone who disagrees with their views. Claiming "anti-religious bigotry" is a device used by the religious right to deflect criticism, as well as to devalue the language of oppression used by other groups. Religious freedom, however, flourishes in the United States. Voluntary religious activity, even in public schools, has always been, and remains, legal.

The far right holds that steps to social equality made by members of minority groups and women have come at the expense of the white male. Groups like David Duke's National Association for the Advancement of White People (NAAWP) claim they are not motivated by hate, but are simply trying to redress what they perceive as discrimination against whites. (David Duke, former Grand Wizard of the Ku Klux Klan, was elected to the Louisiana House of Representatives in 1989.) Yet such cries of "reverse" discrimination do little to mask the hateful ideas that form the core of the white supremacist movement.

"Just like what Nazi Germany did to the Jews, so liberal America is now doing to the evangelical Christians. It's no different. . . . It is the Democratic Congress, the liberal-biased media and the homosexuals who want to destroy all Christians. Wholesale abuse and discrimination are the worst bigotry directed toward any group in America today. More terrible than anything suffered by any minority in our history."

—Pat Robertson[7]

*"White people now face the most extensive racial discrimination in American history. It is true that some blacks faced discrimination in the past, but the discrimination was limited as it was primarily practiced in the private sector. Today the federal government is **forcing** an across-the-board racial discrimination in employment, promotions, scholarships and in college and union admittance."*

—from a NAAWP flyer on
affirmative action programs[8]

- **Censoring other voices.** The anti-democratic right has launched strident campaigns to stifle views that are in opposition to its own. Public schools serve as the most visible battlegrounds, as religiously motivated activists seek to ban literature, textbooks, sex education, and other curricula they deem anti-Christian or un-American. Television programs, films, and works of art have also been the target of censorship. The right is leading a campaign to stop federal funding for the National Endowment for the Arts, the National Endowment for the Humanities, and the Corporation for Public Broadcasting.

"I am aware that America is and must always be a land of freedom including freedom of speech. But there is a right time and place for everything."

> —BEVERLY LaHAYE, president of
> Concerned Women for
> America, on censorship[9]

"What we are up against is not dirty words and dirty pictures. It is a philosophy of life which seeks to remove the influence of Christians and Christianity from our society."

> —DONALD WILDMON, president of
> the American Family
> Association[10]

- **Belief in absolutes.** Both religious and far right groups claim to be purveyors of absolute truth, offering warped interpretations of the Bible and the Constitution to back up their inflexible ideas. Their blind allegiance to political absolutes is destructive to democratic dialogue.

"This [opposition to gay rights, abortion, and feminism] is really the most significant battle of the age-old conflict between good and evil, between the forces of God and the forces against God."

> —PAUL WEYRICH, founder of the
> Heritage Foundation and the
> Free Congress Foundation[11]

"We were here first. You don't take our shared common values and say they are biased and bigoted. . . . We are the keepers of what is right and what is wrong."

—LOU SHELDON, founder of the
Traditional Values Coalition[12]

- **Anti-government hostility.** With the end of the Cold War, the traditionally anticommunist crusaders of the radical right have discovered an enemy within—the U.S. federal government. The government is held in contempt for a variety of reasons: far rightists view federal gun control legislation as a plot to take away liberties from U.S. citizens; religious rightists view welfare policies as promiting sloth, promiscuity, and illegitimacy; new rightists view environmental regulations on industry and private property as an infringement of their rights. Overall, the radical right seeks to transfer power from the federal government to the states or private institutions.

"Something is just going on that is just very unwholesome in this nation and you look for an explanation of this craziness in Oklahoma City and a lot of it goes back to what happened with the Branch Davidians, Randy Weaver . . . This is a shocking abuse of federal power. It's reminiscent of the Nazis, and something has got to be done."

—PAT ROBERTSON[13]

"We don't see any difference between Bill Clinton, Bob Dole and Newt Gingrich. Anybody with entrenched power is suspect."

—State Senator CHARLES DUKE of
Colorado[14]

"Go up and look legislators in the face, because someday you may have to blow it off."

—SAMUEL SHERWOOD, leader of the
United States Militia Association[15]

- **Belief in conspiracies.** The worldview of the radical right is haunted by bizarre and paranoid conspiracy theories. The federal government, the United Nations, and international bankers (understood by many as code words for supposedly Jewish economic elites) are often implicated in a demonic plot to create a dictatorial one-world government—or, in conspiracy-speak, a "New World Order." Conspiracy theory breeds distrust and fear among its believers, preparing them for desperate measures.

"Indeed it may well be that men of goodwill like Woodrow Wilson, Jimmy Carter, and George Bush . . . are in reality unknowingly and unwittingly carrying out the mission and mouthing the phrases of a tightly knit cabal whose goal is nothing less than a new order for the human race under the domination of Lucifer and his followers."

> —PAT ROBERTSON, in his best-
> selling book *The New World Order*
> (1991)

"The UN Charter in full operation would mean: The end of the United States as a nation, making it a mere province in a New World Order, with one vote among 186, mostly hostile, nations. States and counties merged into regions, with UN appointed officials enforcing UN orders, while practicing extortion on us helpless serfs."

> —JACK McLAMB, militia organizer
> and founder of Police Against
> the New World Order[16]

- **The ends justify the means.** Some individuals, seeing no hope of prevailing within the democratic process, have resorted to violence, harassment, and even murder. Terrorist attacks have been directed at abortion providers, government employees, people of color, gays, immigrants, and environmentalists.

"If abortion is murder—act like it is murder."

> —RANDALL TERRY, founder of
> Operation Rescue[17]

"Where ballots fail, bullets will prevail."

—LOUIS BEAM, spokesperson for
Aryan Nations[18]

2

The Religious Right:
The Battle for Dominion

"If Christian people work together, they can succeed during this decade in winning back control of the institutions that have been taken from them over the past 70 years. Expect confrontations that will be not only unpleasant but at times physically bloody. . . . This decade will not be for the faint of heart, but the resolute. Institutions will be plunged into wrenching change. We will be living through one of the most tumultuous periods of human history. When it is over, I am convinced God's people will emerge victorious. But no victory ever comes without a battle."

—PAT ROBERTSON, *Pat Robertson's Perspective* (newsletter), October/November 1992

The original recruiting video for the Christian Coalition, entitled *America at a Crossroads*, opens with a brisk montage of child pornography, gay marches, and ominous close-ups of the American Civil Liberties Union logo. As these calculated images of "chaos" saturate the viewer's mind, televangelist Pat Robertson leans into the camera to assure us that all is not lost, stating in a cheerful yet clenched tone: "Christians founded this nation. Christians built this nation. And for three hundred years they governed this nation. And we can govern again. And that's why I founded the Christian Coalition."

Robertson's prediction in 1989 of imminent dominion over the United States by ultraconservative Christians was scarcely taken seriously. But today, the Christian Coalition's meticulous grassroots organizing is changing the face of American politics. The Coalition is part of a sprawling alliance of politically conservative religious groups and individuals—all working to translate biblical morality into public policy. This movement is known as the "religious right" or "Christian right." Though the religious right is a relatively small part of the electorate, its activists reap results disproportionate to their numbers.

The grassroots activists of the religious right are mostly evangelical Protestants—including fundamentalists and Pentecostals—along with a small number of Catholics. Evangelicals generally stress the inerrancy of the Bible, which they believe is an infallible source of religious and moral authority. It should be remembered, however, that the majority of evangelicals are not affiliated with the religious right.

In the eyes of the Christian right, many social problems can be blamed on the severing of government from religion. Crime, divorce, unwanted pregnancy, illiteracy, AIDS, even the national debt are perceived to be products of moral decay. The so-called "anti-Christian" forces which have fostered the decline of American civilization include the United Nations, the American Civil Liberties Union, Planned Parenthood, the National Education Association, the National Organization for Women, the National Council of Churches, the media, Hollywood, gays, and *Sesame Street.*

The movement's ultimate goal is to establish a theocracy, whereby "Christians" (i.e., its adherents) take dominion over the political and social institutions of America, and ultimately the world. Pat Robertson's vision of a "Christian Nation" is as follows:

> I want you to imagine a land where little children pray in schools, and they read the Bible to them and they're taught the things of God . . . there are no more abortions . . . *church members have taken dominion over the forces of the world.* . . . Imagine a time when . . . the people of God will be the most honored people in society . . .[1] (italics added).

To some, this may describe an ideal world—but in a diverse society it could only be achieved by coercion. Imagine an America where faith is enforced, not embraced willingly; where preferences are given to one religious group over all others; where the separation between church and state has been torn down; where the few dictate policy for the many; where biblical law has replaced secular law; and where any voice of opposition is extinguished.

In its quest to establish a government that is steeped in its

The Impact of the Religious Right in the 1990s

Sixty percent of candidates supported by the religious right in the 1994 national elections won their campaigns, including forty-four representatives, eight senators, and seven governors.[2] Before the election, the Christian Coalition distributed voter registration packets along with 35 million supposedly nonpartisan voter guides to 250,000 conservative churches. According to Republican pollster Frank Luntz, 33 percent of voters in 1994 were religious conservatives, compared to only 18 percent in the 1988 presidential election.[3]

The religious right controls the Republican party apparatus in eighteen states, and is a substantial presence in at least thirteen others, according to *Campaigns and Elections* magazine. Extreme party platforms have resulted. In 1992, for example, Washington state's GOP committee under the control of religious right activists recommended a platform that included a ban on gays in health care, day care, and teaching occupations, a return to the gold standard, corporal punishment in the public schools, the withdrawal of the United States from the United Nations, and the banning of all abortions, witchcraft, and the occult.

The Christian Coalition's *Contract with the American Family*, a ten-point legislative proposal, helped set the congressional agenda in 1995. The Contract's proposals include restricting abortion, defunding the arts, dismantling the Department of Education, and replacing welfare with a system of private charities.

highly intolerant version of Christianity, the religious right combines model democratic tactics—such as organizing, lobbying, demonstrating, and voting—with undemocratic ones—such as censorship, violence, scapegoating, stereotyping, intimidation, deception, and unjust claims of religious persecution.

Since 1989, an estimated 12,625 religious right candidates have been elected to school board seats, according to Robert Simonds, president of the religious right group Citizens for Excellence in Education.[4] Many candidates won by "stealth" campaigns in which they concealed their affiliations and true platform from voters.

Anti–gay rights initiatives have passed in nearly thirty cities since 1993. Statewide initiatives that would permit discrimination on the basis of sexual orientation have been introduced in Colorado (passed), Oregon (twice defeated), Idaho (defeated), and Maine (defeated). Anti–gay rights legislation was planned in at least eight other states, but failed to get on the ballot.

Eighteen percent of reported challenges to school curricula in the 1994–95 school year charged that materials were "anti-Christian" or endorsed a religion other than Christianity, according to People for the American Way, a constitutional liberties organization that monitors the radical right. In 50 percent of the total reported censorship incidents, challenged materials were removed or restricted in some fashion.

Throughout 1990–1995, 56 abortion clinics were subjected to arson, 372 clinics were vandalized, and 254 clinics were the site of antiabortion blockades, according to the National Abortion Federation. Since 1993, assassination attempts against abortion clinic personnel have left five dead, and five seriously injured.

Reconstructing America

"Democracy is the great love of the failures and cowards of life."

—R. J. RUSHDOONY[5]

The theocratic goal of the religious right movement is most uncompromisingly expressed by Rev. Rousas John Rushdoony. Rushdoony, eighty, with his long white beard and meditative gaze, cuts a figure not unlike that of an Old Testament patriarch. Reportedly descended from an unbroken succession of Armenian priests dating back to the year 320, he has spent his life studying and writing voluminous religious texts (in longhand, with pen and ink pot). Rushdoony's work, most notably the nine hundred-page tome *The Institutes of Biblical Law,* has defined the most intolerant ideological strain of the religious right.

In the world according to Rushdoony, homosexuals, adulterers, blasphemers, atheists, and children who verbally disrespect their elders would be subject to execution by stoning, as mandated in the Old Testament. Criminals with lighter offenses who escaped capital punishment wouldn't go to prison, they'd become part of a slave class. Rushdoony insists that "Christianity is completely and radically anti-democratic; it is committed to a spiritual aristocracy."

Rushdoony's militant doctrine, known as Reconstructionism, is disseminated through the literature of his Chalcedon Institute. Though hard-core adherents of Reconstructionism number only around forty thousand (including Randall Terry, founder of the aggressive anti-abortion group Operation Rescue), aspects of its teachings have influenced the broader religious right movement. Rushdoony is a member of the New Right coordinating body, the Council for National Policy, along with Pat Robertson and many senior Republican politicians (see p. 47).

EVANGELICALS ENTER POLITICS

After earning his law degree from Yale and graduating from New York Theological Seminary, Pat Robertson recalls receiving some divine inspiration in prayer: "[God] said to me, 'Pat, I want you to have an RCA transmitter.'"[6] Robertson bought a two-bit TV station and radio outlet in 1960, and started the Christian Broadcasting Network (CBN). Exempt from restrictions on the amount of airtime that could be given over to advertisements, religious television was a lucrative boom industry by the 1970s. CBN, along with the Trinity Broadcasting Network and a number of individual stations, rapidly became multimillion-dollar money spinners.

Media ministries have been a major factor in the development of the religious right. Robertson's program the "700 Club," in particular, has shaped the political views of traditionally apolitical evangelicals, and continues to be a guiding light for the religious right. The Family Channel, spun out of CBN in 1990, currently offers the "700 Club" twice daily to some 59 million homes.[7] Today Robertson's operations have an estimated value of $1 billion, all working toward fulfilling his religious/political goals.

Yet despite their media ministries, evangelical leaders would not have been so successful if it hadn't been for their alliance with young conservative strategists within the embryonic New Right. Christian fundamentalists promoted the economic conservatism of that movement during the late 1970s, and in return their moral concerns were taken on board by the think tanks being built up in Washington. Out of this fusion grew the religious right.

The first four political organizations of the religious right—the National Christian Action Committee, the Religious Roundtable, the Christian Voice, and the Moral Majority—were established in 1979. These groups successfully mobilized 2 million new fundamentalist voters in the 1980 elections. Throughout the 1980s, despite only tepid support from many Reagan administration officials, the religious right worked to place its social concerns at the center of the political agenda. But by the late 1980s, its reputation went into a tailspin with the exposure of the tawdry sex scandals of televangelists Jim Bakker and Jimmy Swaggart.

Pat Robertson, whose father had been a U.S. senator, ran unsuccessfully for the Republican presidential nomination in 1988. Robertson lost out on his bid to become President, but his backers very successfully penetrated state and local GOP organizations. The "700 Club" founder keenly shifted his focus from the national to the local level, taking the key contacts from his campaign and training them as the core of what would shortly become the Christian Coalition.

ONWARD CHRISTIAN SOLDIERS

The Christian Coalition is a modern-day political machine, built from the ground up. "The Christian community got it backwards in the 1980s," explained the then 29-year-old Ralph Reed, executive director of the Coalition, to *The Washington Post* in March 1990. "We tried to change Washington when we should have been focusing on the states. The real battles of concern to Christians are in neighborhoods, school boards, city councils and state legislatures." The Christian Coalition blankets the fifty states with 1,700 chapters, each working on its own local issues. Action alerts from the national or state headquarters quickly reach the grassroots, galvanizing the chapters to influence Washington.

The organization claims 1.7 million members, but its outreach is in fact much larger. "Pat Robertson is in constant contact with Beverly LaHaye [president of Concerned Women for America], with Jim Dobson [president of Focus on the Family], with Don Wildmon [founder and president of the American Family Association], and a lot of the national abortion groups. So it's really hand in hand," Jodie Robbins, a former assistant to Reed has said.[8] The leading Christian right organizations are united by a shared agenda and a considerable amount of overlap in membership and leadership.

In addition to serving as an umbrella group for other religious right organizations, the Christian Coalition sends liaisons from local chapters as ambassadors to area churches to solicit support. "What we're endeavoring to do in Christian Coalition is get the Christians out of the churches and into the precincts. We build a conduit into the churches where we can funnel information in

Good Cop/Bad Cop

There is a disparity between the "moderate" statements of Christian Coalition executive director Ralph Reed, which are meant for mass public consumption, and those of founder Pat Robertson, which are directed at hard-core supporters. An unwary public is at risk of accepting the Coalition as a mainstream political group. But as the following inconsistencies reveal, the group has a hidden agenda.

Reed: "There are two things that have made America great. One is her essential moral goodness . . . but you also have to acknowledge diversity and pluralism."[9]
Robertson: "You say you're supposed to be nice to the Episcopalians and the Presbyterians and the Methodists and this, that and the other thing. Nonsense! I don't have to be nice to the spirit of the Antichrist."[10]

Reed: "We affirm our belief in the notion that church and state should be separate institutions."[11]
Robertson: "They have kept us in submission because they have talked about separation of church and state. There is no such thing in the Constitution. It's a lie of the left, and we're not going to take it anymore."[12]

Reed: "We don't oppose homosexuals having jobs, running for office, being involved in the civic process, owning and renting property. . . . It's not a matter of being against or hating homosexuals."[13]
Robertson: "Many of those people involved in Adolph Hitler were Satanists, many of them were homosexuals—the two things seem to go together."[14]

Robertson's New World Order

Pat Robertson's best-selling book *The New World Order*, published in 1991, is an exercise in paranoia. It recycles centuries-old conspiracy theories, implicating a cabal of economic and political elites in a demonic plot to create a one-world government. Robertson traces the plot back to 1776, originating with an obscure Masonic society known as the Order of the Illuminati. Robertson asserts that "European bankers," a well-known euphemism in conspiracist literature for Jews, began funding the Illuminati in an attempt to control world finance. The long-defunct League of Nations, the Federal Reserve, the Council on Foreign Relations, and especially the United Nations are all claimed to be bastions of one-world conspiracy in the book. Robertson's speculating can be traced back to such anti-Semitic classics as Eustace Mullin's *Secrets of the Federal Reserve* and Nesta Webster's *Secret Societies and Subversive Movements*.[15]

and funnel people out," says Guy Rodgers, former national field coordinator of the Christian Coalition.[16]

Though its nonprofit tax exempt status legally prevents it from endorsing candidates or a political party, the Coalition has routinely fudged these restrictions. Backed by a $25 million budget, this "nonpartisan" group is working to take control of the Republican party from the grassroots up. Pat Robertson has asserted that he wants to see a working majority of the Republican party in the hands of "pro-family" Christians by 1996.[17]

Senator Arlen Specter and other party moderates set up the Republican Majority Coalition to take the GOP back from the religious right. "We believe issues such as abortion, mandatory school prayer, homosexuality, the teaching of creationism and other similar questions recently inserted into the political context should be left to the conscience of individuals," says the group's statement of purpose. Other groups such as Republicans for Choice, Republicans for Environmental Protection, and Log Cabin Republicans (a gay organization) are also fighting the religious right. But the Republican party as a whole is wary of alienating the Christian Right, well aware of its ability to harness the voting power of its supporters. In 1995, the Coalition's annual Road to Victory conference featured Speaker of the House Newt Gingrich, several members of Congress, and most of the Republican presidential candidates.

Organizing Tactics of the Religious Right

Combining information age know-how with the successful organizing, research, and training methods pioneered by the labor movement of the 1930s and the civil rights movement of the 1960s, the religious right teaches its adherents the nuts and bolts of how to win widespread support for its candidates and promote its policies.

- **Hi-tech communications.** Christian right activists receive political prompting from the Christian Coalition's monthly full-color tabloid, as well as by accessing the Coalition's Internet site for up-to-date "action alerts." Phone trees and fax networks, by which one member contacts ten "pro-family" voters, who each contact ten more, and so on, help get the word out. Once a month, *Christian Coalition Live* conducts a meeting via satellite with chapters throughout the country.

- **Training workshops.** Leadership schools, which offer a "crash course in mountain moving," are held throughout the country. They teach Coalition members how to lobby, track legislation, canvass, raise funds for a candidate, run for office, and represent their views appropriately to the media. Over 1,700 have been held in the United States.

- **Pegging voters.** The Coalition controls the nation's largest computerized file of "pro-family" voters, which has approximately one million names. There are 175,000 precincts in the United States, with an average of five hundred to one thousand registered voters in each. The Christian Coalition's goal is to place one "precinct coordinator" and five to ten "helpers" in each to identify voters. The Christian Coalition claims to have fifty thousand precinct coordinators.

Local chapters painstakingly build databases of sympathizers precinct by precinct, using church membership and voter registration lists, which are then cross-referenced with census data, telephone directories, and donation lists. Voters are surveyed, by either phone or door-to-door canvassing, to determine the issues they consider important. They are then contacted during an election or a lobbying campaign, or targeted as volunteers for the Coalition.

After the specific concerns of voters are gleaned from surveys, they can be manipulated in direct mail appeals. During a campaign in Virginia Beach, Virginia, otherwise generic letters included one of a variety of seemingly personalized paragraphs on issues ranging from pornography to zoning laws. Letters sent to pro-choice voters purposefully did not mention the candidate's antiabortion views. Consequently, the Coalition, despite its fervent opposition to abortion, was able to win the support of an overwhelmingly pro-choice electorate, helping to elect conservative Republicans in seven out of nine races.

• **From the pews to the polls.** Voter registration drives are held before elections to ensure that "pro-family" supporters get out and vote. In some cases, activists direct in-pew registration drives at sympathetic churches.

• **Rating Congress.** Congressional scorecards give a score of up to 100 percent to Congress members, based on their agreement with the Coalition's positions. Though the scorecards contain a disclaimer that asserts a nonpartisan nature for the Coalition, they clearly favor Republicans, whose names appear in capital letters and who generally receive higher scores.

• **Delivering votes.** Voter guides, for elections ranging from school board to national races, are also widely distributed by the Coalition, often misleadingly portraying the views of candidates on a half dozen or so issues. An individual who supports the National Endowment for the Arts, for example, is labeled as someone who supports "tax-funded obscene art." Coalition activists give out the guides in Christian bookstores, church parking lots, and polling places, usually on the Sunday before a Tuesday election.

In 1990, with barely a week to go before the election, Senator Jesse Helms of North Carolina was trailing in the polls. He called Pat Robertson for help. Ralph Reed boasts in *Church and State* magazine about how the Coalition came to the rescue: "I had access to the internal tracking, and I knew [Helms] was down by 8 points. So Pat called me up and said, 'We've got to kick into action.' Bottom line is . . . five days later we put three-quarters of a million voters' guides in churches across the state of North Carolina and Jesse Helms was re-elected by 100,000 votes out of 2.2 million cast."

• **Stealth strategy.** "Stealth" strategy represents a serious threat to the democratic process. Religious right candidates have been coached by the Coalition and by Citizens for Excellence in Education to run campaigns in local elections under false pretenses. By not revealing their true platform and affiliations to voters, Christian right candidates have been elected to school boards, hospital boards, water districts, community planning boards, city councils, county supervisory boards, state legislatures, land use boards, and Republican Party committees across the country.[18] In 1990, Ralph Reed gloated about the success of stealth tactics in San Diego, where two-thirds of the religious right candidates won: "I want to be invisible. I do guerilla warfare. I paint my face and travel at night. You don't know it's over until you're in a body bag. You don't know until election night."[19]

FIGHTING BACK

"The Christian Right Is Neither." This terse slogan of protest sums up the concern many Americans have about the divisive and authoritarian religious right movement. Unfortunately, bumper sticker wisdom isn't enough to counter this growing phenomenon.

There's no question that religious individuals have the right to hold and promote their beliefs—a healthy democracy is sustained by ongoing discussion among divergent voices. Constitutional principles are undermined, however, when individuals translate religious absolutes into political absolutes.

Despite their claims, the religious right hardly represents the views of America's tens of millions of Christians. In fact, some of the most steadfast activists fighting the religious right are people of faith. Dr. Gardner Calvin Taylor, a member of the board of directors of the Interfaith Alliance, a national coalition of clergy and laypeople committed to countering the religious right, compares the leaders of groups like the Christian Coalition to priests in the Book of Numbers who followed a false religion: "What we are really dealing with are people using strange fire. They are using the language of religion, the language of our democracy. But they are using it for untoward and selfish purposes. And they will subvert everything we hold dear unless we take heed."[20]

3

The Far Right:
Up From the Underground

A lethal brew of 4,800 pounds of fuel oil and ammonium nitrate exploded the Alfred P. Murrah Federal Building in Oklahoma City on the morning of April 19, 1995. The FBI soon announced that the prime suspect was a red-blooded American, a veteran of Operation Desert Storm. As people tried to make sense of the 168 deaths caused by the explosion, the mass media dug up the frightening story of a homegrown movement that had mushroomed under our noses—a movement that, while wrapping itself in the flag, seemed to be planning the violent overthrow of the U.S. government—the militia movement. Within days, two suspects said to have been associated with the Michigan Militia had been arrested.

The militias are armed paramilitary groups that have sprung up across the country to resist what they see as a hostile federal government. Connections have been revealed between the militias and other groups and individuals on the far right, some of them openly racist and violent.

All too often, these racist groups—Aryan Nations, the National Alliance, Liberty Lobby, the Ku Klux Klan, and others—have been dismissed as marginal, insignificant fanatics. However, the militia movement represents one part of an attempt by white supremacist leaders to reach a more mainstream audience, drawing support not by explicit racism, but by exploiting "bridge" issues like gun control, taxes, abortion, homosexuality, school prayer, and anti-environmentalism. At least one Ku Klux Klan activist in Billings, Montana, for example, was involved in the formation of a chapter of the Young Republicans on the Eastern Montana College campus. An individual may unwittingly join a group because he is concerned about taxes, only to be exposed to poisonous ideas about people of color, Jews, gays, women, and immigrants.

"The new strategy is to combine old hatreds with new rhetoric," writes Loretta J. Ross, former program director of the Center for Democratic Renewal (CDR), an Atlanta-based clearinghouse for information on white supremacist groups and hate crimes in the United States. "Broadening the issues and using conservative buzzwords attracts the attention of whites who may not consider themselves racist, who in their own mind are just patriotic Americans . . ." [1] This strategy is parallel to the religious right's use of such issues as crime, welfare, and taxation to attract support from people who wouldn't necessarily side with their antigay or antiabortion agenda.

WHAT IS THE FAR RIGHT?

"Far right" is a blanket term that describes approximately three hundred groups on the extremist fringe, characterized by racist, anti-Semitic, antigay, antifeminist, and antigovernment philosophies. These groups are working to create a "racially pure" society, dominated by straight white Christian males. They seek to tap into a backlash against social liberation movements and gains made by racial and ethnic minorities, gays, and women—a backlash fueled by rising economic uncertainties. The federal government is the target of the far right's wrath, in part because it is seen as the mechanism through which oppressed groups have asserted their rights.

Hard-core ideological activists for the white supremacist movement, some 25,000, are only a small fraction of the population. But, according to the CDR, about 150,000 to 200,000 people subscribe to their racist publications, send contributions, and attend periodic meetings, marches, and rallies throughout the United States.

Sophisticated technology allows the message of far right groups to spread fast and far. Recruiting is done using a multiplicity of media, such as direct mail, fax, and phone networks, radio, public access TV, satellite TV, videocassettes, and the Internet. Shortwave talk radio has been an especially powerful organizing tool for the far right. With $1,000 worth of equipment, and $100 to $250 an hour for airtime, ultra right-wingers can broadcast to an estimated 17 million shortwave radios in the United States and more than 660 million worldwide. In the past four years, six out of the seventeen private shortwave broadcast stations in the United States have switched to what Radio for Peace International calls "political far right" programming.

THE VIOLENT UNDERGROUND

As the far right's influence spreads, the occurrence of violent hate crimes is rising: The Department of Justice reported 7,684 in 1993 (the latest year for which figures are available), the highest number ever recorded. Hate crime, provoked by racial and homophobic anger, most frequently takes the form of assault.

Liberty Lobby

The Liberty Lobby, founded by Willis Carto in 1955, is the largest and best financed far right organization in the United States, with a $4 million-a-year budget. Its weekly tabloid, *The Spotlight,* is known as the bulletin board of the extreme right. With a circulation of 100,000, it is far more widely read than any comparable periodical. The Liberty Lobby also controls the Sun Radio Network, which has 130 affiliates. Its *Radio Free America* and *Editor's Roundtable* are broadcast by dozens of stations. Carto is well known as an anti-Semite and Nazi apologist.

The Spotlight devotes much space to conspiracy theories. Between January 1994 and June 1995, the publication featured twenty-six pro-militia articles, forty about International Jewish Bankers, and seventy-five about the New World Order or "Global Plantation."

These crimes not only target individuals, but are designed to intimidate the group to which the individual belongs. Antigay crime is the fastest-growing hate-crime category. According to the National Gay and Lesbian Task Force, there were 2,064 homophobia-motivated acts of violence in nine U.S. cities in 1994, committed not just against gays and lesbians or those perceived to be gay or lesbian, but also against those who support their rights.

In the neo-Nazi skinhead movement, with about 3,500 members in forty states (mainly aged between thirteen and twenty-five), committing a hate crime is usually required as part of the initiation into a gang. Between 1990 and 1994, skinheads murdered over twenty-five people.

PENETRATING THE MAINSTREAM

In 1989, David Duke, a former Klansman, won a seat in the Louisiana House of Representatives. In 1990, Duke campaigned for the U.S. Senate and won 44 percent of the vote, largely by employing racially coded antiwelfare and anticrime rhetoric. Although Duke lost the election, he won 60 percent of the white vote.

Duke represents the far right's attempt to tap into the prejudices of the mainstream. But he's not the only politician to do this. Pat Buchanan, political pundit and sometime presidential candidate, has built a career out of misdirecting blame for society's problems—his typical targets being immigrants, gays, welfare recipients, Jews, and minorities. Buchanan has stirred up white resentment by making the claim that Hispanics living in America did not send people to fight for America in World War II and Korea, and thus do not deserve the same social protections as whites.

In Congress, Rep. Helen Chenoweth (R-ID), a longtime John Birch Society sympathizer, supports the causes of the far right more than any other politician. According to Sidney Blumenthal, writing in *The New Yorker,* these include "those of the antienvironmentalists and the religious right, the advocates of states' rights, the citizens' militias, the gun owners and the 'county sovereignty' anarchists, the home-schoolers and the property rights libertarians."

After the Oklahoma City bombing Chenoweth declared, "While we can never condone this, we still must begin to look at the public policies that may be pushing people too far."[2] A videotape of her comments is sold by the Militia of Montana. Chenoweth has linked environmental activism with the New World Order.

Larry Pratt is characterized by the CDR as "the most visible link between the white supremacist movement and Congress."[3] Pratt is founder of English First—a 250,000-member group that sponsors efforts to block bilingual education—and executive director of Gun Owners of America (GOA)—the self-described "no-compromise alternative to the National Rifle Association (NRA)." With approximately 100,000 members, GOA represents the crossroads for various segments of the far right: white supremacists, militia organizers, and the religious right. Pratt is also a former member of the Virginia state legislature, and an advisor to a congressional task force to repeal gun control. He co-chaired Buchanan's 1996 presidential campaign until his far right connections were revealed by the media.

THE SNOWBALLING OF THE MILITIA MOVEMENT

Throughout 1994, militia meetings spread like wildfire across the country, attracting hundreds in rural small towns. According to the Anti-Defamation League, militia membership is estimated at fifteen thousand hardcore activists and tens of thousands more hangers-on. As of 1995, Klanwatch's Militia Task Force had found 224 militias and support groups in the United States.

The gun issue has been the militia's most effective draw. Militia promoters point to Congress's restrictions on assault rifles and the Brady Act—which imposed a waiting period and background checks on handgun buyers—as signs the government is trying to disarm its citizenry. "Our consitutional liberties are systematically being eroded and denied," warns a widely circulated militia manual. A militia motto is "Gun control is for only one thing . . . people control."

Two specific incidents have also driven the dramatic upsurge of militia activity in the 1990s. The first was the eleven-day siege at Ruby Ridge, Idaho, in August 1992. Federal law enforcement officers came in massive force to arrest white supremacist Randy Weaver on a weapons charge after Weaver refused to give himself up. His wife Vicki, his fourteen-year-old son Sam, and a deputy marshal were killed before Weaver finally surrendered. Then, on February 28, 1993, federal agents attempted to arrest David Koresh, the leader of the Branch Davidians, for stockpiling illegal weapons at the sect's compound in Waco, Texas. The compound resisted, resulting in a shoot-out that killed four ATF agents and six members of the sect. The standoff ensued, ending fifty-one days later in a fiery assault that killed eighty Davidians, eighteen of whom were children.

The Weaver family and the Branch Davidians are seen by far right organizers as martyrs to their cause. After the standoff at Waco, the front page of a special NRA report featured a photo of the Davidian compound in flames with the caption "Your rights and your home next?"

Federal law enforcement agencies may well have reacted with excessive force in the Waco and Ruby Ridge incidents. But their mistakes must be put in context. Like others on the far right, Weaver and Koresh were extremely well armed and partial to violent rhetoric. Officers had already lost their lives. And federal officials remember the 1980s, when far right groups such as the Order killed several law officers.

In response to the Weaver killings, Pastor Pete Peters, a preacher of the racist doctrine of Christian Identity, called a summit meeting. It took place on October 23–26, 1992, in Estes Park, Colorado. The flamboyant Louis Beam, former grand dragon of the Texas Klan, was at Peters's meeting. So was Richard Butler, a leader of the white supremacist Aryan Nations. In all, over 160 people affiliated with Aryan Nations, various Klan groups, and the Posse Comitatus, a loosely knit survivalist movement of white supremacists founded in California in 1969, attended.

At the meeting, Larry Pratt, executive director of Gun Owners of America, suggested forming militias as a tactic in the battle against gun control. He gave the example of armed militia units in Guatemala and the Philippines—that is, death squads that had killed thousands of innocent people.[4] Pratt had already offered this idea in his 1990 book, *Armed People Victorious*.

The leaders at Estes Park resolved to organize militias struc-

Christian Identity

Christian Identity is the most significant far right religious theology, being explicitly white supremacist and anti-Semitic. Its teachings underpin the ideology in some militias. Identity doctrine holds that white people of northern European ancestry, sometimes called "Aryans," are the chosen people, descended from the Lost Tribes of Israel, and that America is the Promised Land. Satan is said to have implanted his seed in Eve before Adam did, a seed that grew up to be Cain, while Adam's became Abel. The descendants of Cain are the Jews, who are not the true Israelites, but impostors; the Aryans are descended from Abel. All other races are considered to be "mud people," and are held to lack souls. Armageddon, it is believed, will be a race war pitting the Aryans against the Jews and the nonwhites.

tured around the "Leaderless Resistance" concept promoted by Beam in the February 1992 issue of his newsletter, *The Seditionist*. Beam asserted that right-wing groups should consist of a number of small, autonomous cells. "Utilizing the Leaderless Resistance concept, all individuals and groups operate independently of each other, and never report to a central headquarters or single leader for direction or instruction, as would those who belong to a typical pyramid organization. . . . No one need issue an order to anyone."[5]

The dangers of letting the foot soldiers command themselves are obvious. Francisco Duran, the man who fired a semiautomatic weapon on the White House in an attempt to assassinate President Clinton, is one of many examples of what can happen when people are encouraged to take the law into their own hands. Duran belonged to the Save America Militia and other paramilitary groups. The Leaderless Resistance strategy allows

Militias of Montana

John Trochmann, a retired maker of snowmobile parts, founded the Militias of Montana (MOM) in January 1994. A wiry man with a thick white beard, Trochmann was among those who held a vigil at the Weaver standoff in 1992. Trochmann runs MOM with his wife, Carolyn, brother David, and nephew Randy out of an isolated mountain valley.

Trochmann has said, "We want to use the ballot box and the jury box. We don't want to go to the cartridge box. But we will if we have to."[6] MOM claims 12,000 members, but probably has only about 250 active members. However, its base of soft support is much broader: MOM's mail-order operation fills hundreds of requests for merchandise and information per week.

Like many militia organizers, John Trochmann has recently made an effort to distance himself from the racist right. But according to the Montana Human Rights Network, the Trochmanns have been active in the far right and racist movement for years. They have a long-standing relationship with Aryan Nations and other followers of Christian Identity.

figures like Beam to promote violence and confrontation, while denying responsibility for the actions of their followers.

CONSPIRACY THEORIES

"*Americans see it happening but few understand the cause. They are angry over taxes, debt, inflation, crime, godless schools, inferior education, health and insurance costs, unemployment, government interference in business—101 deplorable conditions. Angry at the President, Congress, the courts, elected officials . . . angry at every-*

Bo Gritz

Col. James "Bo" Gritz mediated between federal agents and Randy Weaver at the Ruby Ridge siege. Riding on his fifteen minutes of fame, the seasoned Gritz, who had previously led commando raids into Vietnam in search of MIAs, began running a lucrative traveling military training course called SPIKE (Specially Prepared Individuals for Key Events). According to SPIKE literature, "Both street confrontation and deliberate shooting will be taught along with instinctive 'Quick Kill' skills. All guns and ammo will be furnished."

Gritz has bought two parcels of land to develop as survivalist communities in the remote Idaho panhandle. They have been christened "Almost Heaven" and "Shenandoah." Asked to comment on the Oklahoma bombing, Gritz described it as a "Rembrandt—a masterpiece of science and art put together."[7]

Though he now tries to project a softer image to the national media, Gritz has long-standing ties to the racist right. In 1988, he was the vice presidential running mate of former Klan leader David Duke. They were backed by the Populist Party, founded by Nazi sympathizer Willis Carto of the Liberty Lobby. Gritz ran for president on the Populist Party ticket in 1992.

one, except *the real culprits. . . . They don't suspect that all this is planned and carried on through UN programs."*

—JACK McLAMB, founder of Police
Against the New World Order[8]

One unifying characteristic of the far right, going back to the John Birch Society of the 1950s, is the readiness to believe in conspiracies, many of which implicate the federal government and the United Nations.

The establishment of a New World Order or a Global One-

Linda Thompson

Linda Thompson, a former lawyer for the liberal American Civil Liberties Union in Indianapolis, has become a media darling as one of the few highly visible female militia leaders. Already well known for her videos—*Waco—the Big Lie* and *Waco II—The Big Lie Continues*—Thompson's most notorious exploit was the call she put out over the Internet for a nationwide militia march on Washington on September 19, 1994. Militiamen were to arrive "armed and in uniform." Thompson wrote, "The militia will arrest congressmen who have failed to uphold their oaths of office, who will then be tried for treason by citizens' courts." Francisco Duran, who attempted to assassinate President Clinton, was reportedly inspired in part by this call. However, with Thompson's cyberspace cohorts failing to support the march, the event came to nothing.

World Government are perennial themes in these theories. Conspiracists believe that a secret cabal of elites is controlling society and plotting to disarm American citizens so that it can take away their freedom and constitutional rights. Domestic and foreign military equipment is said to be moving across the country by rail and flatbed truck, in preparation for an invasion by U.S. and United Nations troops. According to John Trochmann, there is a conspiracy to reduce the world's population to 2 billion by the year 2000. Trochmann also believes a plan to divide the United States into ten regions has been printed on the back of a Kix cereal box.

Jack McLamb, a retired policeman from Arizona, heads a group called Police Against the New World Order. He believes the United Nations wants to make the United States "a mere province in the New World Order," to abolish the "traditional family," and to reduce living standards to "bare subsistence or starvation levels."[9]

Many believe the sign of the Mark of the Beast—the number

666, according to the Book of Revelation—is found in supermarket bar codes, proposed designs for paper money (a view propagated by Pat Robertson's "700 Club"), and implantable microchips. According to Bob Fletcher, a former toy manufacturer from New Jersey who has been a spokesperson for the Militia of Montana, "Six thousand people in Sweden have already been implanted with transponder chips in the backs of their hands. It's unbelievably biblical."[10] Jewish bankers are often implicated as the financiers of the global plot—white supremacists refer to the federal government by the name "ZOG," which stands for "Zionist Occupation Government."

As far-fetched as such a plot may seem to most Americans, "New World Order" theories have had an effect on mainstream policy making. The Conference of the States, a meeting for leaders of state governments which was to take place in October of 1995, was called off because far right conspiracists saw it as part of the plot to nullify basic American rights, and generated an aggressive telephone and fax campaign pressuring legislators to back out of the conference.

Crude conspiracy theories are even spouted by some elected politicians. According to the *New York Times,* State Senator Charles Duke of Colorado is among a handful of state representatives who believe that the federal government planted the bomb that blew up the Federal Building in Oklahoma City. During an interview in the summer of 1995, Duke said, "You have to ask: 'Who had the motive? Who had the means? Who had the opportunity?' It's self-evident that the Government had all three of those."[11]

CONSTITUTIONAL THEORIES

Also swirling around the far right is a welter of creative legal and historical revisionism, mostly jumping off from the U.S. Constitution. The gist of these theories is that the Constitution with its ten original amendments is a sacred, divinely inspired document. Adherents hold that the later amendments to the Constitution—which, among other things, granted civil rights to newly freed slaves, allowed the federal government to impose an income tax, and ensured women the right to vote—are travesties that were forced on America by an evil conspiracy.

Many constitutionalist theories are race-based. White, Christian men are called "organic citizens," having received their rights from God through the Preamble and first ten amendments of the constitution. All other men are "Fourteenth Amendment Citizens" deriving their rights from the Fourteenth Amendment or equal protection clause. According to constitutionalists, these rights were granted by men and therefore may be revoked by men. This theory originated with the far right Posse Comitatus, active in the 1970s and 1980s, which promoted the idea of Christian Common Law. Posse members were taught that blacks were "illegally" granted their rights by the Fourteenth Amendment, while whites were simultaneously enslaved by it.

Numerous movements propound such theories, with names like the freemen, tax protesters, the sovereignty movement, the county movement, and the Tenth Amendment movement. "Freemen" claim to have set up their own parallel court system in which they will bring government officials to trial. Tax protesters believe that the current tax system is illegal, and thus refuse to pay taxes. The county movement holds the county sheriff to be the highest legal authority.

Fringe-dwellers aren't the only ones who believe in constitutionalist theories. These ideas have entered a more mainstream political discourse. Millions of people are now linked by "patriot" or "constitutionalist" fax networks. Many are former Ross Perot followers who have moved ever farther to the right as their anxiety about the economy has grown. The new "patriots" are more suburban and white-collar than the militias. But like the militias, these patriots see a conspiracy of politicians, corporations, media, and the U.N. to institute a one-world government.

Linda Liotta, an artist and homemaker in Potomac, Maryland, who runs a patriot fax network, says, "The global socialists want the U.N. to have all the power, and the global capitalists want the multinational corporations to have it, and in the meantime my kids can't get jobs and my friends' kids can't get jobs and the standard of living is going down for Americans and I'm angry about it." [12] Impeached ex-governor of Arizona Evan Mecham chairs the Constitutionists' Networking Center, made up of more than 2,500 smaller fax networks like Liotta's.

SEEING THE CONNECTIONS

The influx of far right thinking into the mainstream—from David Duke's and Pat Buchanan's political campaigns to the passage of anti-gay initiatives; from the dismantling of affirmative action programs and the linkage of race and intelligence championed by Charles Murray to the support of militia activity by members of Congress—is a disturbing trend. Increasingly, racism lurks barely beneath the surface of much political discourse, particularly around welfare reform, immigration, and crime.

Anti-abortion groups (some of which, like Missionaries to the Preborn, have encouraged the formation of militias among their members) have shown that a minority can win through terrorism what it could not win through elections, and this lesson is now being applied by the anti–gun control and anti-environmental movements, among others. In many parts of the world an inside/outside strategy of terrorists allied to mainstream groups has been very effective. If this becomes the rule in America, it will be at the expense of the very values which the far-rightists pretend to cherish.

4

The New Right:
Behind-the-Scenes Players

The New Right bestrides the landscape of reactionary politics, linking the social agenda of the religious right with the economic agenda of more traditional conservatives. Originally consisting of a few ambitious individuals disillusioned with cautious Republicanism, the New Right (hardly "new" anymore, but the term has stuck) has worked behind the scenes over the last thirty years to translate extreme ideas into the more soothing language of "conservatism" and "traditional family values," shifting the political debate onto its own terrain. The New Right has mushroomed to include thousands of organizations, including some with multimillion-dollar budgets.

The New Right is distinguished from traditional conservatism by its openly divisive tactics. In the 1970s, strategists such as Paul Weyrich, Howard Phillips, Richard Viguerie, and the late Terry Dolan began to infuse the political dialogue with a language of resentment and a right-wing "morality" as a way of mobilizing popular support for conservative economic and social policies that would reverse the progressive changes of the 1960s. They founded groups like the Heritage Foundation, the Conservative Caucus, the National Conservative PAC, and the Free Congress Foundation to shape public debate and policy. By the 1980s, these organizations had become the country's wealthiest and most influential think tanks and political action committees.

The same strategists also founded some of the key bodies of the religious right. In the late 1970s, the New Right leaders—men who had cut their teeth as young activists during the Barry

Goldwater candidacy of 1964—spied an opportunity to mobilize millions of apolitical individuals. They turned their attention to the burgeoning evangelical community and targeted abortion as the pivotal issue around which to politicize it. As author Sara Diamond writes in *Spiritual Warfare: The Politics of the Christian Right,* "Viguerie and company realized that the kind of sentiments aroused by the abortion issue could be used in the same way that the 'personal politics' of the 1960s and early 1970s had galvanized the feminist and progressive movements."[1] Sparked by this realization, Weyrich and Viguerie helped two evangelical activists, Paul and Judy Brown, to set up American Life Lobby—and the anti-abortion movement was in full swing.

In 1979, as a discontented country geared up for a Presidential election, Weyrich, Phillips, and Viguerie, along with Ed McAteer, approached televangelist Jerry Falwell. They suggested he form an organization that would tap into the potentially vast well of religious opposition to abortion and convert it into a potent political movement, one built around anti-communist militarism, moral orthodoxy, and economic conservatism. He agreed and, at Weyrich's suggestion, called the new group the Moral Majority. By 1984, Falwell's organization boasted of six million supporters.

In the year leading up to Ronald Reagan's electoral victory, and in the opening years of his presidency, the religious right and the New Right fused together. During this period, Weyrich's movement began to wedge its ideas into the mainstream political discourse, as several fundamentalists, including Secretary of the Interior James Watt, were appointed to leading government positions.

THE TRIUMPH OF THE RIGHT IN '94

The New Right is not loyal to one political party, according to Howard Phillips, but to a set of political principles. Nevertheless the New Right has effectively captured much of the Republican Party's decision-making apparatus. By the 1992 Republican convention, at which Pat Buchanan delivered his notorious "Cultural War" speech, New Right ideas had thoroughly soaked into the Grand Old Party. During the election that followed, religious

Paul Weyrich: The Master Strategist of the New Right

Paul Weyrich, an arch-conservative Catholic known for his hardball tactics, founded and/or heads a dozen rightist organizations. In 1973, the young Weyrich started the Heritage Foundation with a $25,000 grant from beer magnate Joseph Coors. Today, the Heritage Foundation, with an annual budget of around $25 million, is the most influential think tank in Washington. Heritage's quarterly journal, *Policy Review*—with regular contributors including Ralph Reed, executive director of the Christian Coalition, and House Majority Leader Dick Armey—acts as a sounding board for policies that, at the time of writing, are often outside the realistic political discourse, but which, as the culture moves farther to the right, are entering the general legislative arena. Heritage has generated dozens of other groups, including the Center for the Defense of Free Enterprise and the American Legislative Exchange Council.

Weyrich's Free Congress Foundation (FCF) has long served as a coalition builder and training ground for religious right groups in the United States. FCF is a key architect of anti-gay political strategies.

In 1993, Weyrich founded National Empowerment Television, a twenty-four-hour interactive satellite TV network that is unabashedly ideological. Programs include *Direct Line with Paul Weyrich*, a daily call-in show with the populist motto "Cut the Baloney"; and *The Progress Report with Newt Gingrich*, a weekly call-in show. Religious right groups participating in NET include the Christian Coalition, the Family Research Council, the Eagle Forum, the National Right to Life Committee, and Concerned Women for America. The network reaches more than 11 million homes, and is growing.

The Council for National Policy

The kingpin coordinating body of the New Right is the secretive Council for National Policy (CNP). This group meets four times a year to decide strategy for promoting right-wing politics. All of the New Right hierarchy attends these meetings and participate in policy-making sessions via a number of working committees.

The CNP was founded in 1981 by wealthy Texas businessmen T. Cullen Davis and Nelson Bunker Hunt, both linked to the far right John Birch Society. The Council was initially presided over by Tim LaHaye, one of the religious right leaders initiated into the Reagan inner sanctum. More recently ex–Attorney General Ed Meese has led it. Within this coordinating body, the New Right began mapping out its agenda for the last twenty years of the twentieth century.

The club roster of the Council for National Policy reads like a virtual Who's Who of the Right. In the CNP can be seen the overlapping interests of economic conservatism, cultural conservatism, and biology/race-based conservatism.

CNP's five hundred members include Weyrich, Viguerie, Phillips, Pat Robertson, Ralph Reed, Phyllis Schlafly of the Eagle Forum, James Dobson of Focus on the Family, the reconstructionist leader R.J. Rushdoony and his millionaire sponsor Howard Ahmanson, Oliver North, Edwin Meese, John Sununu, Jack Kemp, Alan Keyes, Gov. Tommy Thompson, Sen. Jesse Helms, Sen. Trent Lott, House Majority Leader Dick Armey, Rep. Robert Dornan, Rep. Steve Stockman, Rep. Helen Chenoweth, Marion Magruder (the CEO of McDonald's), members of the Coors family, Richard DeVos of Amway, Larry Pratt of Gun Owners of America, and a number of people linked to Sun Myung Moon's Unification Church. CNP's second president was Tom Ellis, who had previously headed the Pioneer Fund—a body long at the forefront of the eugenics movement.

right activists passed out hundreds of thousands of guides that warned that a vote for Bill Clinton was a sin against God.

In the 1994 election, the religious right mobilized its forces, including the one-third of the state Republican parties now under its control, expertly. For the first time in forty years, the Republicans took control of both the House of Representatives and the Senate. At last, the New Right ideologues could implement their agenda.

Newt Gingrich and the House Republicans authored the *Contract with America*, which, Gingrich wrote, "fleshes out the vision and provides the details of the program that swept the GOP to victory." The *Contract's* proposals reflect the long-sought goals of the New Right. By early 1996, most of the Contract had breezed through the House but was bogged down in the Senate. It remains very much on the national agenda.

In 1983, Richard Viguerie had published a book called *The Establishment Versus The People*. At the time, the ideas contained in this book were considered far outside the mainstream. Many of the themes that Viguerie covered, however, anticipated the xenophobic and homophobic rallying cries raised by Pat Buchanan and the conspiracy theorists, and now dominate the *Contract with America:*

• **Replace the income tax with a flat tax.** This proposal is supported in varying incarnations by House Majority Leader Dick Armey, Jack Kemp, Steve Forbes, and several other leading politicians.

• **Abolish the capital gains tax.** Cutting this tax—which is predominantly paid by the wealthy—has become part of the Republican platform.

• **Eliminate any Social Security benefits for non-U.S. citizens.** The passage of Proposition 187 in California wrote this proposal into law in 1994. Proposition 187 bars illegal immigrants from public schools, public assistance, and medical care; it also encourages public employees to turn in people whom they suspect of being illegal immigrants. The enforcement of this anti-immigration measure is suspended pending an investigation of its constitutionality.

• **End affirmative action.** This idea was taken up by all the leading Republican presidential candidates in the 1996 race. California Governor Pete Wilson endorsed the California Civil

Rights Initiative, which would ban all state-enacted affirmative action programs—some signed into law by his own hand. This initiative, which headed for the ballot in 1996, is the first major move by any state to end affirmative action.

• **Family cap—limiting cash welfare payments to three children per family.** The House went beyond Viguerie's suggestion and passed a total family cap on welfare payments; the Senate rejected it. Several states are considering similar measures.

• **Reduce food stamps by over 50 percent.** Supported by most House Republicans and several senators. Many Congress members advocate complete federal abandonment of food stamps, and their replacement with block grants to the states.

• **End public housing programs.** Supported by House Majority Leader Dick Armey and the right wing of the Republican party.

• **Abolish the Federal Reserve; return to the Gold Standard.** This is supported by a handful of U.S. representatives. In New World Order conspiracy theories, the Federal Reserve and the decision to leave the gold standard are signs of the domination of world finance by economic, often Jewish, "elites."

• **End funding for National Public Radio, the Corporation for Public Broadcasting, and "homosexual, pro-abortion, anti-nuclear, radical feminist and thousands of other liberal groups."** Supported by the religious right, House Republicans, Senator Phil Gramm, Pat Buchanan, and the radical right talk-radio mob.

• **Life sentences without parole for drug dealers.** The Clinton crime bill created over fifty federal capital offenses, including large-scale drug smuggling. In August 1995, Newt Gingrich called for the mass public execution of drug smugglers.

• **Oppose gay rights legislation.** The Christian Right has made this a central organizing principle.

• **Constitutional Amendment "protecting the right of the unborn to be born."** This is also at the heart of the religious right agenda and has been part of the Republican grassroots platform for years.

POLITICS OF RESENTMENT

The New Right strongly denounces most facets of government, and misleadingly poses as an "outsider" movement: "We are no

longer working to preserve the status quo. We are radicals, working to overturn the present power structure in this country," said
Paul Weyrich, mimicking the liberation rhetoric of the 1960s.[2]
They generally look back to an era lacking a guaranteed social
safety net, a social Darwinist world in which the rich flourish
while the majority flounder, and advocate rolling back nearly a
century's worth of social and regulatory legislation.

An attack on social programs can only be effective if backed
by popular support. The New Right promotes a message that the
supposedly immoral poor are bankrupting the hardworking
blue- and white-collar classes. This demonization effort identifies
welfare recipients as unworthy of public support, immigrants as
moochers or job-stealers, and prisoners as living a life of luxury.
In 1993, Paul Weyrich wrote in *Policy Review,* the journal of the
Heritage Foundation, "Most of our economic problems have cultural roots. . . . The American people realize that things are
going badly because people are behaving badly." The New Right
insists that if society were to re-embrace "traditional values," economic success would follow.

Meanwhile, billions of dollars a year are lost through tax loop-
holes for the rich and subsidies for big business: lost to corporate welfare. A massive reverse redistribution of wealth has
occurred in the past twenty years in this country. Using statistics
compiled by Michael Lind in his 1995 book *The Next American
Nation,* the scale of this redistribution can be seen clearly. Between 1973 and 1992, the wealthiest tenth of the population saw
its real income rise 18 percent, while the bottom tenth saw its decline 11 percent. A series of reports has suggested that the average blue-collar wage, when reduced benefits, increased health
insurance copayments, and fewer paid holidays are factored in,
has fallen by as much as 20 percent in real terms over the past
two decades. And while the extremes of poverty and wealth are
growing farther apart, the middle class is shrinking.

This economic squeeze was accelerated during the eighties by
a deliberate assault on the tax base of this country. During the
decade of the 1980s, the top 1 percent saw its federal tax burden
fall 14.4 percent, while the poorest 20 percent saw its taxes rise
16.1 percent. This tax cut for the wealthy, coupled with a bal-
looning defense budget, contributed significantly to today's
enormous national debt.

Those left hurting are looking for answers. They are vulnerable to the easy solutions offered by the New Right, solutions hawked as being in the best interest of the hard-working, God-fearing small-timer, but which in fact primarily benefit large monied interests. Given this context, it is not surprising that the movement to balance the budget has focused primarily on cutting social programs, welfare safety nets, and government regulations rather than, for example, defense spending and corporate tax breaks, or raising taxes for the wealthy. It is a political discourse based on myths and misinformation, one that scapegoats in lieu of addressing the real economic problems facing the country.

PART II
Understanding the Issues

5

Public Education: Under Siege

"We have a plan to take our entire education system back and put it in God's hands. And the way we're going to do it is to take control of every school board in America."

ROBERT SIMONDS, founder and
president of Citizens for
Excellence in Education [1]

In May 1994, the sleepy town of Merrimack, New Hampshire, elected Shelly Uscinski to the five-member school board. Uscinski, who won by only three votes, stressed "improving the quality of education" during her campaign. But once in office, she and two other recently elected council members pushed through a moment of silent prayer in all schools, despite substantial opposition from the community (several middle school students walked out in protest on the first day the moment of silence was implemented). They also banned Planned Parenthood literature and unveiled a measure to forbid teachers from presenting homosexuality "in a positive light" and counselors from referring gay students to gay organizations. The controversy escalated when Uscinski and company backed a proposal to teach creationism alongside evolution in the science curriculum of the Merrimack schools. One pro-creationism board member told the *Boston Globe,* "If you're only going to teach evolution, then your God is King Kong. I'm sorry—my children and grandchildren did not come from apes."

All over the country the religious right is attempting to impose its views on the public school system: the classroom is one of the key battlegrounds in the "culture war." Since 1989, the National Association of Christian Educators/Citizens for Excellence in Education (NACE/CEE) claims to have played a role in securing the election of over 12,625 conservative Christians to school boards across the nation, with the help of groups like the Christian Coalition and Concerned Women for America. Once in office, religious right activists attempt to push public schools to teach the absolutes of biblical morality.

Looming over the entire debate is the ultimate goal of the religious right—to dismantle the public education system. Pat Robertson has said that "tax money spent on public education instills atheism in our society."[2] It is here that the religious right vision merges with that of the secular rightists. New Right think tanks such as the Heritage Foundation and the Cato Institute, arguing that education, like health care, should be allocated according to the principles of a free market, favor privatizing the country's education system. Both the secular and religious right support the idea of "school choice": replacing the public school infrastructure with a network of private and parochial schools funded by tax dollars through a voucher system.

TACTICS OF THE RELIGIOUS RIGHT

Censorship

In 1982, in Calhoun County, Alabama, a minister formed a coalition of fifty parents and religious leaders to pressure the libraries to ban Doris Day's autobiography for containing objectionable language. While they were at it, they also banned *A Clockwork Orange* and all of John Steinbeck's works. The books remained forbidden until members of the community organized themselves to get them reintroduced.

Since that time, People for the American Way (PFAW), a nonpartisan constitutional liberties organization, has documented a steady rise in censorship activity. Library books, sex education, counseling programs, self-esteem programs, environmental education, school plays, and student newspapers have all come under attack. Some of the most frequently challenged materials in public schools include such literary classics as *The Catcher in the Rye, The Adventures of Huckleberry Finn,* and *I Know Why the*

Caged Bird Sings. According to PFAW, most censorship challenges originate from individuals or local groups affiliated with national organizations such as the Christian Coalition, NACE/CEE, Focus on the Family, and the Eagle Forum.

In Texas, Mel and Norma Gabler have spent over three decades organizing the censorship of school books and material. The Gablers have stated that they oppose teaching about the Great Depression, because it "will only succeed in raising doubts about our system." In the same vein, they also want to ban the study of archaeology, slavery, the Watergate scandal, the Equal Rights Amendment, and pollution. Since Texas is a big market for textbooks, and publishers can't afford to develop multiple editions for different states, the Gablers' influence in Texas has resulted in a watering-down of textbooks nationwide.

A Composite Model of a Religious Right Censorship Campaign

- a local group distributes materials in churches and throughout the community to mobilize opposition to a particular book or program;
- the group demands the book or program be removed, usually appealing directly to the school board;
- members lobby intensely and often threaten legal action against the board;
- the group often responds to school board rejection of their demand with costly lawsuits, school board recall campaigns, or attempts to defeat school tax levies;
- if these strategies fail, religious right groups often sponsor candidates to run for local school boards and, once elected, to carry out their agenda.

SOURCE: "The Freedom to Learn: Fact Sheets on Fighting School Censorship," People for the American Way.

Taking Over School Boards

Like other religious right leaders, Robert Simonds of NACE/
CEE has trained supporters to campaign using stealth tactics,
whereby candidates hide their true agenda from voters: "There
are two ways you can run. You can say: 'I'm a Christian. I believe
in traditional values. I believe in teaching both viewpoints, creationism and evolution.' The other way is [to run] as a conservative parent who says: 'I'm running because I love my children.'
You don't have to say up front that you're a Christian."[3]

The 1990 elections in San Diego County became the blueprint
for successful stealth campaigns. Candidates avoided public ap-
pearances and often refused to fill out questionnaires detailing
their views and backgrounds. Church directories were used for
get-out-the-vote phone drives, and 200,000 voter guides were distributed in church parking lots the Sunday before the election,
giving the impression that the candidates were church-endorsed.
Sometimes tactics such as résumé-doctoring and distributing of
materials under fictitious names were used to defame incum-
bents.

After all the votes were counted, two-thirds of the religious
right candidates (sixty out of ninety) had won their races for
low-level state and local positions. Newly elected board members
in a number of San Diego school districts opposed counseling
for pregnant teens, federally sponsored breakfast programs for
poor children, and the release of students for confidential doctor's appointments during school hours.

While Pat Robertson and Ralph Reed later rejected the notion
that the Christian Coalition encourages stealth campaigns, Reed
unabashedly claimed victory at the time. "Stealth was a big factor
in San Diego's success," he was quoted as saying by the *New York
Times* in 1992, "but that's just good strategy. . . . If you reveal your
location, all it does is allow your opponent to improve his ar-
tillery bearings."

Taking over school boards is only a means to an end. Many in
the religious right are intent on using these local positions of influence to abolish the public school system. Robert Thoburn, of
the religious-right Thoburn Press, wrote in 1986:

Christians should run for the school board. . . . Our goal is not to make the schools better. . . . The goal is to hamper them, so they cannot grow. . . . Our goal as God-fearing, uncompromised . . . Christians is to shut down the public schools, not in some revolutionary way, but step by step, school by school, district by district.[4]

DISTORTIONS ABOUT PUBLIC EDUCATION

"Public schools discriminate against Christians."

Nowhere is the religious right's grab for victim status clearer than in the area of public education. Attacking the California Teachers Association, Simonds wrote in 1987: "The left-wing union's intolerance toward parents, board members and Christian views has become alarming." He added, "We are helping parents stand up against this bigoted anarchy."[5]

The religious right presents such measures as reinstating school prayer as part of a restoration of religious freedom in America. But in fact, they are seeking not to gain religious freedom, but to impose their religion on others. The religious right's attempts to force the Bible into public schools circumvent two important Supreme Court rulings: the 1962 *Engel v. Vitale* case that declared organized school prayer in New York to be unconstitutional and the 1963 *Schempp v. Abington School District* case that ruled mandatory reading of the Bible in Pennsylvania's schools unconstitutional. These two rulings were the culmination of a half-century court fight to truly separate church and state in schools. Neither rulings outlawed school prayer; what they did forbid was *organized* school prayer, and religion mandated by the school authorities.

"The separation of church and state is not in the Constitution."

Ironically, the very safeguard that guarantees religious freedom, the separation of church and state established under the First Amendment of the Constitution, is blamed by the religious right for so-called "anti-Christian" bigotry. This separation was designed as a protection against government interference with religion, and religious interference with government.

David Barton, founder of Wallbuilders, is leading the crusade to tear down the wall between church and state. Barton contends that before the Supreme Court rulings in the 1960s, the United States was a "Christian Nation," established as such by the founding fathers. The revisionist history he presents in his popular books and lectures is aptly described by the Anti-Defamation League as "little more than a compendium of anecdotes divorced from their original context, linked harum-scarum and laced with factual errors and distorted innuendo."[6]

While it's true that the literal phrase "separation of church and state" does not appear in the Constitution, there is no doubt among most historians that the concept is ingrained therein. Eminent church-state scholar Leo Pfeffer writes in his book *Church, State and Freedom*, "[I]t was inevitable that some convenient term should come into existence to verbalize a principle so clearly and widely held by the American people. . . . [T]he right to a fair trial is generally accepted to be a constitutional principle; yet the term 'fair trial' is not found in the Constitution." The religious right interprets the Constitution by the same narrow means they do the Bible: reading the letter, not the spirit, of the text.

"Schools teach secular humanism."

"Secular humanism" is a term used by the religious right to describe all forces that have supposedly undermined Christian faith in America. "*The centers of power in our culture—government, education, media, business, and philanthropy—are firmly in the hands of secular humanists,*" cautions Pat Robertson, "*who are exerting every effort to debase and eliminate Bible-based Christianity from our society* [italics in original]."[7]

Christian right attacks on public school curricula often charge that secular humanism, as opposed to Christian principles, is being taught to children. Included is the study of other cultures, world religions, foreign languages, environmentalism, or any topic that the religious right views as subverting moral absolutes or the supremacy of Western Christian civilization. In contrast, most educators agree that a diverse curriculum does not brain-

wash young people into embracing amorality; rather it intro-
duces a broad spectrum of ideas to them in an effort to help
them think critically.

"Schools encourage children to be homosexuals."

Efforts on the part of schools to deal with gay and lesbian issues
are opposed by religious right activists. Realistic discussions of
gay issues are attacked as "promoting" homosexuality—whether
it be a health class dealing with AIDS, or an English class presenting information about the contributions of notable gay writers, or a guidance counselor giving advice to gay teenagers.
While schools attempt to teach tolerance, the religious right
tries to scare parents into thinking their children are in danger.
Pat Robertson has said, "This gang of idiots running the ACLU,
the National Education Association, the National Organization
for Women, they don't want religious principles in our
schools. . . . Instead of teaching the 10 Commandments, they
want to teach our kids how to be homosexuals."[8] Lou Sheldon, a
leading crusader against gay rights, simply warned in a 1991
fund-raising letter: "They Want Your Children."

In 1994 and 1995, the religious right pushed Congress to pass
legislation that would cut off federal funding to school districts
that "promote, condone, accept or celebrate homosexuality."
Several state legislatures have considered similar measures. They
would be particularly destructive coming at a time when an estimated one-quarter of teenage suicides are committed by gay and
lesbian youths, and when antigay violence is on the rise.[9]

"Sex education encourages immorality."

The religious right claims that comprehensive sex education
teaches children to have sinful sex. Phyllis Schlafly, a leading opponent of sex education, has written, "The major goal of nearly
all sex education curricula being taught in the schools is to
teach teenagers (and sometimes children) how to enjoy fornica-
tion without having a baby and without feeling guilty."[10] In truth,
comprehensive sex education emphasizes abstinence, while also
providing vital information on contraception and disease pre-

vention for those teens who do not abstain. This information will be equally important when teens reach adulthood.

Polls demonstrate that eight in ten parents support the providing of sex education in public schools, and more than nine in ten support HIV/AIDS education, according to the Sexuality Information and Education Council of the United States.[11] But the minority that opposes sex education is extremely vocal.

Themes of fear and retribution, underpinned by a narrow religious morality, run throughout the teaching and philosophy at the heart of the alternative abstinence-based sex education curricula developed by the religious right. One of these programs is *Sex Respect,* which several fundamentalist school boards attempted to introduce in California before backing down in the face of Planned Parenthood, ACLU, and parental opposition. One scene from a *Sex Respect* video counsels as follows:

> Student: "What if I want to have sex before I get married?"
> Teacher: "Well, I guess you just have to be prepared to die. And you'll probably take with you your spouse and one or more of your children."

Another program being pushed is *Free Teens,* produced by an organization of cult leader Sun Myung Moon. A slide picture of an emaciated man is accompanied by the words "This is what Magic Johnson could look like in ten years when he develops full-blown AIDS." *Free Teens* has been approved for use in New York City schools.

"Creationism is a science, and should be taught in schools."

Going back to the 1925 Scopes "monkey" trial in Tennessee, fundamentalists have fought against the teaching of the theory of evolution in schools. First, they attempted to prevent Darwin's theory from even being discussed; now some want to present it as merely one of several equally valid theories of human origins.

Groups such as NACE/CEE and the Rutherford Institute (a legal institute promoting "religious freedom") are pushing hard for the creation story in the Book of Genesis to be taught as a valid alternative theory to evolution, though so far without much success. The Supreme Court has ruled that the theory of creationism constitutes a particular religious doctrine, and thus is not allowed to be taught in public schools.

"The occult is being taught in schools."

Another charge against the public schools is that they have become hotbeds of "new age" and occult thinking. Concerned Women for America has opposed students reading King Arthur's legends, *The Wizard of Oz,* and *Cinderella* because of their references to the supernatural. There have also been numerous attempts to censor the celebration of Halloween.

The Rutherford Institute has brought a number of cases to court claiming that teaching "new age" religion in the school infringes on the separation of church and state. According to a NACE report, Alabama banned progressive relaxation, guided imagery, and yoga from its classrooms in 1994.[12] A similar resolution was passed in New Mexico, and another is currently being debated in Colorado.

"Liberal educators are rewriting history."

The religious right is outraged by history curricula that encourage students to look at the negative as well as the positive aspects of American history, and to explore other cultures and civilizations.

Lynne Cheney, the former head of the National Endowment for the Humanities (who is now leading the fight for its abolition), writes in *Telling the Truth* (1995) that children should be taught "objective truths." Yet, her idea of objective truth is blatantly biased. In her book, Cheney defends the history curricula voted in by a Christian right school board in Lake County, Florida, in 1993. This curriculum, which was successfully challenged in the courts by the ACLU and teachers' unions, mandated that students be taught that American culture was incontrovertibly superior to all others, both contemporary and historic.

The *Phyllis Schlafly Report* devoted the March 1995 issue to the subject "How Liberals Are Rewriting History." Schlafly states that "academic organizations are now dominated by left-wing radicals who are determined to drop the DWEMs (Dead White European Males) down an Orwellian Memory Hole and to replace history with 'Oppression Studies,' featuring third-rate feminist and minority writers who attack Western Civilization as sexist, racist, and oppressive." Schlafly, like other critics of multicultural education, advocates a candy-coated approach to U.S. history that doesn't tackle some of the more serious deficiencies in the U.S. experience.

RIGHT-WING PROPOSALS

"School Choice" or Vouchers: Abolishing Public Education

Both the religious and secular right support dismantling the public education infrastructure and replacing it with a system in which public tax funds are used for the payment of tuition at private and parochial schools. The theory is that once the law of the marketplace is applied to education, it will encourage competition and thus raise standards—particularly in impoverished areas. However, it is assumed that all parents have access to information about better schools, and the opportunity to choose them. For those unable to make this choice, we can envision a system of second-class schools separating the haves from the have-nots.

A voucher system would subsidize further middle-class flight from city schools. The problems faced by student populations made up disproportionately of poor children would be exacerbated within the public school system. Poverty, and its accompanying pathologies, would not have been removed from the education system, but merely increasingly ghettoized. In the name of helping the poor, the radical right pushes a policy that would primarily subsidize better schooling for those who already have the money to send their children to good private schools, while offering no real guarantee of better schooling for those currently caught within an impoverished inner-city education system. Despite these dire problems with a voucher system, the 104th Congress has been very receptive to arguments to dismantle the public school system.

Add a Religious Equality Amendment to the Constitution

The "crown jewel" of the Christian Coalition's *Contract with the American Family* is the misleadingly named "Religious Equality Amendment." Under the proposed amendment "all citizens, including students, would be free to express their faith in noncompulsory settings and in ways that affirm their convictions without infringing upon the rights of others."

Taken literally, such an amendment would only reaffirm what was ruled constitutional by the Supreme Court in its 1985 *Wallace v. Jaffree* ruling, which stated that while states couldn't introduce legislation that explicitly declared that moments of silence were to be used for voluntary school prayer, they were permitted simply to introduce moments of silence, which the students could choose to use as they pleased. Moreover, in 1990 the Supreme Court upheld the Equal Access Act, which allowed students to form religious clubs (including bible studies clubs) at school and to use school property for their events after hours.

The agenda behind the REA is more coercive than it appears. Supporters seek to overturn the limit the Supreme Court has placed on how far states can go in "suggesting" that students pray. They also want to pave the way for prayer at public student gatherings such as commencements and sporting events. While students wouldn't actually be coerced into prayer, they would in effect be corralled into a religious ceremony at which students and teachers prayed aloud to a God not everyone believed in. More incidents would occur like the one in Utah, where a Jewish high school student fled her graduation ceremony after classmates launched into a Christian hymn.

The Coalition to Preserve Religious Liberty, an alliance of over fifty national religious, educational, and civil liberties organizations, including the Baptist Joint Committee and Evangelicals for Social Action, is campaigning against the REA. The Clinton administration has also come out against the amendment by publishing guidelines that stress that students already have a right to engage in prayer, to wear religious clothing to school, and to carry the Bible with them.

Defund Head Start

The United States has fewer publicly provided preschool places for children than other industrial democracies—and many fewer than the Scandinavian countries, the Netherlands, and Germany. Many children do not begin their education until kindergarten. Yet modest proposals to increase the number of state-funded preschool places, such as Head Start, have met with furious opposition. The religious right opposes Head Start because they believe it represents a further governmental push to indoctrinate children with "secular humanism." The secular right opposes it because they dislike any governmental expansion in the social arena. The current Congress is attempting to defund the program.

Repeal Goals 2000

Goals 2000 is a federal program created in 1994 which provides for a voluntary national system of standards and certification to enhance workforce skills. Goals 2000 encourages local districts to involve parents, businesses, and the community in the development of standards for local schools, and in the cultivation of workplace-related skills for youngsters unlikely to progress onto college. Although the standards contained in Goals 2000 are voluntary, states that refuse to implement them forfeit some federal funding.

The Goals 2000 legislation has been relentlessly criticized by the religious right for the content of the standards, particularly the standards for U.S. and world history. During their campaign to repeal Goals 2000, religious right leaders have erroneously claimed that Goals 2000 establishes school-based health clinics required to give out condoms, and that students would be forced into community service. Responding to pressure from the right, California, New Hampshire, and Virginia have passed legislation barring implementation of Goals 2000. A few other states are also considering such measures.

POSITIVE ALTERNATIVES

Innovations in education *are* needed. In critiquing the radical right's agenda, we are not defending all aspects of the existing system, a system that often produces poorly educated youngsters who graduate from (or drop out of) dilapidated schools, after being taught by overworked teachers in intolerable social environments. There is no reason for Armchair Activists not to use their dissatisfaction with the education system to push for other alternatives, and every reason not to let right-wingers seize the initiative on this issue.

Many of the advances made in education this century have been due to experimental techniques and classes, pioneered by Elisabeth Montessori, and seen more recently in the Alternative School movement. In the last few years, a number of alternative schools, often specializing in certain subject matters—art, science, media technology, and so on—have emerged around the country and attained encouraging results. Some inner-city magnet schools have been set up specifically to attract back into the city students whose families have migrated to the suburbs.

Anne Dodd, a Maine-based education theorist, offers the model of the Mast Landing Elementary School in Freeport, Maine. This single school offers three different education approaches within the one institution, from which parents can choose: traditional education, single-age-group non-graded learning, and multigrade classes. Parents and students have a say in what type of education children receive, without all being herded into a single system.

Dodd believes this type of education should be extended throughout the school system. In the meantime, state-funded schools that specialize in certain subject areas and experimental teaching techniques should be encouraged and expanded, Dodd says. Model schools include the Bronx High School of Science, the High School of Performing Arts in Manhattan (of *Fame* fame), the Boston Latin School, and El Puente in Brooklyn (see profile below). These schools remain within the public sector, and hence do not have the destructive impact of private and parochial schools supported by vouchers, yet they offer exceptional educational opportunities.

How This Issue Affects You

At some stage education directly affects everyone—whether you are in school, teach in a school, have kids in school, or know someone who does. The sour fruits of right-wing reform would

El Puente: An Alternative in Public Education

Based in an old church building, El Puente Academy for Peace and Justice exudes a more friendly atmosphere than the surrounding public schools in Brooklyn, New York. There are no metal detectors and no bars on the windows. The classrooms are separated from the teachers' common room area only by a flimsy divider. The walls are covered in student-painted murals, including one of Martin Luther King, Jr.

Originally a community center serving the mainly immigrant community of South Side Williamsburg, El Puente (The Bridge) was converted into a school in 1992 as part of New York City's New Visions School Project, a program to establish alternative schools within the public sector. In turn, New Visions is part of a national project, known as the Coalition for Essential Schools, which is trying to reform public education by reaching out to students through innovative teaching techniques and curricula that integrate the youngsters' experiences into the classroom. These schools often concentrate on one particular area of learning, and provide environments that depart from the coercive, bureaucratic ones of large urban high schools.

Because the school is small, teacher-student relationships are far more personal than in most schools, and the hours more flexible—many of the kids stay for after-hours classes, some until 9 P.M. Teachers (most of whom are themselves fresh out of college) have the time to work with individual students on specific projects, some of which involve community research, such be a culture truly dumbed down, with no understanding of other societies and belief structures, and intolerant of diversity within its own borders. In a modern world where information is power, such a culture would not flourish. Destroying the public education infrastructure of this country may be easier than re-

as tracking pollution levels in the area the youngsters live in and compiling photography exhibits of the locality.

El Puente combines a traditional academic approach (math, science, English, social studies, and Spanish are mandatory) with a more participatory, inventive curricula. The school specializes in media studies and has state-of-the-art computer and video technology. Students have access to over thirty computers and spend much time doing research over the Internet, studying how the modern media functions, and working on projects that explore inner-city realities often ignored by much of the press.

According to Miriam Greenberg, a teacher at the school who coordinates its media studies program, "The ideal is to have these schools arise organically out of communities, to have very active parent groups, and a sense that the school is embedded in its surroundings, and to have what is taught in schools relevant to the lives of the students—which came out of the multicultural approach." Quality education, she stresses, should be "an experience that speaks to the needs and the history of the community we're in."

Although the school is new, the students are already scoring higher on their Regents tests than those in other schools in the area. El Puente's success shows that with some positive innovations, public education can be reformed—even in areas where the odds are against the kids.

pairing it, but it would have devastating long-term consequences.

Censorship, the forced imposition of religion, and the abandonment of innovative classroom techniques all would render
education a more coercive experience. An overtly rigid system
would cause students' capacity for critical thinking to atrophy. In
addition, the replacement of medically accurate sex education
with fear-based abstinence curricula in the age of AIDS would
have serious private and public health ramifications.

We all benefit by sharing a commitment to the best possible
education for America's children. They are the leaders of tomor-
row and will mold the society of the future—something of which
the radical right is well aware. For those who don't subscribe to
the worldview of Pat Robertson, Robert Simonds, and Phyllis
Schlafly, it is time to spring into action!

What You Can Do: Action Sampler

Get Involved in School Board Elections

One of the more effective ways of countering the radical right is
to prevent or overturn their electoral successes, especially at the
school board level. The right's strategy of taking over the school
boards across the country is built on the assumption that the majority of people do not vote. When confronted with religious
right candidates, form active coalitions with other community
members to generate alternative candidates and platforms. And
the next time election season rolls around, don't pass up the opportunity to ensure that quality candidates are elected. You may
even consider running for the office yourself.

Fight Censorship

Parents, educators, and concerned citizens can effectively mobilize to support the freedom of expression when it is in jeopardy.
The law is on your side, as the Supreme Court has ruled that
schools may remove materials based on educational criteria
only—but not on ideological, political, or religious grounds.

Organizing strategies vary, but your role in a censorship battle can be to send out a "censorship alert" to potential community allies: librarians, bookstore owners, school personnel, members of the clergy, arts organizations, senior citizen groups, and business organizations. You can contact your local library or county government for a list of community organizations in your area.

If vocal protest from the community is not enough to counter the censors, People for the American Way, a nonprofit organization committed to countering the radical right, offers further resources.

Technical assistance. People for the American Way has created the Freedom to Learn Project, which monitors school censorship activity and provides communities confronting such efforts with materials, guidance on organizing, and logistical and legal assistance. Its hotline number is 1-800-326-PFAW.

An Activist's Guide to Protecting the Freedom to Learn ($13.95). This kit published by People for the American Way provides information and tools for organizing public education advocates to combat censorship efforts, defend public schools from political attacks, and participate in school board elections. To order, contact:

People for the American Way
2000 M Street, NW, Suite 400
Washington, DC 20036
(202) 467-4999

Support Quality Sex Education Programs

If you are experiencing controversies over sex education in your community, the Sexuality Information and Education Council of the United States (SIECUS) offers a Community Action Kit to support comprehensive sex education. It includes strategies for community organizing, analyses of comprehensive versus fear-based sex education, and guidelines for evaluating sex education materials. It also includes reproducible materials for handouts or posters. Action Kits are $19.95. Technical assistance is also available to activists. Contact:

SIECUS
130 West 42nd Street, Suite 350
New York, NY 10036
(212) 819-9770

Sample Letter

The following letter is to a local school board president in response to a censorship campaign.

Dear [Name of School Board President]:

It has come to my attention that my daughter will no longer be able to borrow one of the classic American novels by John Steinbeck from the River District School's library. I understand that *Of Mice and Men* has only been removed temporarily, in response to a series of attacks by critics who claim that the book "undermines traditional values." As the fate of this book will be

---

Questions to Ask School Board Candidates

1. Describe your personal experience and involvement with the public schools within the past five years that qualifies you as a school board member.
2. What would be your highest priorities for the school district?
3. What do you see as the school district's role in educating students who face the problems of poverty, family problems, and/or lack of the English language?
4. If elected, what changes would you seek to make in school district policies and/or programs?
5. Do you support the constitutional provision for a separation between church and state?
6. As individuals, children are allowed to pray now in all public schools. Should this right be expanded in any way?
7. What is your position on the use of public tax funds, currently supporting public schools, for the payment of tuition at private and parochial schools (a "voucher" system)?
8. What is your position relative to teaching creationism as an alternative to the theory of evolution to students in public schools?

decided pending an investigation by the school board in the upcoming months, I wanted to express my concern.

The views of the small group of people pushing the ban do *not* represent the views of the entire community, yet they are intent on deciding what all students should not read. This suppression of ideas is clearly an act of censorship. I ask that the book be returned to the shelves as soon as possible.

It may be that these censors have a right to prevent their children from reading *Of Mice and Men,* but under no circumstances should they be allowed to deny my daughter the opportunity to do so. If the school board caves in to their sectarian demand, I fear that more intolerant requests will soon follow.

9. What do you think is an appropriate breadth of content for sex education courses? Do you support including a wide range of preventative techniques to prepare students to protect themselves against AIDS, sexually transmitted diseases, and unwanted pregnancies?

10. Are you affiliated with any organizations? Please name those who sponsor or endorse you and those from which you have requested endorsements.

11. What role should the school board play in the selection and approval of text and library books?

12. What do you see as the primary role of the school guidance counselors? To what degree should they be free to make decisions based on their experience, professional knowledge, and understanding of district policies and philosophy?

SOURCE: Adapted from Frederick Clarkson and Skipp Porteous, *Challenging the Christian Right: The Activist's Handbook* (Great Barrington, MA: Institute for First Amendment Studies, 1993), pp. 137-140.

Let's show our children that ideas, even controversial ones, have free rein in our school—and indeed, in our country.

Sincerely,

Armchair Activist

6

Welfare:
The War on the Poor

When one visualizes the Great Depression of the 1930s, a stark and tragic poverty comes to mind. One thinks perhaps of an isolated street scene in a Walker Evans photograph, revealing a man in a worn overcoat down on his luck, standing gaunt-faced in a weather-beaten doorway. It's an almost romantic notion of hard times—when the poor were deserving but deprived; when the poor wanted to work but couldn't. Much of the debate in contemporary America seems to be stripped of such sympathy. It has become commonplace to blame the least powerful, the poorest, and the unluckiest for all the ills facing the country today.

During the Depression, it was believed that society, not the huddled masses, had failed. The federalization of relief initiated in the 1930s was a dramatic shift from the previous "hands off" strategy. Programs such as the Civilian Conservation Corps, Federal Emergency Relief, and many public works schemes, designed to provide the able-bodied with employment, were enacted. In addition, social insurance policies were created to act as a safety net for times of need. Many of these, notably unemployment insurance, Social Security, Aid to Dependent Children (later renamed Aid to Families with Dependent Children, or AFDC), and Aid to the Aged, Blind, and Disabled (later to become Supplemental Security Income, or SSI), are still with us.

Although conservatives fought against the New Deal, and against the growth of welfare during President Johnson's Great Society, over time many came to accept safety net programs as both inevitable and even socially desirable—serving to appease those excluded from the economic mainstream. Nixon expanded several programs, as did Reagan—though at the same time, they cut others. The compromise between capitalism and the realities of a mass industrial society with certain democratic expectations has been labeled by Michael Lind and other political commentators a "Social Market."

The New Right, however, rejects the Social Market and embraces the thinking of Austrian theorist Friedrich A. Hayek, who argued in the 1940s against welfare policies because they preempted competition and put society on a "road to serfdom." Current House Majority Leader Dick Armey wrote in the winter 1993

Facts Most People Don't Know About Welfare

Assumption: Teen mothers make up a large percentage of the welfare caseload.
Reality: Only 8 percent of mothers on welfare are teenagers. Less than three percent of poor families are headed by women younger than nineteen.[1]

Assumption: Families on welfare have lots of children.
Reality: The typical welfare family includes two children, about the same as the average American family.[2]

Assumption: Welfare checks are larger than they should be.
Reality: The average welfare mother receives $366 a month. Even with food stamps worth $295, this is still 31 percent below the poverty line for a family of three.[3] AFDC benefits alone have lost about a third of their value since 1979.[4]

Assumption: African-Americans make up most of the welfare caseload.
Reality: Although minorities are significantly overrepresented, the welfare caseload is not dominated by any one race. 39 percent of AFDC parents are white, 37

issue of *Policy Review* of soon being "able to advance a true Hayekian agenda, including . . . the elimination of the family-destroying welfare dole. . . . History is now on the side of freedom."

In other words, a person is truly free only if there is a near-complete absence of mediating public institutions between him/herself and the market. This is radically different from the idea that has dominated social thinking for the better part of this century: that at some point, the government has to intervene to ensure the population has food to eat, shelter, education, and access to health care.

To convince people that taking away this basic safety net is in their best interest, the New Right scapegoats poor people and

---

percent are black, 18 percent are Latino, 2.8 percent are Asian, and 1.4 percent are Native American.[5]

Assumption: Welfare recipients stay on the rolls indefinitely.
Reality: 70 percent of women applying for welfare receive benefits for less than two years; only 8 percent remain for eight years or more.[6]

Assumption: People on welfare could find work if they wanted to.
Reality: There just aren't enough jobs for workers with little or no skills that pay a living wage. Full-time year-round work at minimum wage puts a woman and two children $3,000 below the poverty line—with no health care or child care coverage.[7]

Assumption: The existence of welfare encourages out-of-wedlock births.
Reality: Research has found that AFDC benefits do not influence a single mother's decision to have a child; nor do they influence mothers already on welfare to have more children.[8]

antipoverty programs, and accuses the welfare state of promoting illegitimacy, abortion, promiscuity, the disintegration of the family, and sloth. Single mothers are called "welfare queens," their children "welfare tickets."

The War on Poverty has turned into a War on the Poor. Proposals to introduce strict limits on the aid available to single mothers—especially teenage single mothers—have all passed in the House. But it should be emphasized that two-thirds of AFDC recipients are children. Denying parents benefits because of their "immoral" behavior denies food, shelter, and clothing to the millions of impoverished children who are dependent on these parents. You can't punish one and not punish the other. A real debate on welfare reform should concentrate on eradicating poverty, not on eliminating public assistance and punishing the poor.

DISTORTIONS ABOUT WELFARE

"Welfare is a giant tax burden."

A common tactic of the radical right is to pit the middle class against the poor. Welfare, however, is not a major tax burden to the middle class. A family earning $50,000 annually typically contributes $615 a year—a mere $1.69 a day—to federal programs that support poor people, including the elderly and disabled.[9] These programs are designed to provide protection against economic hardships for *everyone* in America. Social Security and Medicare, unemployment insurance, Medicaid, food stamps, and AFDC are a critical safety net in time of need—for an economically squeezed middle class as much as any other group.

"Welfare is bankrupting the country."

"Welfare is killing us! . . . It's going to kill our nation!" Star Parker, radio personality and founder of the Los Angeles Coalition on Urban Affairs, yelled to a room packed with four thousand of the Christian Coalition's members in 1995.[10] With so much attention focused on the cost of welfare, most people are surprised to learn that only 1 percent of the total federal budget is spent on Aid to Families with Dependent Children.[11] Total federal spending on AFDC, food stamps, Medicaid for AFDC recipients, and other programs known as welfare, make up a mere 6 percent of all federal entitlement spending and only 3–4 percent of the total federal budget.[12] No matter what the right wants you to think, this percentage of the budget is not responsible for the country's deficit.

In contrast to the $12 billion spent by the federal government yearly on AFDC—which recipients urgently need to pay for food, clothing, and housing for themselves and their kids—there is the enormous defense budget: $242 billion in 1996, a figure $7 billion higher than the Pentagon itself had asked for. When it comes to arguments for balancing the budget, it seems that the New Right is far more concerned with cutting social programs than with a numerical balancing of revenues with spending.

"Welfare promotes illegitimacy."

The welfare debate is dominated by the idea that public assistance encourages women to have children out of wedlock. "I don't think we can deal with welfare in this country without dealing with illegitimacy," said Texas Senator Phil Gramm, who has proposed some of the most drastic cuts in funding, to the *Los Angeles Times* (August 3, 1995). "This problem has reached crisis proportions. We've got to eliminate financial incentives for people to have babies out of wedlock." The system's problems are primarily framed as female-created, with "welfare queens" labeled promiscuous, selfish, and deceptive.

Arguing that the government's role is to restore "traditional family values," the welfare debate has shifted from how to deal with poverty to how to modify the "immoral" behavior of the poor. A letter to Congress signed by the Family Research Council, the Eagle Forum, the Traditional Values Coalition, the Christian Coalition, and Concerned Women for America states that "A major change in the behavior of young men and women will occur only when the prospect of having a child out of wedlock bears such immediate, tangible economic consequences that those concerns override all other considerations."

While the increasing number of single parents is a cause of expanding welfare rolls, this does not mean that the existence of

AFDC is the major explanation for the increase in unwed child-bearing. That most welfare families are headed by single women signifies not that these women had their children just because a federal safety net exists to support them, but rather that families headed by single mothers are the ones most eligible for benefits. The women do not become single parents *because* of welfare.

In addition, women receive about 4C percent less in inflation-adjusted dollars in AFDC benefits today than they did twenty years ago—hardly a child-bearing incentive.[13] Monetary incentive theories are further debunked by the fact that in Idaho, Montana, Maine, and New Hampshire, states with some of the more generous welfare payments, the illegitimacy rate is low; while states with low welfare payments, such as those in the Deep South, have high illegitimacy rates. As noted conservative James Q. Wilson writes about illegitimacy, "Clearly, there is some important cultural or at least non-economic factor at work, one that has deep historical roots and that may vary with the size of the community and the character of the surrounding culture."[14]

"Welfare encourages teen pregnancy."

"The welfare state and its programs have the effect of encouraging 12-year-old girls to have children and 15-year-old boys to promiscuously impregnate them," Newt Gingrich has said.[15]

Gingrich's comment is a product more of an overactive imagination than of fact: Only 1 percent of all mothers on welfare are under the age of eighteen, according to the U.S. Department of Health and Human Services. Even when eighteen- and nineteen-year-olds are figured in, the percentage of teen mothers on welfare is still a low 8 percent.

Ironically, religious right groups who attack single teenage mothers are also the most active in limiting their access to sex education and to abortion.

"Welfare fosters the breeding of inferior people."

Charles Murray, peddler of controversial social theory and hero of New Right thinkers, believes welfare is bad policy not only because it encourages women to have children out of wedlock but because it encourages the "wrong" women to do so. In 1994

Murray and Richard Herrnstein published *The Bell Curve,* presented as a work of science but considered by many as a deeply racist tract. In it, they argued that the government should take away welfare benefits so as to prevent the breeding of genetically inferior people. The thesis, writes Charlotte Allen in the *Washington Monthly:* "Take away the check and you will shrink the size of the 'underclass,' [not by spurring them on to self-sufficiency] . . . but by ensuring that they won't be born." [16]

Murray condemns welfare by asserting that "The United States already has policies that inadvertently social-engineer who has babies, and it is encouraging the wrong women. . . . The technically precise description of America's fertility policy is that it subsidizes births among poor women, who are also disproportionately at the low end of the intelligence distribution." *The Bell Curve* argues that "undesirable" social traits the authors link with low IQ—such as poverty—are in turn associated with being African-American.

Murray's idea that poor people with low IQs—particularly African-Americans—shouldn't have children ought to have no place in the welfare debate. Poverty doesn't equal stupidity. On average, the poor are less educated than those who are not, but this is a product of lack of opportunity, not genetic inferiority. Furthermore, the "underclass" isn't procreating at a greater rate than any other group in society. The birthrates of mothers receiving AFDC and those not receiving it are nearly identical. [17]

"The welfare system has caused an increase in poverty and traps people in a dependency culture."

"Government programs designed to give a helping hand to the neediest of Americans have instead bred . . . more poverty," states the *Contract with America.* [18]

The fact is that in 1964, the year President Johnson declared the Great Society's War on Poverty, the poverty rate was 19 percent. Today it is 14.5 percent. [19] It is logical to conclude that had Johnson not called for new programs to help the poor (and had those programs not continued and expanded during a time when the *New York Times* ran regular articles reporting starvation in the United States), there would be an even greater poverty gap, especially as the "full employment" of the 1960s no longer exists.

Nevertheless, during a House debate on welfare, Representative John Mica (R-FL) held up a sign stating *Don't Feed the Alligators.* "Unnatural feeding and artificial care creates dependency," said Mica. "I submit that with our current handout, non-work welfare system we've upset the natural order." Moments later Representative Barbara Cubin (R-WY) compared people on welfare with pen-reared wolves unwilling to leave their cages.[20]

Dependent behavior is blamed for the breakup of the family structure, particularly within the black community. John Perkins, publisher of the Mississippi magazine *Urban Family* (and an African-American) writes: "Programs like AFDC, combined with food stamps and housing assistance, although meant for good, have broken up more families than slavery ever did."

It is often suggested that people choose welfare instead of work, and that they then grow dependent on it. But, while there is evidence of long-term reliance on welfare, it is not usually continuous dependency. Rather, families seem to go through cycles of being on and off of government aid. Ninety percent of all welfare "spells" end within five years, seventy percent within two years, and fifty-six percent of welfare recipients are able to get off of welfare within one year. But, the return to welfare is often equally swift. According to the Urban Institute, at the end of five years, seven out of ten of those who left have returned.

These figures suggest that people are trying to get off public assistance, but can't. Four out of five current recipients state that they would leave AFDC if they had a minimum wage job that provided health care. But even if they do find a job, the current minimum wage is $1.75 under the $6 an hour needed to keep a family of three out of poverty. Welfare mothers with limited skills find it nearly impossible to earn enough to support their families. The right's proposals, such as limits on benefits and work requirements, and the outright abolition of some programs, are geared not toward making the poor self-sufficient, but simply toward removing them from welfare rolls.

A more positive response would be to make it more practical for the poor to work—by providing child care, health care, job training, and counseling. This was the thinking behind many of the experimental state reforms approved by the Clinton administration. For example, under current federal law, women with children lose almost $1 of benefits for every $1 they earn after four months of employment. More than thirty states have obtained permission from the federal government to relax this rule, so as to create incentives for self-sufficiency. About twenty states have received permission to expand child care and Medicaid for women on welfare who find jobs.

"People on welfare are living the easy life."

In a speech to the Christian Coalition, Star Parker described her experience on welfare fifteen years ago, before she got "saved": "I was just fine, living in my modern apartment, with my subterranean garage, a fireplace in my unit and a Jacuzzi in the back. I had no problem taking my daughter and dropping her off at a government subsidized day care, selling off a few medical stickers a month to buy drugs, and hanging out at the beach all day. And when people try to tell you that people like me don't exist, you can tell them they're lying—because everyone else I knew that was on welfare was just like myself."[21]

But while right-wing figures may spout anecdotes of individuals taking advantage of the welfare system, Parker's life on welfare is not the norm. Their rhetoric is meant to fire up people's anger toward the poor, not present an accurate picture of poverty in America.

Only a dozen states meet the standard that allows a family on welfare to live above the poverty line. Average monthly AFDC benefits range from $923 in high-cost Alaska, down to $120 in Mississippi. On average, a family with one parent and two children receives $366 a month in AFDC benefits and a food stamp allowance of $295. This combined payment still leaves a family of three (a mom and two children) well below the poverty line.[22] The food stamps provide for food, but after paying rent, utilities, and telephone (which is a necessity for job-hunting), the mother has little if any money left for clothing or transportation.

RIGHT-WING PROPOSALS

Proceeding from myths about welfare, the following proposals for "reform" reflect the radical right's two-fold goal of cutting social spending and modifying social behavior.

Family Caps

The presumption that a woman on welfare has additional children for a few extra dollars a month in welfare has led to the family cap reform, which denies the small automatic increase in benefits a welfare family receives when a new baby is born. (On average, this amounts to $79 a month.) The family cap penalizes poor children while ignoring the root causes of illegitimacy. This measure, championed in the House by Rep. Clay Shaw (R-FL), is supported by Newt Gingrich and some of the leading religious right groups—although others disagree with the penalty because they fear that restricting a woman's benefits in this way will lead to more abortions.

Since employers do not give raises on the basis of family size and need, ask proponents of family caps, why should the government? But means-based programs are supposed to be based on need, and by definition a family with three children has more need than a family with two. Moreover, Congress has passed a $500-per-child tax credit to aid working families as they have more children.

The first state to implement family caps was New Jersey. There is no evidence that there has been any effect upon the birth rate, notwithstanding a preliminary study by June O'Neill, an economist at Baruch College, which found lower birth rates among women on welfare in the months following its passage. Nine states had copied New Jersey's plan by July 1995, the month Rutgers University released a study showing that the reduction in the birthrate was *not* attributable to the family cap, and that O'Neill's results were best explained by a general decline in births, a slight decline in "illegitimacy," and most importantly, a delay in reporting new births: "It seems that many women mistakenly thought they'd be cut off from welfare altogether if they had another kid," said Michael Laracy, who has studied New Jersey's welfare policy for seventeen years. "When they realized they'd only lose the additional cash payments but could still get food stamps and Medicaid, they reported the additional births." [23]

Fingerprint 'em

To contain welfare fraud, fingerprinting has been suggested to discourage recipients from registering for benefits in more than one state—a measure critics claim would cost more than it would save. This draconian sanction implies that nobody on welfare can be trusted. Applying for welfare is degrading enough for people down on their luck; fingerprinting would mean treating them as if they were criminals.

Give Control to the States

Proposals for state autonomy, which would allow states to design their own welfare systems with "block grants" from the federal government, have been passed by both houses of Congress, on the assumption that individual states are better equipped to detect welfare fraud and distinguish the deserving from the undeserving. The proposed block grants allocated for welfare would include no requirement to continue federal protections that provide a safety net for all of those in need.

Block grants would be capped at specific sums. The result would be many benefit denials to needy families during recessionary periods when welfare applications would increase but funding would remain fixed. Logically, welfare programs should expand during an economic downturn; with block grants, the reverse would occur.

If state autonomy becomes a reality, we may also see a "race to the bottom" as states attempt to outdo one another in the harshness of their policies, in order to provide a disincentive for people to participate in their welfare systems.

Cut Teens Off

Despite the fact that only 1 percent of single mothers on welfare are under the age of eighteen, punitive provisions to stop "children having children" have been at the center of the welfare debate. Gingrich's proposed Personal Responsibility Act (PRA) bars single mothers under the age of eighteen from receiving AFDC unless they live at home, marry the biological fathers, or marry individuals who legally adopt the child. These restrictions don't take into account that many teens who get pregnant have a history of family abuse and neglect, and many are impregnated by adults unconcerned with the girls' future. The rise of teen pregnancy in the United States is a concern, but there is no evidence that cutting welfare will curb this. Senator Daniel Moynihan (D-NY), voicing the opinion of most researchers, has said: "We really don't know what to do [about illegitimacy], and anyone who thinks that cutting benefits can affect sexual behavior doesn't know about human nature."[24]

Administer Welfare through Private Charities

In the *Contract with the American Family,* the Christian Coalition advocates "enactment of legislation to enhance contributions to private charities as a first step toward transforming the bureaucratic welfare state into a system of private and faith-based compassion."

The Bible provides a clear calling to minister to the poor—and indeed, church-based charities do perform an invaluable service helping the needy in communities across the country. However, a system of private philanthropy is economically unrealistic, and socially undesirable. Yet it would serve the religious right's agenda in two ways: It would shift power from the federal government to the church, and it would allow the church to control the behavior of the poor.

The evangelical purpose of this proposal is clear. An article about local charitable organizations in the May/June 1995 issue of *Christian American,* the magazine of the Christian Coalition, states: "Private programs . . . offer an element that no government program could possibly give: faith in God."[25]

While religion may motivate a person to climb out of poverty, it should not be forced upon those in need. Nor should private charities determine who is and who isn't deserving of aid, which would be the case if all welfare projects were admininistered by the Christian right. This kind of discrimination can be seen in a church charity set up by hard-core reconstructionist George Grant. Food was distributed only to nuclear families, excluding single mothers. To receive food, individuals were required to work at the church and report weekly for counseling from the church's "shepherds."[26]

Build Orphanages

If mothers are left destitute after welfare cuts, how are they going to raise their children? The Personal Responsibility Act suggests a simple solution: the benefits denied to mothers can be used to "establish and operate orphanages." It's an idea that led *Time* magazine to ask on its front cover, "Is Newt Gingrich's America really that heartless?"[27]

Offering orphanages as a "solution" assumes that if a woman doesn't have the means to raise her child, she is an unfit parent and her child should be taken away. Putting a woman in this predicament is perhaps the cruelest of punishments, and the proposal met with general public outrage.

Workfare and Participation Mandates

Since the late 1960s, Congress has taken steps to change AFDC from a no-strings-attached entitlement (where all poor single mothers were eligible) to a program where people would have to participate in some kind of work-related activity in order to get full income support. In 1981, Congress for the first time allowed states to require welfare recipients to work for their benefits in unpaid community service jobs (known as "workfare"). In the 1988 Family Support Act, Congress reaffirmed that work should replace welfare, and provided added funds for states to run work-directed activities and to provide child care.

States have expanded the share of people participating in work-directed activities, but funding constraints have limited the numbers. As the Congressional Budget Office has shown, providing training or requiring workfare is expensive: day care has to be provided; supervisors have to be paid; administrators must design and manage the program; welfare recipients have to be convinced to go.

When asked about welfare, Pat Robertson, who in his youth

worked among the poor, now quotes Paul's advice: "If anyone
will not work, neither let him eat." [28] This attitude has spawned
some unrealistic measures for workfare. Gingrich's proposed
Personal Responsibility Act mandates workfare, but would provide no money to initiate it or the supporting programs—such as
meaningful job training and education—that would be needed.
It simply gives states a limited sum of money (less than they have
under the current system) and decrees that increasing percent-
ages of recipients work. It pledges not to increase the block
grant funding if more people apply for the program. People receiving assistance would thus confront a work requirement without any of the tools to make a successful transition to
employment.

Workfare *could* be positive if it were intended to help welfare
parents gain independence, rather than simply push people into
job markets where they are not needed, wanted, or supported.
Many progressive reformers support workfare if it includes education, training courses, and job search activities, if funding for
child care and transportation is included, and if it is part of a
broader transformation that provides health coverage to low-
wage earners.

POSITIVE ALTERNATIVES

Some states and counties have demonstrated that they can conduct effective, large-scale welfare-to-work programs that both
increase the earnings of participants and save money for taxpayers. Model programs, like Greater Avenues for Independence
(GAIN) in Riverdale, California, strive to improve the lives of
people on welfare. GAIN boosted the incomes of those who participated while reducing AFDC payments, showing a "50 percent
increase in earnings and a 15 percent decline in welfare outlays,
thereby returning to taxpayers nearly $3 for every $1 spent to
run the program." [29]

Unfortunately, most workfare programs haven't been this effective. Experts agree there is no silver bullet to enable success
among the impoverished. In the short term, it is, in fact, less expensive for the government simply to give the poor money than

to provide them with the training and education they need to get meaningful, quality jobs. Thus welfare and poverty traps cannot be eradicated if the politicians' first priority is budget cutting.

"Does [our] mixed experience suggest that it is time to abandon the basic compromise of the welfare-to-work strategy?" asks Judith Gueron, president of Manpower Research Demonstration Corporation, which evaluated the GAIN program. "I argue that the answer is a compelling 'no' and that, quite to the contrary, our nation should now redouble its efforts to make this transformation succeed." [30] Unless a substantial number of people get off welfare and into jobs that pay a realistic salary before reaching proposed welfare time limits, the country will be faced with ever greater poverty.

It's the individual success stories of people who have achieved self-sufficiency through taking advantage of government education and social programs who provide the greatest hope. Alexa James grew up on welfare in California, but when she had a child of her own, she was determined to get off. Reading at a seventh-grade level at the age of twenty-two, she earned her GED with the help of New Chance, a government program designed specifically to help young mothers on AFDC who are school dropouts. Alexa was provided with child care, and within a few weeks she began working at a Summer Youth Employment Program job. She went on to complete a three-month nurse's aide training program at a local technical school and eventually got a job at a nursing home. Her certificate earned her a raise, from $6.70 an hour to $7.20 an hour, with benefits including medical and dental coverage, sick leave, and a two-week paid vacation.

Had Alexa been on welfare with food stamps, she would have received $6,924 a year plus medical benefits; had she been forced to work at minimum wage, she would have received $6,132 and no benefits. "Now I'm making enough to pay the bills and have a little bit of extra money I can put to the side. I can actually afford to do things with my daughter, or buy something for the house," says Alexa.

Helping people with low or very low income to escape no-hope, dead-end, minimum-wage employment is also the goal of a group called Working Capital, in Cambridge, Massachusetts. Working Capital is a nonprofit program that encourages self-employment through loans, business training, and group-based support to persons with limited access to resources, who wouldn't qualify for traditional business loans or credit. Over half of the borrowers are women, with most living in rural communities or inner cities.

Each participant joins a business loan group of four to ten business owners. Members then apply directly to their group for loans, which start at $500 and can increase to $5,000 (loan capital is obtained by Working Capital from regional and local banks, national foundations, and government agencies). All group members must be up to date on their loan payments before *any* group member can apply for another loan—this ensures that members pay their loans on time. (The loan repayment rate is over 97 percent.) Each business loan group serves as a base of support for members, who meet regularly to exchange ideas, share customer contacts, and build their business skills. Participants have included child care providers, taxicab owners, dressmakers, bakers, mechanics, and craftspeople.

Since October 1991, Working Capital has assisted more than 1,700 small businesses, distributing nearly 2,100 loans totaling over $1,800,000 in six states. Collectively, borrowers reported a 40 percent average increase in sales and 20 percent average increase in income after one year in the program.

"Social programs provide Band-Aids," says Jeffrey Ashe, founder and executive director of Working Capital, "while the root cause is lack of dignified employment. This program allows for dignified employment . . . and working through your own initiative . . . in your own community."

How This Issue Affects You

If you have a stable income, welfare is something to which you probably don't give much thought. Why, then, is this an issue to which you should pay attention?

Welfare is the ultimate insurance policy for Americans in time of need. You hope you'll never require it, but you just might. What if some tragedy pushes you down below the poverty line? You could be laid off from work; your marriage could break up; you could lose your health insurance; your job could be exported to another country. The purpose of welfare is to provide protection when hardship strikes, and to help people recover from life's hard knocks. And if this social safety net were removed, the psychic cost of allowing millions of its citizens to remain destitute and hopeless would be enormous to a wealthy society.

If the cuts currently proposed are implemented, more American children will suffer from hunger, malnutrition, homelessness, abuse, abandonment, and poor health. They will grow up in circumstances that pose grave risks to their future as adult citizens, thus impairing the next generation of American workers.

This debate isn't just about welfare, it's about poverty. The poor don't deserve to be scapegoated for the problems of this country. Your activism can help dispel the myths surrounding the issue, converting the current demagoguery on how to punish the poor into a democratic debate on how to eradicate poverty.

WHAT YOU CAN DO: ACTION SAMPLER

Get Involved with Community Poverty Programs

Working to alleviate poverty in your own community can be one of the most rewarding experiences you will ever have. You'll most likely find that volunteer opportunities in your area are plentiful—churches, synagogues, and civic organizations often run much-needed soup kitchens, literacy programs, and homeless shelters. If you've never personally experienced poverty, giving your time to such programs will put some faces on a problem that is often dehumanized in political discourse.

Speak Up

Perhaps the most helpful action you can take to clear the air for a constructive debate on welfare is to counter the misconceptions about the poor and poverty programs. Armchair Activists should take the opportunity to correct distortions about welfare whenever they are voiced: in a newspaper, in Congress, or on talk radio shows.

Sample Letter

The following is a sample letter to the editor written in response to a series of stories on welfare fraud.

Dear [Name of Editor]:

I'm writing in response to your exposé of the welfare system as a haven for swindlers. Welfare fraud does exist, but it is not the norm. Moreover, it occurs on a far smaller scale then the routine tax evasion that occurs throughout society. Most people on welfare are genuinely suffering from dire poverty, and they don't deserve to be stereotyped as cheaters making a profit off government support.

The typical person on welfare is a woman in her late twenties with two children who needs assistance for about two years. She isn't out to take advantage of the system, but to get back on her feet. She is by no means living a life of luxury.

If you ask this woman whether she chose to be on welfare, she'll tell you she had no other choice. And if you ask her how it feels, she'll probably tell you the shame is crushing: dealing with caseworkers who treat you like a number, getting funny looks in the supermarket checkout line when you pull out your food stamps, not being able to afford new shoes for your children. The stigma that is attached to being on welfare is enormous.

The poor are losing their champions in politics and government. Their plight will only worsen if they lose the compassion of their fellow citizens. Let's treat them with dignity, not disdain. We must find ways to make the welfare system more efficient and to prevent fraud, but not at the expense of those in need.

Sincerely,

Armchair Activist

7

Abortion:
Chiseling Away at Choice

Motherhood, according to the religious right, is the primary role of women—it is what God intended for the female sex. The writings of figures like Beverly LaHaye demonstrate an obsession with women who seek to avoid motherhood, particularly those who terminate pregnancy through abortion. Abortion is viewed by the religious right as an abomination, with pro-life groups around the country working to eliminate a woman's legal right to choose this procedure (a right affirmed in the 1973 *Roe v. Wade* Supreme Court decision). The abortion issue galvanized the religious right in the late 1970s, and it continues to do so today.

Opponents of abortion focus the debate on the sanctity of human life. However, the abortion issue is not only about the life of the fetus; it is also about the newfound independence of women. Having secured both contraceptive devices and the backup option of medically sound abortions, women, like men, are now free to have sex on their own terms. It was a twenty-six-year-old former used-car salesman named Randall Terry who in 1986 founded Operation Rescue, one of the most militant direct-action groups against abortion. Many of the die-hard members of the group were men in their twenties and thirties. Though "rescuers" portrayed themselves as heroic defenders of unborn babies, feminist writer Susan Faludi recalls an Operation Rescue protest in which "the spokesmen of the militant anti-abortion movement called feminists 'child-killers' and berated them for triggering 'breakneck' abortion rates. But more revealing was what they said under their breath: their whispered 'whores' and 'dykes' were perhaps their more telling epithets. Sexual independence, not murder, may have been the feminists' greater crime."[1]

With the rise of these militant groups like Operation Rescue, violence against clinics became common. Anti-abortion terror escalated during the 1990's, resulting in the murder of five abortion clinic workers. Clearly this movement is not simply about the sanctity of human life.

The defense of traditional paternal authority is at the heart of the anti-abortion movement. John Wilke, former president of the National Right to Life Committee, proclaimed that pro-choice women "do violence to marriage [because they] remove the right of a husband to protect the life of the child he has fathered in his wife's womb."[2] Randall Terry believes that an ideal society would enforce the submission of women: "God establishes that the man is the head of the home. . . . I'm here to tell you God created patriarchy."[3] Eleven states have laws on the books requiring a husband's consent or notification for a woman's abortion. However, these laws are unenforceable due to rulings such as a 1992 Supreme Court decision *(Casey v. Planned Parenthood of Southern Pennsylvania)* which held that spousal notification was an undue burden in obtaining an abortion, particularly for women in abusive or otherwise dysfunctional marriages.

Abortion is a legal right—but the overall strategy of the anti-abortion movement is to create a situation where this legal procedure is virtually impossible for women to obtain. Whether through legislation, litigation, and government regulation, or through intimidation, harassment, and terrorist violence, anti-abortion forces are making it harder and harder for women to gain access to abortion services—especially low-income, young, and rural women. There is a severe shortage of abortion providers today, and at least one out of ten women who want an abortion cannot get one.[4]

Although surveys reveal that most Americans are pro-choice, many are not strongly opposed to "small" restrictions upon that choice, such as limiting Medicaid funding for the procedure, imposing parental consent laws, mandating waiting periods, or prohibiting women in the United States armed forces from obtaining the procedure in military hospitals overseas. David Frum, author of the book *Dead Right,* explains:

> Republicans in favor of legal abortion . . . tend not to see abortion as a right that women must possess in order to achieve their full personhood. We think, instead, that, on balance, legal abortion produces less human misery than outlawing abortion would.[5]

Pro-choice Republicans may not like their party advocating restrictions on abortion, but they generally do not feel strongly enough about the issue to leave the party. Many pro-lifers, however, feel so strongly about the issue that they would abandon the party in the event the GOP abandoned its right-to-life platform. Since the Republican Party has become more reliant on the religious right's support, efforts to restrict access to abortion have been stepped up. As Representative Nita Lowey (D-NY) phrased it, "The Speaker [of the House, Newt Gingrich] won't take a sledgehammer to *Roe* when a chisel will do the trick instead."[6]

The 1994 elections saw a stunning loss in pro-choice seats in Congress. Anti-choice candidates gained 5 seats in the Senate and 38 seats in the House of Representatives. This created a clear anti-choice majority in the House, with 218 pro-life members, 146 pro-choice members, and 71 who have mixed records on the issue. Among Senators, 45 are anti-choice, 38 are pro-choice, and 17 have mixed records.[7] In addition, such anti-choice leaders as Jesse Helms, Orrin Hatch, Dick Armey, and Henry Hyde now hold leadership positions in Congress.

THE FAR RIGHT'S USE OF THE ABORTION ISSUE

A significant political convergence between the extreme faction of the antiabortion movement and the far right has occurred in recent years. While most pro-lifers are not affiliated with far right groups, white supremacist leaders use abortion as a bridge issue to reach those who may not at first be attracted to their ideology.

The racist right's take on abortion, as phrased by Planned Par-

enthood researchers, "resurrect[s] that most vicious piece of historical anti-Semitism: child-killing Jews."[8] Tom Metzger, leader of
the neo-Nazi skinhead group White Aryan Resistance, has said,
"Almost all abortion doctors are Jews. Abortion makes money for
Jews. Almost all abortion nurses are lesbians. Abortion gives
thrills to lesbians. Abortion in Orange County [California] is
promoted by the corrupt Jewish organization called Planned
Parenthood. . . . Jews must be punished for this holocaust and
murder of white children along with their perverted lesbian
nurses."[9]

There is also a convergence between antiabortion militancy
and militia activity. In 1994, Planned Parenthood released a
video of Matthew Trewhella, director of the fanatical "rescue"
group Missionaries to the Preborn, speaking at a U.S. Taxpayers
Party (USTP) convention in Wisconsin. "What should we do?"
Trewhella asked. "We should do what thousands of people across
the nation are doing. We should be forming militias."[10] The
USTP—founded in 1992 by the ultraconservative Howard
Phillips with a platform that claims, "The U.S. Constitution established a republic under God, not a democracy"—sold at the
conference a "Free Militia" manual on how to form an underground army. First on the manual's list of reasons to take up arms
is to defend the "right to life" against "legalized abortion."[11]

Howard Phillips ran for President on the USTP ticket in 1992.
During his campaign, Phillips produced antiabortion television
advertisements so gory that many TV stations requested that the
FCC permit them to broadcast them only during late-night
hours. One such ad showed pictures of dead and aborted fetuses
while a voice stated:

> In his paid television commercials presidential candidate
> Howard Phillips has shown graphic, grisly pictures of unborn
> children whose lives were extinguished intentionally with pre-
> meditation by hired killers described in the media as abortion-
> ists. Well, it is time to end the coverup. Here are some of the
> names, addresses, and faces of the abortionists who kill for
> money and who commit their grisly deeds in our state.

The photographs, names, and home addresses of a former
and current medical director of Planned Parenthood of Greater

Iowa were then shown while the narrator stated: "Howard Phillips urges you to contact these baby killers and urge them to mend their ways." "A vote for Howard Phillips," the narrator continued, "is a vote to prosecute the baby killers for premeditated murder." [12]

Randall Terry now stumps for the USTP. When he isn't doing that, his newest endeavor is the Christian Leadership Institute in upstate New York, which he bills as a "Christian retreat for male leaders" that will generate "fierce, militant, unmerciful warriors." [13]

Though the USTP has attracted few Republican politicians so far, Pat Buchanan and former members of Congress William Dannemayer (R-CA) and Ron Paul (R-TX) have spoken at USTP events. [14]

TACTICS OF THE RADICAL ANTIABORTIONISTS

Clinic Demonstrations and Blockades

Direct blocking of entrances to women's health care clinics and doctors' offices is the hallmark technique of Operation Rescue, which hopes, by doing this, to force these establishments to close their doors. Demonstrators chain themselves to the doors of a clinic or form a human chain around the building. This form of disruption peaked in 1989, with a total of 201 incidents of clinic blockades, resulting in 12,556 arrests. [15] Many blockaders are arrested multiple times—twelve members of Missionaries to the Preborn had been arrested a total of 1,123 times by 1994. Women entering blockaded clinics, even if only for a routine health exam, may be confronted by screaming picketers holding graphic photographs of fetuses and signs reading "Don't Kill Me, Mommy," or "Abortion Is Murder."

In response to these blockades, clinic defense groups have been formed. These are groups of pro-choice activists who prevent the clinic entrances from being blocked and allow all women to keep their appointments. They protect the entrances by forming walls with their bodies along the walkways to the clinic. Typically, antiabortion forces remain in the area and attempt to intimidate defenders or physically break through the defense lines.

Clinic Terrorism

Walking into some women's health clinics is like entering a high-security encampment. You'll see video cameras, armed guards, security booths, and locked doors. If the clinic has previously been under attack or there are demonstrators outside, you'll sense fear among the staff and patients: It is well known that hard-core anti-choice activists have engaged in bombing, arson, invasion, vandalism, assault and battery, death threats, kidnapping, burglary, and stalking in their crusade for the "unborn." In the 1990s five people who worked at clinics have been murdered. Several others have been wounded in shootings.

Violent and intimidating anti-choice actions began as isolated incidents in the late 1970s, but they have rapidly increased in frequency. While there was a total of 149 violent incidents between 1977 and 1983, in 1993 alone there were 434, according to the National Abortion Federation. In 1994, 66.7 percent of all clinics reported one or more types of violence.

Despite its long history, the overarching pattern of threats and violence against women's clinics only began to be investigated by the FBI in 1994, the day after Dr. John Britton and volunteer escort James Barrett were killed by Paul Hill in Pensacola, Florida. This was more than a year after the first murder by an antiabortion activist, Michael Griffin's killing of Dr. David Gunn, also in Pensacola. The media has been similarly reluctant to identify antiabortion violence with organized terrorism: When the New York Times (April 20, 1995) ran its first story covering the bombing in Oklahoma City, it included a list headlined "Other Bombings in America" spanning four decades. None of the forty officially documented bombings of women's health clinics were mentioned.[16]

Some of the more moderate antiabortion groups, like the National Right to Life Committee, have always condemned unlawful actions. However, over two dozen antiabortion leaders signed the public statement of Paul Hill's group Defensive Action, which supports the concept of "justifiable homicide," whereby it is morally acceptable and biblically mandated to kill abortionists and the people who work with them or protect them. Since the murder of Britton and Barrett, there have been two more killings, of Shannon Lowney and Leanne Nichols, both receptionists at women's health clinics in Brookline, Massachusetts. They were killed on December 30, 1994, by John Salvi.

Incidents of Violence and Disruption Against Abortion Providers 1977–1995

VIOLENCE	TOTAL NUMBER OF INCIDENTS FOR 1977–1995
Murder	5 (1 in 1993; 4 in 1994)
Attempted Murder	12 (2 in 1991; 1 in 1993; 8 in 1994; 1 in 1995)
Bombing	41
Arson	104
Attempted Bombing/Arson	69
Invasion	351
Vandalism	616
Assault and Battery	97
Death Threats	266
Kidnapping	2
Burglary	37
Stalking	271

DISRUPTION	
Hate Mail and Harassing Phone Calls	2,088
Bomb Threats	352
Picketing	9,124

CLINIC BLOCKADES	
No. of Incidents	639
No. of Arrests	33,719

SOURCE: National Abortion Federation

The Army of God Guide to Terrorist Tactics

Circulating among antiabortion terrorists is the Army of God manual, an underground handbook on how to conduct violent protests. The how-to guide gives the fundamentals of "improvised explosives" among its sixty-five tips on destroying or damaging clinics. Other tips include:

- Never make a bomb threat from anywhere but a pay phone.
- Put holes through clinic windows. The problem with .22 [-caliber weapons] is the noise—the Fourth of July and New Year's Eve are great times for gunshots.
- Hot-wire a bulldozer at a construction site, drive it to a clinic, jump off and let the bulldozer crash through a clinic wall.
- Be sure to wrap duct tape around any tools you use; it will not hold fingerprints.
- Extract Freon from the clinic's air-conditioning system. This repair is gonna cost major $$$!
- Dump a load of cow manure in front of the clinic.
- Block sewer pipes with concrete.
- Use a high-powered rifle to fire bullets into the engine block of a doctor's car.
- Look up survivalist magazines such as *Soldier of Fortune* or *Survivalist*. Guaranteed that you will be amazed, if not shocked, by the materials available!
- If terminally ill, use your final months to torch clinics; by the time the authorities identify you . . . you will have gone to your reward.[17]

RIGHT-WING PROPOSALS

Make Abortion a Crime

Banning abortion is, of course, the ultimate goal of all antiabortion organizations. The Christian Coalition has called in its *Contract with the American Family* for a constitutional amendment to "enshrine protection for unborn children." In Congress, Representatives Dornan (R-CA), Emerson (R-MO), Oberstar (D-MN), and Volkmer (D-MO) have introduced measures intended to amend the Constitution with "respect to the right to life."[18]

According to the National Abortion Rights Action League (NARAL), of the 99 state legislative bodies and the District of Columbia City Council, "37 oppose legal abortion and can be expected to enact virtually any obstacle to abortion." However, 42 can be expected to reject bills outlawing abortion, and 21 are closely divided. Though states are prohibited from banning abortion, the willingness to enact a ban demonstrates how vulnerable women's reproductive rights would be if the federal guarantees legalizing abortion were ever overturned.

The banning of abortion would have dire consequences for women. Prior to the *Roe v. Wade* decision, obtaining an abortion illegally was dangerous and expensive. Deaths from the procedure, often performed in unsanitary conditions with no anesthesia and inadequate precautions against hemorrhage or infection, were a major factor in maternal mortality before 1973. While affluent women could sometimes obtain an abortion from a private physician who was willing to certify a medical need for the procedure, or by traveling abroad or to a state where it was legal, this was not an option for the poor. Of low-income women surveyed in New York City in the 1960s, 77 percent said they had attempted a self-induced procedure.[19]

Stop Public Funding of Abortion

Three years after *Roe v. Wade,* Congress enacted the Hyde Amendment, barring Medicaid funding for abortion unless a woman's life was in danger. This legislation, upheld by the Supreme Court, was altered in 1993 to allow payment for abortions for women who are the victims of rape or incest. Before the

Hyde Amendment, one-third of all abortions (260,000 per year) were funded by Medicaid. After the amendment, many states followed the federal government's lead and also stopped funding "medically unnecessary" abortions.

The cost of an abortion represents nearly two-thirds the amount of the average monthly AFDC payment for a family of three. Raising money can take time, and often puts off an abortion by as much as two or three weeks. An estimated 22 percent of Medicaid-eligible women who have second-trimester abortions would have had first-trimester ones if not for the lack of public funds.[20] Twenty to 35 percent of Medicaid-eligible women who want to have an abortion are forced to carry their unplanned pregnancy to term, according to the Alan Guttmacher Institute. A few attempt self-induced abortions.

Congress, with the support of the Christian Coalition and the National Right to Life Committee, passed legislation denying payment for abortions in federal employee health plans except when the woman's life would be endangered by a full-term pregnancy, or in cases of rape or incest. President Clinton signed the bill in November 1995. Legislation denying abortion services to women in federal prison except in cases of life endangerment or rape has also been introduced, and measures have been passed that forbid women enlisted in the armed forces to obtain an abortion at military hospitals when stationed overseas, even if they pay for it with their own money.

Ban Abortions in Public Health Facilities

In *Webster v. Reproductive Health Services* (1989), the Supreme Court found that states could ban all abortion procedures from public hospitals and prohibit public employees from performing the procedure, except in cases where an abortion is necessary to save the life of the mother. Even private hospitals, which almost always have some involvement with the public sector—either by leasing land from local government or by participating in Medicaid/Medicare—can be considered "public" under the ruling. Five states currently have laws prohibiting the use of public facilities for the provision of abortion services.

Even though 93 percent of all abortions take place in clinics or doctor's offices, limiting hospital participation could still have devastating effects for some women. A restriction on in-hospital abortions prevents high-risk women who should have the procedure in a hospital, such as those with cancer, diabetes, or HIV, or those having a late-term abortion, from doing so. It would also block care in the case of severe fetal defects, which are almost always treated in hospitals. This in-hospital ban particularly affects low-income women, who often utilize hospitals—sometimes the only source of care in a community—for most of their medical care.

Prohibit Abortion Counseling

In *Rust v. Sullivan* (1991), the Supreme Court upheld "gag rules" that prohibit counselors and physicians in federally funded facilities from providing information or making referrals about abortion. When counseling a pregnant woman, employees in federally funded hospitals, family planning clinics, community health centers, migrant health centers, and sexually transmitted disease clinics would not be allowed even to mention abortion as an option—though critics argue that this violates medical ethics codes which enshrine the patient's right to full information. The Court approved a requirement that workers at family planning clinics tell women who ask about abortions that abortions are not an acceptable method of family planning, and refer them to prenatal care providers who promote the life and health of "mother and unborn child." Today, Louisiana, Montana, and North Dakota have gag rules, although the latter's has been ruled unconstitutional.

A federal gag rule, created by President Reagan in 1987, was kept in effect by President Bush, despite two attempts by Congress to overturn it. One of President Clinton's first acts in office was to eliminate the gag rule by executive order. The Christian Coalition, the NRLC, and the House Pro-Family Caucus have pushed Congress to overturn this order.

Enforce "Informed Consent" and Waiting Periods

Thirty-one states have abortion-specific "informed consent" laws, many of which require doctors to give women seeking abortions lectures and materials on fetal development, prenatal care, and adoption. Many of these laws prohibit a woman from obtaining an abortion for at least twenty-four hours after receiving the state-mandated lecture. According to NARAL, waiting period laws are currently being enforced in eleven states and have recently been considered in twenty-two others.

Anti-abortion activists rationalize these laws by saying that women need one last chance to think things through. However, these laws simply put one more barrier between a woman and her right to choose. Because of a shortage of doctors who perform abortions, many women have to travel hundreds of miles to a doctor's office. Mandatory waiting periods mean that women often have to make two trips, or stay overnight, which especially affect low-income women, single mothers, and young women, as well as inflict serious hardship on women who work and women who do not have access to cars or public transportation. Women may have to take multiple days off from work, and many are forced to leave families unattended or arrange for costly child care. Waiting periods also endanger women by increasing their exposure to harassment: In some cases, anti-choicers harass women at their homes (which they track down through license plate numbers) during the state-mandated delay.

In addition to these problems, the laws are demeaning, as they imply that women cannot make responsible decisions. Moreover, existing standard medical practices and informed consent requirements already ensure that clients have weighed the consequences and made an informed decision by the time they reach a hospital, clinic, or physician's office for a medical procedure.

Require Parental Consent

It is the hope of every parent that his or her child will turn to the parent when there is a crisis. And most do. In fact, NARAL reports that in the absence of specific legal requirements, more than three-fourths of all minors under sixteen involve one or both parents in their decision to have an abortion. But while positive relationships between parents and children are a good thing, they cannot be legislated. Nevertheless, states have attempted to do just that through mandatory parental consent and notification laws, now in force in twenty-nine states.

Some young women do not tell their parents that they are

pregnant because there is physical or emotional abuse in the home, or because their pregnancy is the result of incest. According to NARAL, 30 percent of minors who did not tell a parent about their abortion have experienced violence in the home or fear being forced to leave home. Studies show that family violence is often harshest during a family member's pregnancy. In an especially horrific case, a thirteen-year-old sixth grader from Idaho was shot to death by her father after he learned she intended to terminate a pregnancy caused by his acts of incest.

The Supreme Court has ruled that parental consent and notification laws are acceptable so long as the young woman has an alternative to telling her parents; under most state laws, she has the opportunity to attempt to obtain permission from a judge. But this judicial bypass is no guarantee of freedom of choice for young women. In many states, judges routinely refuse to grant abortions. One seventeen-year-old, an A student in Toledo, Ohio, who planned to attend college, testified that she was not emotionally or financially prepared for motherhood. She was denied permission for an abortion by a judge who stated that the girl had "not had enough hard knocks in her life."

Limit Abortion Training for Doctors

Eighty-four percent of all U.S. counties offer no abortion facilities, and the number of abortion providers declined by 8 percent between 1988 and 1992 (from 2,582 to 2,380), according to the Alan Guttmacher Institute. Despite this shortage, Rep. Tom DeLay (R-TX) has introduced legislation to undermine the Accreditation Council on Graduate Medical Education's new requirement that OB/GYN residency programs provide training in abortions.

Ban Late-Term Abortion

"The Partial Birth Abortion Ban of 1995," passed by the House and Senate, is an outright challenge to the legality of abortion. This broadly drafted bill would ban a late-term abortion procedure known as "dilation and extraction." This procedure is performed typically when a woman's life or health would be jeopardized if the pregnancy is continued or if there is a severe fetal abnormality—it is generally limited to pregnancies that are in the 20th to 24th weeks. Abortions performed late in a woman's pregnancy are difficult, and not taken lightly by patients or the medical team. They are also extremely rare—according to the Alan Guttmacher Institute, only slightly more than 1 percent of all abortions take place after 20 weeks gestation.

Those promoting the bill have given grotesque testimony to Congress regarding the procedure, illustrated with sensationalized drawings. The misleading phrase "partial-birth abortion" is not a medical term; it was invented solely for use in promoting this legislation. The legislation defines "partial-birth abortion" as one in which a woman "partially vaginally delivers a living fetus," a definition that is bizarre and vague, according to physicians who have reviewed it. President Clinton has vetoed this bill.

POSITIVE ALTERNATIVES

The promotion of policies to help prevent unintended pregnancies is one positive alternative in this debate. More effective use of contraceptives would lessen the need for abortion, yet right-wing forces are also trying to ban sex education in the schools and to cut federal and state funds for family planning services. As it is, the cost of contraceptive drugs such as the pill is substantial, and subsidized services are not available to all women. In most other developed countries contraceptive care is generally available to all women at little or no cost through their national health insurance plans. The Title X federal family-planning program provides education and contraception to low-income women. This successful program should be fully funded.

We should also support comprehensive sex education. The religious right demonizes sexuality in order to cultivate abstinence. But this only results in ignorance. Comprehensive sex education emphasizes abstinence, but also teaches young adults how to take responsibility when they do have sex, whether as a teen or as an adult.

Because of the lack of abortion providers, women must travel long distances to obtain the procedure, or be deprived of access altogether. North Dakota and South Dakota, for example, only have one abortion provider each. The Reproductive Rights Network of Boston formed the Abortion Access Project in 1992 to make abortion services more accessible in Massachusetts and elsewhere.

After the Abortion Access Project lobbied medical institutions in Massachusetts, one community hospital hired staff to perform abortions, and five hospitals changed their intake procedures to enable women to more easily schedule abortions without having a primary physician at the hospital. The project successfully pressured a publicly funded medical school to set up a course on abortion procedures, and supports changing the law to allow midwives, nurse practitioners, and physician's assistants to carry out first-trimester abortions.

The lack of abortion providers is due in part to the fact that many residency programs do not provide abortion instruction in their core curricula, with some offering it only as an elective. The National Abortion Federation along with other pro-choice organizations has launched a nationwide campaign to change medical school regulations and curricula with regard to abortion training.

To increase access to abortion services, pro-choice organizations around the country are also fighting against state restrictions on abortions such as waiting period and "informed consent" laws. Many people also support the approval of RU-486, the European "abortion pill," for use in this country. The availability of this drug would dramatically alter the abortion issue, for it would allow a woman to have an abortion at the earliest stage of her pregnancy, rather than waiting until the sixth or eighth week, which is the case for standard abortions.

No individuals seeking medical care or providing medical services should have to endure threats, harassment, or obstruction. And no individuals, no matter how strongly they feel about an issue, should be able to take the law into their own hands and prevent other citizens from exercising their legal rights. In response to violent incidents and disruptive protesters, abortion rights activists supported Freedom of Access to Clinic Entrances (FACE) legislation, which President Clinton signed into law in 1994. Under FACE it is a federal crime to use force, intimidation, or physical obstruction to interfere with reproductive health services. Violent offenders face up to $100,000 in fines and a year in prison for a first conviction, and up to $250,000 and three years in prison for subsequent offenses. The law does not restrict lawful and nonviolent demonstrations. Pro-choice activists continue to work to stamp out clinic violence by supporting the enforcement of FACE and raising public awareness about the issue.

How This Issue Affects You

Abortion is safe and legal, and a majority of Americans want to keep it that way. Reproductive health care is good medical and societal sense, affirming a woman's basic right to control her own body. Abortion has become part of mainstream medical practice, and to reverse this would be a giant step backward. Banning abortion won't prevent women from having the procedure; it will merely return us to the days of "back alley" abortions.

If you support a woman's right to choose, your activism is needed now more than ever. The 1994 elections—in which only 44.9 percent of eligible women voted—virtually undid the significant pro-choice electoral gains in Congress of the past, establishing a solid anti-choice majority in the House of Representatives. Electing pro-choice legislators is crucial to protecting women's reproductive health and their constitutional right to choose.

What You Can Do: Action Sampler

Raise Your Voice for Choice

Attend pro-choice rallies or demonstrations. Make your pro-choice sentiments visible through bumper stickers or buttons. Send a message to your community by writing a letter to the editor or an op-ed piece for your local newspaper, or by calling in to talk radio shows. Speak up for sexual freedom for all people. Link the attack on a woman's right to choose to right-wing attacks on people of color, gays, and immigrants. Most importantly, cast your vote for pro-choice candidates.

Support Abortion Providers in Your Community

The National Abortion Federation offers suggestions to activists on how they can support choice in their area. Some tips include:

- Volunteer as a patient escort when clinics are blockaded or picketed.
- Sponsor a "clinic watch" program: If you live near a clinic or drive by one regularly, make a point of scanning for anything or anyone unusual on the premises, especially late at night. You can even set up a schedule if enough people are interested and the clinic agrees.
- Offer your professional services pro bono—legal work, accounting, graphic design, or other skills.
- Provide transportation for patients or staff, especially in bad weather.
- Send the staff of the clinic holiday cards, and write supportive notes of encouragement and concern if you hear of an incident of blockading or vandalism.
- Host a fund-raiser. Many clinics and nonprofit organizations have funds to help women who cannot afford to pay for abortions or birth control, and these funds are usually stretched to the limit.

Increase Access to Abortion

Encourage local doctors to provide it on their list of services. Call your own family physician or OB/GYN and ask if she or he performs abortions. Call your local hospital and do the same. If the people you call do not provide these services, encourage them to do so. If they do provide these services, send them supportive letters. Encourage the medical school near you to teach these medical procedures.

Tell It to Washington

Call or write your representatives and senators and let them know about your pro-choice beliefs—and that you will vote according to their records on the issue. Anti-choice groups are phoning, faxing, and writing in force, to all members of the

House and Senate. They provide moral support for the anti-choice legislators, they intimidate and demoralize pro-choice elected officials, and they influence those in the mushy middle. Pro-choice Representative Nita Lowey (D-NY) says, "I get many more anti-choice letters from constituents than pro-choice letters, and I'm the chair of the pro-choice task force!"

Join a Pro-choice Group

Encourage friends and family to sign up, too. The following organizations publish newsletters and reports that will keep you well informed about reproductive rights and pro-choice activities. Contact these groups for membership information and their publications lists.

- **American Civil Liberties Union (ACLU)**
  Reproductive Freedom Project
  132 West 43rd Street
  New York, NY 10036
  (212) 944-9800, ext. 618
  Involved in litigation relevant to abortion rights. Publishes the quarterly Reproductive Rights Update.

- **National Abortion Federation**
  1436 U Street, NW, Suite 103
  Washington, DC 20009
  (202) 667-5881
  An association of abortion providers, individuals, and organizations working for abortion rights. NAF distributes informational publications.

- **National Abortion Rights Action League (NARAL)**
  1156 15th Street, NW, Suite 700
  Washington, DC 20005
  (202) 828-9300
  The largest U.S. organization working exclusively for the right to legal abortion. It has a campus organizing project that assists students who want to get involved with pro-choice activism. Membership includes a subscription to NARAL News, which will keep you updated on several abortion-related issues. Other publications available.

- **National Organization for Women**
  1000 16th Street, NW, Suite 700
  Washington, DC 20036
  (202) 331-0066

- **Planned Parenthood Federation of America**
  810 7th Avenue
  New York, NY 10019
  (212) 541-7800

- **ProChoice Resource Center, Inc.**
  174 East Boston Post Road
  Mamaroneck, NY 10543
  (914) 381-3792
  (800) 733-1973
  This group helps grassroots activist groups identify pro-choice voters in their community and inform others about which candidates support reproductive freedom and which do not. Publishes the quarterly newsletter ProChoice IDEA.

- **The Religious Coalition for Reproductive Choice**
  1025 Vermont Avenue, NW, Suite 1130
  Washington, DC 20005
  (202) 628-7700
  An ecumenical coalition of thirty-six religious denominations and organizations working for reproductive choice.

8

Civil Rights or "Special Rights"?: Racial and Ethnic Minority Rights— Women's Rights— Gay and Lesbian Rights

The quest for civil rights is a struggle to bring full civic equality and economic opportunity to groups of people who have traditionally been disenfranchised, marginalized, and discriminated against by individuals and, often, by the laws of the land. Though tremendous gains have been made over the last thirty years, full equality has not yet been achieved for ethnic minorities, women, or gays. Historical patterns of racism, sexism, and homophobia have proven hard to break.

The civil rights movement injected the idea into the broader American culture that social roles are not static. African-Americans fought against discrimination, often with success, but also with some disappointments. Following their lead, women and then gays joined the fight for equal rights, reconstructing their place in society. Meshed with these social shifts was the counterculture of the 1960s, which rebelled against political and cultural authority and rejected a "traditional" lifestyle, in favor of one that was more open to experimentation. It was in reaction to these cultural changes that much of the radical right coalesced.

Discrimination against racial and ethnic minorities, against women, and against gays has very different sociological roots and is expressed in different ways. However, these biases do share an important underlying common principle: Those who falsely claim underqualified African-Americans are taking jobs from qualified Caucasians, those who declare that women should return to the subordinate role of housewife/mother, and those who attempt to ban gays from teaching and health professions all share an exclusionary vision of society. Moreover, they generally see our society as a zero-sum game: If one group advances, another must fall back. Women claiming the right to work for the same wages as men are thus seen as promoting discrimination against men. African-Americans and Hispanics who decry housing, banking, and employment discrimination are accused of undermining the economic and social integrity of the white race. And gays wanting civil rights protections are held to be undermining the rights of "genuine" and "deserving" minorities. Bigotry, oppression, and economic deprivation, along with hate violence committed against individuals because of their race, religion, national origin or sexual orientation, are all tools of social control.

Not surprisingly, many of the groups opposed to gay rights also oppose the feminist movement, believing that both subvert "traditional values." And while much of the right has made a concerted effort to embrace what has been termed "transtolerance"—bringing together conservative whites, blacks, Hispanics, Asian-Americans, Protestants, Catholics, Jews, and Muslims in a massive coalition against those who challenge traditional religious/cultural values—many right-wing organizations and leaders are sympathetic to reactionary racial theories.

CIVIL RIGHTS FOR RACIAL AND ETHNIC MINORITIES

In the years following the victory of the Union in the Civil War and the emancipation of the slaves, Congress passed seven civil rights acts. The Fourteenth Amendment, which established the rights to personal liberty and equal protection for all citizens, was ratified in 1868. Although the civil rights acts promised newly freed slaves the privileges and rights guaranteed by the Constitution, these were quickly negated by several Supreme Court rulings. Despite the abolition of slavery, its legacy—in particular Jim Crow segregation, violence, and poverty—persisted.

Like the acts passed after the Civil War, the Civil Rights Act of

1964 supposedly represented sweeping change; but again there was the problem of implementation. The enforcement agencies were weak—acting only after complaints were filed—and by 1971 the Equal Employment Opportunities Commission reported that "discrimination continues largely unabated." Even today, male African-American college graduates, on average, still earn only three-quarters as much as their white counterparts.

In 1965, during his famous Montgomery speech, Martin Luther King, Jr. told his audience that poor whites had been fed Jim Crow instead of bread. And the same could well be said today: blue-collar workers (of all races) have seen their real wages and benefits fall by up to (and in some cases by more than) a fifth in the last twenty years, according to a number of estimates.[1] As anger over economic downtrends grows, the radical right has been quick to target affirmative action, "quotas," and the much-trumpeted "black underclass" as lying at their source.

DISTORTIONS ABOUT RACIAL AND ETHNIC MINORITIES

"Poor blacks and Latinos constitute an incorrigible underclass."

In the last fifteen years, barely veiled racist rhetoric has found its way back from extremities such as the Nazi Party into the heart of the political process. The race button is repeatedly pressed even by mainstream politicians. We saw it in the election of David Duke, an ex-Klansman, to Louisiana's state legislature in 1989. We saw it in Ronald Reagan's campaign ads featuring a black welfare cheater who rolled up to the AFDC office in a limousine to pick up her multiple checks. We saw this when Harold Washington, an African-American, ran for mayor of Chicago (a race he eventually won) and his opponents ran attack ads that stated simply "Before it's too late . . ." We saw it with George Bush's scurrilous Willie Horton ads in 1988, using a black rapist to portray his opponent, Michael Dukakis, as soft on crime. And we see it today in the opportunistic onslaught against affirmative action by politicians such as Senator Bob Dole and California Governor Pete Wilson who previously supported such programs, and with the more nakedly racist rhetoric of Pat Buchanan.

Racial Violence

Over seven thousand hate crimes were reported in 1993 in the United States, according to the FBI, with 62 percent directed toward people because of their race or ethnicity. The following are a few examples of such crimes from the recent past:

- In Georgia, a disgruntled mother, who felt her son had been unfairly passed over to give a high school valedictorian speech in favor of an African-American, called in the Klan to picket the school.
- Skinheads incited by White Aryan Resistance (WAR) beat an Ethiopian immigrant to death in Portland, Oregon.
- In Sacramento, California, Nazi skinheads bombed the NAACP offices, a synagogue, and several Asian-American targets.

The labeling of the poor, particularly the urban black and Latino poor, as an "underclass" complete with a number of deviant behavioral pathologies has been of particular use to those seeking to steer social policy away from an emphasis on a universal safety net and expanded access to education and job training, and toward a more coercive and punitive social policy. Herbert Gans writes in *The Underclass and Antipoverty Policy: The War Against the Poor* that "the labeling of the poor as moral inferiors . . . blames them falsely for the ills of the American society and economy, and reinforces their mistreatment, increases their misery, and further discourages their moving out of poverty."[2]

Once the poor have been assigned to an "underclass," it is that much easier, according to Gans, "to emasculate them politically, thus excluding them, and their needs, from political institutions that are supposed to serve all citizens."[3] Politically motivated labeling—which often has a racial bias—strips labeled persons of other qualities. "That a welfare recipient may be a fine mother becomes irrelevant; the label assumes that she, like all others in her category, is a bad mother."[4] The political debate is now so dominated by race stereotypes that poor African-Americans are being further excluded from the political process, while their living conditions continue to decline.

"Society is no longer racist, therefore affirmative action is no longer necessary."

On a radio station in Weatherford, Texas, a Rush Limbaugh devotee remarked: "You know, Rush is right: Racism is dead in this country. I don't know what the niggers have to gripe about now."[5] Clearly, society is not yet as color-blind as some pretend.

In an open letter to the public, California's Governor Pete Wilson, who is attempting to dismantle his state's affirmative action programs, wrote: "In the 1960s and 1970s, great societal guilt was felt in America for the wrongs of past discrimination. . . . But however natural this compensatory urge may have been in the immediate post-discrimination period of the 1960s and 1970s, the validity of the need for such compensation has steadily faded ever since."[6]

Taking on the liberationist rhetoric of the progressive movements from the 1960s, those seeking to eliminate affirmative action quote Martin Luther King, Jr. and his desire to see a "color-blind society." In fact, the anti–affirmative action initiative being pushed in California for 1996 is referred to as the "California *Civil Rights* Initiative." Conversely, those who seek to preserve affirmative action are accused of advocating state-sponsored racism. It is clear, however, that genuinely equal opportunities for individuals and groups do not exist. As Michael Novick writes in *White Lies, White Power,* "We do not become color-blind by simply declaring ourselves so."[7]

RIGHT-WING PROPOSALS

The punitive measures suggested by right-wingers on the issues of welfare, crime, immigration, and education have a particularly great impact on racial and ethnic minorities. These proposals are detailed in their respective chapters.

End Affirmative Action

Affirmative action programs were devised as a quick fix to create a labor picture that more accurately and fairly reflected the racial, ethnic and sexual makeup of the country. First, these programs are intended to level the playing field, that is, to assure that qualified minorities and women are included among the candidates for jobs. Secondly, these programs assure that minorities and women have the same developmental opportunities as white males, so that they can move onto the playing field with equal preparation.

Affirmative action programs take a variety of forms. Some employers actively seek out minorities and women to apply for jobs. Some programs will give a job to the minority or female candidate when he or she has essentially the same qualifications as the competition. In others, a woman or minority person will get the job if he or she meets the minimum qualifications, even if there is a more qualified white male candidate. This practice has been upheld in some court cases, particularly regarding federal and private sector programs, and struck down in others at the state and local level.

Most controversial is the situation when the search to fill a position continues until an acceptable woman or a member of a minority group can be found, regardless of whether a qualified white male is available. Despite critics who harp on such programs, this type of rigid quota has not been upheld in the courts, does not constitute legal affirmative action, and rarely occurs. While 23 percent of white men say they've been personally affected by "reverse discrimination," according to a 1995 Gallup/CNN/*USA Today* poll, reverse discrimination complaints account for only one hundred of approximately three thousand discrimination cases heard in the years 1990 through 1994. Of these, only six cases were found to have merit. Many accusations of reverse discrimination stem from the erroneous assumption that when a minority or a women gets the job, it is invariably because of their race or sex, not their qualifications.

Both Senators Gramm and Dole have pledged that as President they would outlaw affirmative action programs. In July of 1995, Pete Wilson succeeded in getting the University of California regents, led by conservative black businessman Ward Connerly, to repeal the university's affirmative action admissions policy. Opponents of the change predict the number of African-Americans and Latinos enrolled at top campuses such as Berkeley will fall dramatically. Governor Wilson has also signed an executive order barring all further affirmative action hiring policies in state institutions.

Though President Clinton has defended the overall goals of affirmative action, and says it "has been good for America," his administration is reevaluating federal preference programs.

WOMEN'S RIGHTS

The inclusion of women in the Civil Rights Act of 1964 was an afterthought, and initially an act of sabotage. It was introduced by a Virginia senator who believed that the issue of gender rights might divide proponents and serve to kill the bill. It didn't, and a safeguard against sex-based discrimination was included.

Two years later, as more women were reading and being influenced by feminist literature such as Simone de Beauvoir's *The Second Sex* and Betty Friedan's *The Feminine Mystique,* the National Organization for Women (NOW) was founded under Friedan's leadership to push for women's equality. By 1969, polls showed that the majority of Americans approved of married women choosing to work outside the home. Between 1971 and 1991, the total number of employed women rose by 60 percent and the number employed full-time doubled. Alongside this change in the economic realm, which allowed women to be less dependent on men for income, a shift in demographics and attitudes resulted in a modified picture of the average American family. Since 1970, the proportion of "traditional families"—that is, marriage-based two-parent families—has fallen by 35 percent.[8]

The right views America's changing family structure as an assault on the moral foundation of our country, and its ideologues insist that society's problems can only be solved by a return to the traditional patriarchal setup—where children are subordinate to parents, wife to husband, and family to God. As used by the right, the word "family" is intended to conjure up a Norman Rockwell image of safety, security, and control. Yet it also restricts family structure to a single narrow mold, confines women to the role of full-time mothers and housewives, and reasserts male status and power in a changing world. It is in the name of "tradi-

Violence Toward Women

The Center for Democratic Renewal writes: "While violence against women is different in some ways from other forms of bias violence—for example, the majority of assaults and murders targeting women are carried out not by strangers, but by persons known to the victim—the bottom line is that there are more similarities than there are differences. Violence against women is motivated by misogyny and hatred just as gay bashing, and racist and anti-Semitic violence are the result of bigotry."[9]

The staggering levels of male violence against women is linked to the backlash against women's struggle for equality:

- The American Medical Association estimates that 1 in 12 women in the United States will be raped during her lifetime.
- Over 700,000 women are sexually assaulted each year. That's nearly 2,000 every day. That's one woman every 45 seconds.
- Three-quarters of sexual assaults are committed by a friend, acquaintance, intimate partner, or family member.
- Each year, 2 to 4 million women are victims of domestic violence. Domestic violence is the leading cause of injury to women, causing more injuries than muggings, rape by strangers, and car accidents combined.
- Each year roughly 1,500 women are murdered by intimate partners.

SOURCE: The American Medical Association.

tional family values" that the current right-wing attack on women's rights takes place.

DISTORTIONS ABOUT WOMEN AND FEMINISM

"Feminism is anti-family, and unnatural."

Two of the most ardent opponents of the women's movement are Phyllis Schlafly and Beverly LaHaye. Schlafly's *Power of the Christian Woman* associates "the disease called women's liberation" with original sin: "The woman in the Garden of Eden freely decided to tamper with God's order and ignore His rules. She sought her own self-fulfillment. . . . Sin thus entered the world." LaHaye's Concerned Women for America, which leads anti-choice and anti–gay rights campaigns, was established to "oppose everything that NOW favors." [10] CWA's claimed membership, 600,000, is currently twice that of NOW's—though critics charge that this number is inflated.

The condemnation of feminism by the radical right is an attempt to strengthen the traditional role of women as wives and mothers, yet it is based on a multitude of myths. Feminists are not "anti-family"; they are merely asserting the right to choose whether or not to marry, to have children and, if they are lesbian, to live openly as such. Also, it is important to recognize that a woman's satisfaction with her life's work serves her family as well as herself, both monetarily and otherwise. And the reality of the 1990s is that the vast majority of women are motivated by financial necessity to work. In turn, the U.S. economy depends upon women's labor, as women make up 46 percent of the labor force.

"Sexual harassment is an overblown issue."

In the aftermath of the Clarence Thomas/Anita Hill hearings, the number of women joining NOW and other feminist organizations rose rapidly. Many felt sexual harassment was an issue that had been ignored for too long. According to Equal Rights Advocates in San Francisco, at least seven out of ten working

women experience some overt or subtle form of sexual harassment on the job.

Yet Schlafly has said, "If there's no proof, it's all in your mind.
We don't want a policeman at every water cooler, you know."[11] In
fact, sexual harassment policies are needed—they are designed
to give a woman suffering unwanted sexual advances from a
male work superior a legal means of addressing her grievances,
without jeopardizing her job.

"Feminists are putting the country in jeopardy by not having children."

Susan Faludi and other feminist scholars have identified a radical right backlash against feminism that has at its center the assumption that liberated, professional women are undermining
America's world role through postponing childbirth, risking
higher rates of infertility and creating a "birth dearth." Leading
backlasher Charles Murray, author of *The Bell Curve*, writes that
current social policy encourages the poor to have more children, while discouraging the affluent to have as many—in other
words, white middle-class America is being outbred by the
brown-skinned underclass. Faludi sums up this argument perfectly: "The pronatalists' use of the disease metaphor is uninten-
tionally revealing: they considered it an 'epidemic' when white
women didn't reproduce or when black women did."[12]

RIGHT-WING PROPOSALS

Also see the chapters on abortion and welfare, two issues on
which the right's proposals particularly affect women.

Promote Male Dominance

Militant anti-abortion leader Randall Terry told an audience of
U.S. Taxpayer Party supporters that there was a crisis facing America even more serious than the prevalence of abortion and
"sodomites": "We are facing a crisis of righteous, courageous,
physically oriented, *male* leadership!"[13]

The theme of patriarchal revival coincides with the broader attacks on the gains made by feminists, and is in line with the ide-

ology of the phenomenon known as the Promise Keepers, started by University of Colorado football coach Bill McCartney in 1990. Promise Keepers' highly charged events pack football stadiums with all-male audiences who promise to reaffirm their religious faith and return home to reestablish their "natural," God-given role as heads of their families; women must submit to their husbands for the "survival of our culture." In 1995, over 700,000 men attended Promise Keepers rallies; in 1996, it is expected that over a million men will participate, and plans are already in the works for a monumental Promise Keepers rally in Washington, D.C., in 1997. McCartney was also one of the most outspoken supporters of Colorado's overtly homophobic Amendment Two, an anti-gay rights initiative passed in 1992 (see p. 128).

In October 1995, hundreds of thousands of black men participated in the Million Man March in Washington, D.C., organized by Louis Farrakhan's Nation of Islam. While there is no evidence to suggest that the majority of Million Man marchers were racist, sexist, or homophobic (and a good deal of evidence suggesting a serious aspiration to restore unity and pride to a shattered community, and to counter the societal assault on the African-American man), Louis Farrakhan himself is all three. Farrakhan has stated that Jews and Asians setting up businesses in African-American population centers are "parasites." He believes that women should play a subordinate role to men, and he has made public statements advocating the execution of homosexuals. An underlying theme of the march organizers, as identified by women such as activist Angela Davis, was the restoration of a male-led social order.

It is constructive for impoverished and ravaged communities to begin coming together politically—when the disadvantaged articulate political and social goals and seek to realize them, possibilities emerge for halting the right-wing resurgence. Yet, anger and frustration can easily be hijacked and twisted. Farrakhan's message seeks to blame women, Jews, Asians and homosexuals for the plight of African-Americans, rather than examining the economics and ingrained prejudices that trap so many in poverty and violence in the first place.

End Affirmative Action for Women

Parallel to the campaign against affirmative action for racial and ethnic minorities, is the move to repeal programs designed to raise the number of women in the professions, business, and the academy. However, the need for these programs is apparent. Despite women's gains in employment, they still face discrimination in the workplace:

- In 1993, women earned 72 percent of what men earned. (African-American women earned 64 percent of what white men earned, and Hispanic women 54 percent.)[14]
- The median annual income for a family headed by a single black woman in the United States is $12,000.[15]
- Four in five working women still work in traditionally female jobs, such as secretary or sales clerk.[16]
- White men make up only 43 percent of the workforce, yet they hold over 90 percent of senior management jobs.[17]
- Pregnancy continues to be a serious source of workplace discrimination.

GAY AND LESBIAN RIGHTS

As recently as four decades ago, sodomy was a crime in all states, and the police routinely arrested suspected homosexuals. President Eisenhower decreed no homosexuals were to be employed by any federal agency or any business seeking government contracts. Not until the Stonewall riot against police harassment in New York's Greenwich Village in 1969 did a gay liberation movement come to the fore.

Within three years of Stonewall, the number of gay groups in the United States had grown from fewer than 20 to about 1,200. A primary goal of these organizations was the passage of civil rights laws similar to those forbidding discrimination on the basis of race, religion, ethnic origin, and sex. They also worked for the repeal of all laws criminalizing any form of sexual behavior between consenting adults in private. In 1973, the American Psychiatric Association removed homosexuality from its list of psychiatric disorders.

Despite some gains, sodomy (defined as oral or anal sex between any two people) remains illegal in nearly half the states of the union, and although rarely enforced, the penalties that are theoretically applicable in these states are severe: In Idaho, the maximum sentence is life imprisonment; in Georgia, Rhode Island, and Virginia, twenty years; in Michigan, fifteen years; and in Maryland, Mississippi, Montana, North Carolina, and Oklahoma, ten years. In addition, most states still do not have statutes preventing housing and employment discrimination against gays. And without laws that specifically ban discrimination based on sexual orientation, gay people have no legal recourse when they are discriminated against. Moreover, civil rights for gay people are the rights most explicitly under attack by the religious right. During the 1990s the Christian right has invested much energy in organizing anti–gay rights initiatives, such as Colorado's Amendment Two, at local and state levels.

Open homophobia remains in mainstream politics. Politicians such as Senator Bob Dole have swung to the right on the issue of homosexuality as Republican primary voters have become ever more conservative. In 1995, Dole's presidential campaign team

---

Homophobic Violence

In 1993, 1,043 people across the country were victims of violent attacks on their persons or property carried out by people hostile to their sexual orientation. (These FBI figures do not include the numerous cases of verbal abuse, or employment and housing discrimination.) A hate crime is intended to intimidate all gays at least as much as the individual directly attacked. Anti-gay hate crimes are on the rise in areas where anti-gay initiatives have been voted on.

A 1984 survey of more than 2,000 gays, lesbians, and bisexuals, carried out by the National Gay and Lesbian Task Force, found that nineteen percent had been "punched, hit, kicked, or beaten" at least once in their lives because of their sexuality. In a 1989 poll, seven percent reported they had been assaulted within the previous year.

solicited and received a $1,000 campaign contribution from a gay Republican group, the Log Cabin Republicans. But later, in an attempt to pander to his party's right wing, Dole publicly returned the contribution, stating that the group embraced views he neither shared nor sympathized with. (Dole ended up accepting the contribution after a media blitz criticizing his action.)

Homophobia comes through loud and clear on talk radio. Rush Limbaugh has frequently referred to gays as "faggots" and "perverts."[18] After New York's annual Lesbian and Gay Pride celebration in 1994, nationally syndicated broadcaster Bob Grant remarked: "Ideally, it would have been nice to have a few phalanxes of policemen with machine guns and mow them down."[19]

DISTORTIONS ABOUT GAYS AND LESBIANS

"Gays are demanding special rights."

"Special rights" has no legal meaning. Gay and lesbian activists simply want the *same* rights as those guaranteed to all other American citizens. As Robin Kane, Public Information Manager of the National Gay and Lesbian Task Force, writes: "The right to get and keep a job based on merit is not a special right. Equal access to housing is not a special right. . . . The right to walk down a street and not get attacked because of who you are and who you love is not a special right."[20]

In addition, anti–"special rights" agitators imply gays are demanding that affirmative action programs include them. The fact is anti-discrimination codes do not extend affirmative action programs to gay people. Nor have gay advocacy groups campaigned for such.

"Gay rights laws undermine the civil rights of those who are truly discriminated against."

Taking a divide and conquer approach during the campaign for the anti-gay initiative Amendment Two, one of Colorado for Family Value's (CFV) pamphlets was titled "How voting 'Yes!' on Amendment 2 protects Colorado's true minorities." It begins:

If you're African-American, Hispanic, a woman or differently abled, we think you should know about these people. They're called "gay rights" activists. They're dedicated to giving one of America's most affluent, best educated, most advantaged special interest groups—themselves—the same special legal status as, say, a disadvantaged African/American [sic], Hispanic, or handicapped person. And if they get their way, what they call "gay rights" will strip the true Colorado minorities of hard-won gains . . . to subsidize gays' yen for "divergent" sex.[21]

This argument is designed to prevent coalition-building among diverse groups struggling for equality. If a law passes that asserts, for example, that a landlord cannot refuse to rent an apartment to someone because of his or her sexual preferences, this in no way infringes on any other disadvantaged group's civil rights. In reality, the more people who are protected by civil rights ordinances, the harder it is for a discriminatory culture to gain control and impose its agenda on any traditionally oppressed group.

"Homosexuals are child-molesters."

The religious right seeks to demonize homosexuals and to associate them in the public imagination with the ultimate taboo—pedophilia. Stephen Bransford, one of the CFV organizers, claims that "So-called normalization of homosexuality threatens to legitimize what used to be called child molestation."[22]

Despite claims such as this, Dr. Carol Jenny, a specialist in the study of child abuse, informed the court during the hearings on Amendment Two that she had studied 269 child abuse cases in Colorado and had found that heterosexual male family members of children were over 100 times more likely than lesbians or gay men to molest children.[23] Pedophiles are a danger to society; gays who engage in consensual adult sex are not.

"AIDS is a gay plague, brought down on gays by God."

Although AIDS first began spreading rapidly in the United States within the gay community, it has never been confined to homosexual men. The latest Centers for Disease Control figures suggest that the incidence of AIDS is growing six times faster among women than among men in the United States. And poor communities, where intravenous drug use, prostitution, and lack of sex education are commonplace, have seen explosions in heterosexual infection over the last decade. AIDS is now the leading cause of death for men aged twenty-five to forty-four. And in some cities, such as New York, it is also the leading killer for women between the ages of twenty-five and thirty-four. The religious right's ongoing effort to demonize this disease, cut federally funded AIDS research, and eliminate AIDS education in the schools puts the general public at serious risk.

"Gays lead a depraved and disease-ridden life."

Discredited psychologist Dr. Paul Cameron asserts that gays en masse engage in practices that put their and others' health at serious risk. Cameron claims that even after excluding AIDS deaths, gays' life expectancy is only forty-two years. His results have not been reproduced by any other studies. Cameron has not only been denounced by the American Psychological Association, but censured by the Nebraska Psychological Association, the American Sociological Association, and the Midwest Sociological Society.[24] He now runs a fundamentalist organization called the Institute for Scientific Investigation of Sexuality (ISIS).

In *The Gay Agenda,* a virulently homophobic video produced by a group in California known as The Report, Dr. Stanley Monteith, the chairman of the California Republican Party's Health and Human Services Committee and longtime member of the John Birch Society, asserts that the ingestion of feces and urine is a common practice among gay men, and that the "average" homosexual has sex with 20 to 106 partners per year. Monteith's allegations are based exclusively on a study by Cameron. *The Gay Agenda* has repeatedly been excerpted on Pat Robertson's "700 Club," and several thousand copies were used by the leaders of the anti-gay initiative movements in Oregon and Colorado.

RIGHT-WING PROPOSALS

Remove Civil Rights Protections for Gays

Colorado's Amendment Two passed in a 1992 referendum in response to a number of city ordinances barring discrimination against gays and extending domestic partnership benefits to include same-sex relationships. Amendment Two organizers, claiming these ordinances were an infringement of free speech and religious liberty, drafted the measure to ban them. After a long campaign, during which Focus on the Family broadcast national programs in its favor, 53.5 percent of voters supported Amendment Two.

The amendment was promptly challenged in court by a wide alliance of gay rights groups, the ACLU, a number of states and cities, the American Bar Association, several state bar associations, the National Organization for Women, and many other groups. The Colorado Supreme Court ruled the amendment unconstitutional, and the state then appealed this decision to the U.S. Supreme Court. As *The Armchair Activist* goes to press, the Court has not yet ruled on the constitutional status of the amendment.

At the same time, the Oregon Citizens' Alliance promoted Ballot Measure Nine, which attempted to change Oregon's constitution to declare homosexuality "abnormal, wrong, unnatural, and perverse." Thanks to a campaign that included Republicans Against Prejudice, the Catholic church, and fourteen rural political action committees, the measure went down to defeat. Two years later a similar proposal, Ballot Measure Thirteen, was presented to the electorate. It also failed, as did an antigay initiative in Idaho.

Meanwhile, however, voters in Cincinnati, Ohio, chose to repeal the city's gay rights laws, and in Oregon, following the 1992 election, the OCA began targeting counties and localities that had supported Ballot Measure Nine. In 1993, sixteen Oregon localities and counties passed antigay initiatives. The following year ten more did so.

In 1995, antigay activists in Maine organized yet another type of ballot. This one did not mention gays or homosexuality at all. Instead it asked voters to support a measure that defined which groups *did* have access to antidiscrimination protections: ethnic minorities, religious groups, women, the elderly, the disabled, and a handful of others. By default, gays would be excluded from such protections, and local ordinances, such as the one in Portland, that did cover gays in antidiscrimination policies would have to be abandoned. (Paradoxically, so would a wide variety of other antidiscrimination measures, including those protecting veterans.) Again, pro–civil rights groups, supported by Governor Angus King and the business community, mobilized to defeat the initiative.

Ban the Discussion of Gay Issues in Schools

The schools are a prime battleground for the warriors against gay rights. Books such as *Heather Has Two Mommies* have aroused the wrath of religious conservatives. Sex education curricula that include information about homosexuality and counseling services for gay teenagers have also been targeted by the religious right. Anti-gay activists often erroneously connect homosexuality with child abuse in an attempt to frighten parents.

Publicly Identify or Intern Carriers of HIV and People with AIDS

Dr. Paul Cameron is the foremost advocate of interning those with HIV or AIDS and branding their foreheads with a large *A*, clearly an infringement of civil liberties. Cameron's work has been widely distributed by Colorado for Family Values, a group supported by the Traditional Values Coalition, Concerned Women of America, and the Christian Coalition. In addition to this, Paul Weyrich's Free Congress Foundation has called for "mandatory reporting of all intercourse contacts" by male homosexuals.

POSITIVE ALTERNATIVES

Civil rights activists are fighting back. Groups like the ProChoice Resource Center in Mamaroneck, New York, are mobilizing pro-choice voters nationwide. The Center for Democratic Renewal's Georgia Project in Atlanta provides assistance to victims of racially–motivated violance in rural communities throughout the state. And, while anti-gay campaigns have been energetic, the radical right has suffered major defeats on this issue.

But the resurgence and mainstreaming of racism, sexism, and homophobia can not adequately be countered by identity-based politics alone. An effective response to any form of discrimination begins by mobilizing different elements of the community to respond in a cohesive way. For this reason, many single-issue social justice groups in the 1990s are concentrating on coalition building to unify the struggle for equality among people of color, women, and gays.

The Center for Democratic Renewal, for example, was founded to monitor and counter the activity of racist groups like the Ku Klux Klan, but its work now touches on the women's movement, the gay and lesbian movement, and the pro-immigration movement. CDR has investigated the involvement of the Klan and neo-Nazi activists in the antiabortion movement as part of the Women's Watch Project, launched in 1992. After CDR documented over three hundred persons involved in both movements, its research methods were taken up by many women's groups that had not formerly examined white supremacist organizations.

Too often, members of groups that suffer discrimination themselves oppose full civil rights for members of other oppressed groups. For example, Latinos sometimes criticize affirmative action for favoring blacks, or vice versa. A deliberate divide-and-conquer strategy can be seen in the religious right's literature for antigay initiatives. But the strongest way to support equal rights for one group is to support equal rights for all. As the diverse elements of the right have found common ground on many issues, so must women's groups, racial and ethnic justice groups, and gay rights groups come together and stand up to these antidemocratic forces.

How These Issues Affect You

If you are a woman, gay, and/or a person of color, it is obvious how the sexism, homophobia, and racism spread by the various factions of the radical right affects you—your right to live a life free of discrimination is being challenged. However, everyone is affected by these bigotries: the rights of one group cannot be divorced from the rights of all.

Attempts to scapegoat entire sections of the population for society's ills have ramifications for everybody—these distortions prevent positive public policy change. Demonizing women on welfare will not result in more job training or day care; stereotyping black males as criminals will not reduce crime and poverty; censoring AIDS education will only accelerate the epidemic. Moreover, the religious right's open attack on homosexuals and women's reproductive rights is only part of a more sweeping agenda by groups seeking to impose a theocratic morality on society.

And it is obvious that in a society where hate crimes and sexual assault are common, nobody can feel entirely safe, secure, or comfortable. Those committed to freedom and diversity must realize that true democracy cannot coexist with these prejudices.

WHAT YOU CAN DO—ACTION SAMPLER

Support Diversity

Programs in public schools that attempt to meet the challenge of dealing with America's diversity should be encouraged and supported. This includes multicultural curricula, and sex education material that treats homosexuality as a reality, not something to fear. Advocate for diversity training workshops in your workplace.

Help Track Homophobic Legislation

Lambda and the National Gay and Lesbian Task force (see addresses below) both track antigay inititatives and referenda. Notify these groups if petitions are circulated in your community or legislation filed or placed on the ballot. (Lambda also provides legal research to eligible groups.)

Keep on Top of Issues That Affect Women

Political Woman Hotline is an excellent on-line newsletter dedicated to keeping people informed about legislation in Congress—it gives you the facts you need quickly and succinctly. Find out how the latest proposals on reproductive rights, welfare, or education are faring in the House, and who's supporting them and who isn't. To subscribe, send an e-mail of interest to PolWoman@aol.com.

The Body Politic is a newsletter dedicated to exposing right-wing attacks on women's rights, the feminist movement, and abortion rights. Subscriptions are $27 a year. For more information, contact:

The Body Politic
P.O.Box 2363
Binghamton, NY 13907
(607) 648-2760

Join National Organizations Fighting for Equal Rights

Many of the following groups have local chapters, where you can get directly involved with others in your community. Most provide educational resources and publications to keep you updated on current events.

Race and Ethnicity

American-Arab Anti-Discrimination Committee
4201 Connecticut Ave., NW, #500
Washington, DC 20008
(202) 244-2990

Anti-Defamation League of B'nai B'rith
823 United Nations Plaza
New York, NY 10017
(212) 490-2525

Asian American Legal Defense and Education Fund
99 Hudson Street, 12th floor
New York, NY 10013
(212) 966-5932

Mexican American Legal Defense Fund
634 S. Spring Street, 11th Floor
Los Angeles, CA 90014-1974
(213) 629-2512

National Association for the Advancement of Colored People
4805 Mount Hope Drive
Baltimore, MD 21215-3297
(410) 358-8900

National Urban League
500 East 62nd Street
New York, NY 10021
(212) 310-9000

Native American Rights Fund
1506 Broadway
Boulder, CO 80302
(303) 447-8760

Women

The Fund for the Feminist Majority
1600 Wilson Boulevard, Suite 801
Arlington, Virginia 22209
(703) 522-2214

National Coalition Against Domestic Violence
P.O. Box 34103
Washington, DC 20047
(202) 638-6388

National Organization for Women
1000 16th Street, NW, Suite 700
Washington, DC 20036-5705
(202) 331-0066

National Women's Political Caucus
1211 Connecticut Ave., NW, Suite 425
Washington, DC 20036
(202) 785-1100

(For resources regarding reproductive rights, see pp. 110–111.)

Gay and Lesbian

Human Rights Campaign Fund
1101 14th Street, NW, Suite 200
Washington, DC 20005
(202) 628-4160

Lambda Legal Defense and Education Fund, Inc.
666 Broadway, 12th Floor
New York, NY 10012
(212) 995-8585

National Gay and Lesbian Task Force
2320 17th Street, NW
Washington, DC 20009
(202) 332-6483

9

Crime and Punishment: Putting the Teeth Back Into Criminal Justice

Punishment as spectacle is back. Drive along the roads in Alabama, Florida, or Arizona, and you'll see groups of prisoners shackled at the ankles at labor. The chain gang, abolished for over forty years due to public outcry, lives again—a punishment that humiliates prisoners while demonstrating to the public that politicians and prison officials are "getting tough on crime." Some motorists take the opportunity to roll down their windows and bark invective at the predominantly black chained convicts, who work for up to ten hours a day. The imagery seemed to remind one elderly white woman in Alabama (quoted in the *New York Times*) of a previous era: "I love seeing 'em in chains. They ought to make them pick cotton."[1]

America's criminal justice system appears to be rapidly regressing to a point where punishment is again a form of social catharsis rather than a method of removing criminals from society and, hopefully, rehabilitating them. The current debate on crime is dominated by the clamoring for more prisons, longer sentences, lower parole rates, deliberately humiliating discipline, and an increase in executions.

America now locks up more people as a percentage of its population than any other industrial country, having recently surpassed Russia and South Africa. The prison population is increasing spectacularly, especially in the southern states and California. In 1980, the United States' federal and state prison population was about 330,000. By 1992, this population had almost tripled. Today, 1.5 million people are behind bars in federal and state prisons and county jails, with another 3.5 million under some form of correctional supervision.[2] These numbers continue to rise.

Billions of taxpayer dollars are spent each year to support the emerging prison-industrial complex, yet crime and the uncertainty of what to do with those who commit crime remains. Perhaps more than anything else, the fear of crime, and of a criminal underclass, is pushing American culture rightward toward a more repressive future. The political leadership, always keen to press "hot buttons," has jumped onto this bandwagon, and politicians are duking it out to see who can come up with the toughest, harshest responses to criminal justice.

DISTORTIONS ABOUT CRIME AND PUNISHMENT

"Crime is raging out of control."

While it is true that tens of thousands of people are maimed and murdered every year in the United States, and U.S. murder rates are far higher than in other industrial countries, this is not a new tragedy. In fact, according to the Federal Bureau of Investigation, there is an indication that crime rates are receding after they surged in the mid-1980s with the epidemic of crack cocaine and the increasing use of guns by young people.[3] The Bureau of Justice Statistics reveals that current murder and violent crime rates are actually lower (in terms of crimes committed per 100,000 people) than they were in 1993, lower than they were in 1990, and roughly comparable to what they were in 1975. Between 1980 and 1992, the murder rate actually fell 9 percent.[4] Since 1992, it has continued to fall. The rates of robbery and property crime are much lower than they were twenty years ago.

One of the factors fueling America's perception of an escalating "crime wave" is the sensationalist media. According to Jeff Cohen and Norman Solomon, in their book *Through the Media Looking Glass,* a rising trend in sensationalist coverage of crime and the use of gory imagery as news-entertainment, combined with "real-life" crime programs such as *America's Most Wanted* and

Cops, has exacerbated the populace's feeling of vulnerability and risk. Solomon and Cohen write that "what has soared is crime coverage. From 1989 through 1991, the three nightly newscasts on network TV together spent 67 minutes per month on crime. By the end of 1993, 'crime time' had more than doubled—to 157 minutes each month."[5] And, according to a study conducted by the Center for Media and Public Affairs, not only did television coverage of crime more than double from 1992–1993, but murder coverage *tripled.*

"All criminals are immoral."

In the 1995 book *Crime,* sponsored by the Bradley Foundation, a conservative body that funds academic projects, University of Arizona professor Travis Hirschi writes:

> *Child-rearing takes lots of hard work. . . . The goal of such work is to reproduce the family, to produce a healthy, educated child capable of making a good marriage and a good living. Obviously, none of these things is going to happen if crime or immorality intervenes, if the son ends up in prison or the daughter ends up an unmarried parent. . . . Family weakness causes immorality and crime, which cause or perpetuate family weakness. Crime and immorality have the same causes and consequences and are thus the same thing.*[6]

Equating immoral behavior with criminality ignores the role played by poverty and grim living conditions in generating crime. Focusing the entire policy debate on issues of morality leaves little room for rehabilitative or preventative arguments. Punishment becomes the only solution.

Hostile to psychology, sociology, and other attempts to understand individual behavior in a group and cultural context, the religious right sees increased incarceration or capital punishment as the only response to criminal behavior. Speaking at the September 1995 Road to Victory Christian Coalition conference, the born-again broadcaster Star Parker announced her solution to the crime problem:

> Wicked criminals roam the streets. Where are those appointed by God to be the terror to evil?! Where is the electric chair?!

How many murders do we have to read about and experience before we get serious? The Bible said, "Cursed is he who keeps back his sword from blood." . . . And crime? Execute! You all don't want to get me started about crime. . . . We should build one big facility. . . . East St. Louis is a good place to build that one big facility. We'll just ship them all in. Hey, get rid of all that bureaucracy, all the corruption, all the red tape—ship them all in.

The idea of one giant concentration camp for prisoners is not too distant from the Christian Reconstructionist vision of society preached by Rousas J. Rushdoony, which holds that criminals who aren't executed ought to be delegated to a slave class that works to pay off their debt to society or, more immediately, to the victims of their crime.

"Criminal behavior is programmed in the genes."

Recent attempts to find a "crime gene" have focused attention on a biological propensity to crime. Patricia Brennan, Sarnoff Mednick, and Jan Volavka, writing in the right-wing anthology *Crime,* argue that "If a biological factor leads to criminal outcome only in a certain environmental circumstance, then prevention programs can target the biologically vulnerable and change their environment before the criminal behavior ensues."[7] Rather than regarding a poor environment as the primary trigger for crime, they choose instead to target the "biologically vulnerable." Even if this were possible, such groups could only be identified through some nightmarish system of compulsory genetic testing for those living in poor areas—there would be no point testing the affluent, for they would not be exposed to the environmental factors that trigger the "crime gene."

"Prisoners are living a life of luxury."

Likening prisons to hotels is a good—albeit absurd—way to get taxpayers angry. Texas Senator Phil Gramm has pledged to "stop building prisons like Holiday Inns." In 1995, Gramm said, "We're going to take out the air conditioning, take out the TV sets. We'll make our prisons industrial parks."[8]

But, television or not, prison is not the place you'd like to spend your next vacation. "Freedom is a very, very powerful thing to take away from someone," explains Richard Stratton, editor and publisher of *Prison Life* magazine. "That's the punishment that prison is all about: You've broken the law, therefore you're being taken out of society and you're not free anymore. That in itself is enough punishment. To compound that by creating harsher conditions is basically shortsighted."

"It's the old junkyard dog theory," Stratton continues. "If you want to make an animal really vicious, you chain him up, kick him, and treat him badly, and he'll get vicious. It's the same with people. If you're treating them like animals and worse, you can expect that the backlash is going to be horrendous. What do you want these people to be like when they come out? Do you want them to be even worse than they were when they went in?"[9]

California, with more prisoners and prisons than any other state, also has some of the most brutal conditions. At the Calipatria prison, the cells are each six feet by ten, and due to gross overcrowding, most hold two inmates per cell. Super-maximum security, hi-tech prisons called special handling units—such as Pelican Bay in Northern California—provide even harsher conditions. "These are incredibly antiseptic, with all-white cells," says Stratton. "The lights are kept on twenty-four hours a day, with video cameras in the cells, so there's no privacy." SHU's are run electronically, to eliminate the need for a large staff. Prisoners are completely isolated and rarely see other humans.

Prison historian Eric Cummins has called Pelican Bay a "place of pure psychological destruction."[10] It has been cited by Amnesty International and numerous prisoners' rights organizations for atrocious violations of human rights. According to the American Friends Service Committee in Newark, New Jersey, special handling units exist in thirty-six states.

RIGHT-WING PROPOSALS

More Prison Sentences, Longer Prison Sentences

William P. Barr, George Bush's attorney general, is at the forefront of the campaign for more and longer prison sentences. He writes, "The message clearly is that getting tough works. . . . Increasing prison capacity is the single most effective strategy for controlling crime. . . . A free civil society cannot long endure a justice system which returns violent predators to the streets."

Arguments such as Barr's are bolstered by the widely challenged work of economist Edwin Zedlewski. Zedlewski published a report in 1987 estimating that locking up 1,000 additional prisoners would prevent 187,000 crimes a year, saving society $405,000 per year per prisoner. However, an article by Perry Johnson and Bill Kime, in the February 1995 issue of *Focus,* the monthly report put out by the National Council on Crime and Delinquency, bluntly criticizes Zedlewski's analysis. "The problem is that it is not true. Consider the fact that more than 400,000 parolees are supervised in the community each year. If each of these people commits an average of 187 crimes each year as Zedlewski maintains, there would be a total of almost 75 million crimes per year. This is at least five times the number of crimes reported to the police, and more than all the victimizations estimated by the Bureau of Justice Statistics." But such criticism has had little impact. Though longer sentences have not been correlated with a significant reduction in crime rates, incarceration theories are back in vogue.

Truth in Sentencing

Truth-in-sentencing laws mandate that certain criminals serve a set percentage of their sentences, usually 85 percent. The aim is to abolish or severely curtail parole. Over a dozen states have passed such laws, with varying requirements—some, like Virginia, only apply it to violent offenders; others, like Arizona, apply it far more broadly. Increases in prison populations across the country are likely, especially because the federal government has linked the amount a state receives in grants for prison building to the population of inmates subjected to truth-in-sentencing laws.

Three Strikes and You're Out

Three-Strikes-and-You're-Out laws, mandating life imprisonment for conviction of three serious crimes, are now on the books in twelve states. Three-strikes legislation in California counts as a third strike any one of approximately five hundred felonies. Hundreds of people have already been sentenced under this law, including one man who was sentenced on a third strike for stealing a piece of pizza. According to the ACLU's *National Prison Project Journal,* the Los Angeles District Attorney's Office reports that three out of four offenders who get life sentences under three-strikes legislation will be nonviolent offenders. Responding to popular fears, Georgia legislators passed a more draconian two-strikes law in 1994. The problem, as many have pointed out, is that both truth-in-sentencing and three-strikes legislation give enormous discretionary power to prosecutors while taking it away from judges.

While driving up the prison population, three-strikes legislation will also raise costs. In 1994, California prisons housed an astounding 120,000 inmates—in facilities designed for 66,000. The state's new three-strikes legislation is expected to boost the prison population to 211,000 by 1999.[11] California is planning to build ninety more prisons. On prison building alone (not to mention the increased costs associated with feeding and providing health care for thousands more prisoners) the state will spend over $20 billion over the next thirty years, according to a 1995 study carried out by RAND, a conservative, business-oriented think tank.

The War on Drugs

The war on drugs, formally begun in the latter years of the Reagan presidency and continued under both Bush and Clinton, and an array of mandatory sentencing laws are largely responsible for the rising prison populations. Nearly half of all inmates are serving terms for drug offenses, many of them nonviolent. In Florida, where a series of mandatory sentencing drug laws went into effect in the 1980s, the prisons ended up confining thousands of nonviolent inmates convicted of drug offenses—while those convicted of non–drug related violent crimes were released early to make room for them.[12]

The effects of the war on drugs have been more racially skewed than virtually any other social policy this side of Jim Crow. Indeed, as *The Armchair Activist* goes to press, the Supreme

Court is considering whether the laws and penalties against the use and distribution of crack are unconstitutional precisely because they ensnare such large numbers of black youth. According to the U.S. Sentencing Commission, over 88 percent of people sentenced for crack offenses are African-Americans and 4.1 percent, white.[13] And, because those convicted of crack offenses (overwhelmingly black inner-city male youth) face far longer sentences than those convicted of powder cocaine offenses (more often white, suburban youth), a black convict can expect, on average, to spend 41 percent more time in prison than a white convict.[14]

Michael Tonry, University of Minnesota professor of law and public policy, draws devastating conclusions in his comprehensive analysis of this phenomenon in his book *Malign Neglect:* Between 1985 and 1989, the number of blacks arrested for drug crimes more than doubled, while the number of white drug arrests increased by only a quarter. In Minnesota, non-white drug arrests increased five-fold in the 1980s, while white drug arrests rose only 22 percent. In Pennsylvania, sixteen times as many nonwhite males were in prison for drugs at the end of the 1980s as at the beginning.[15] Yet the Bureau of Justice Statistics states that only 10 percent of blacks and 11.5 percent of Hispanics in the country had ever used cocaine (including crack).[16] This is lower than the 11.7 percent of whites who had tried the drug. More whites than nonwhites had also tried marijuana and hallucinogens. Nevertheless, one in twelve American black men aged 18 to 54 are in prison, close to half for drug-related offenses.

Keep Punishment Profitable

The newly emergent security industry lobby is leading the call for right-wing criminal justice reform. The incentive is apparent—there is a vast amount of money to be made on "corrections." The Department of Corrections' nationwide budget is over $25 billion per year, and rising. The *Angolite Newsletter* (July/August, 1994) estimates the total annual cost for the criminal justice system (including prisons, police, judicial proceedings, and so on) at $74 billion.

A number of for-profit private companies are involved in maintaining, staffing, and equipping the growing number of

Increased incarceration rates are having a particularly devastating effect on the African-American community. Adam Walinsky described this in *The Atlantic Monthly* as a culture moving "toward a race behind bars."

- Blacks are seven times likelier to be incarcerated than whites.[17]
- Although African-Americans make up only 12 percent of the general population, they constitute 44 percent of the prison population.[18]
- Over 1.4 percent of the black population are imprisoned.[19]
- In 1989 one of four African-American men between the ages of twenty and twenty-nine was under some form of criminal justice supervision.[20]

prisons. Corrections Corporation of America (CCA) is the largest operator of private prisons, with an income of $60 million a year in Tennessee alone. Private prison firms house 2 percent of the country's prisoners, and the number is growing. Jan Elvin notes in the ACLU's *National Prison Project Journal* (Winter 1995) that defense contractors, hurt by cuts in military spending, are getting in on the opportunities in the corrections industry, and in the process shifting the policy debate. Elvin writes, "The lobbying power of these companies, especially those defense contractors with lobbyists in Washington and long-term relationships on Capitol Hill, distorts the dialogue that should be taking place about the effectiveness of incarceration as a policy and drowns more reasonable voices." Economically devastated communities lobby for prisons as a way of bringing in jobs; some towns in Texas have even offered prison management free country club memberships if they locate there.

1994 federal crime legislation allotted nearly $9 billion for prison building; this figure was subsequently raised by HR3, the crime bill passed by the House of Representatives in 1995. HR3 introduced a system for federal funding of prisons that would grant more money to the states if they either introduced truth-in-sentencing laws or incarcerated prisoners for 10 percent longer than the national average—thus setting into motion an "incarceration race" among the states, as the legislators and criminal justice systems vie with one another for coveted prison building grants.

Exploitation of Prison Labor

A stone's throw from the type of forced prison labor America is so quick to castigate the Chinese government for using is the Prison Industries Act drafted by the American Legislative Exchange Council (ALEC), an association of right-wing state legislators. It provides that "inmates may be assigned to work in a private manufacturing enterprise."

The act specifies that the inmates will be paid minimum wage, but that the money will go to the Department of Corrections. After taxes are taken out, and restitution paid to the victim of the crime, twenty percent will go to the inmate's family. But if the family is on welfare, the state will instead take the money "until that amount of aid or assistance is repaid." Ten percent of the wage will go to the inmate and ten percent will be held for the inmate until his or her release. The rest will go to the state as partial reimbursement to the state for the "cost of the inmate's imprisonment and care." What all of this effectively means is that if a proposal such as this passed, prisoners could be sent to work in the private sector for approximately $15 per week.

Frequent Application of the Death Penalty

The most extreme example of retributive justice is, of course, the death penalty. Cries for the increased use of the death penalty issue from the mouths of many elected officials. Governor Pete Wilson of California promised, "I will put the teeth back into the death penalty."[22] Texas Senator Phil Gramm wants the death penalty to be used "fairly *and regularly.*"[23] In August 1995, Newt Gingrich called for the mass execution of drug smugglers. Not to be outdone, Governor Fife Symington of Arizona urged the creation of stone-breaking chain gangs for the 120-plus prisoners on the state's death row.[24]

Forty states have reintroduced the death penalty since the

Guns Out of Control

In 1991, the National Rifle Association set up a CrimeStrike division designed to oppose gun control while pushing harsher justice for criminals. To back up this initiative, the organization published a "Fact Card" to show how few guns were used criminally. One fact is that there are 200 million firearms and 70 million handguns in the United States. Another is that "Over 99.8 percent of U.S. firearms and 99.6 percent of U.S. handguns will not be involved in criminal activity in any given year." This sounds fairly impressive, until the figures are broken down—then one finds that 400,000 firearms and 280,000 handguns *will* be used in criminal activity every year!

The NRA lobbied intensively for passage of H.R. 1488, the Citizens' Protection from Violent Crime Act of 1995. This act, unlikely to survive a presidential veto, would repeal all the gun restrictions in the 1994 Crime Bill. ALEC also recommends a law that would forbid localities (such as cities) to pass restrictive firearms legislation beyond that passed at a state level.

H.R. 1488 imposes mandatory sentences of up to thirty years for using weapons in a crime. It also, according to an approving NRA summary, "adds serious drug offenses committed by juveniles to the list of prior crimes punishable by the fifteen-year mandatory sentence for 'armed career criminals' "[21] In short, the bill keeps guns on the streets and then severely punishes teenagers tempted to use them: it is a policy guaranteed to waste and destroy young lives.

The NRA and other pro-gun groups also played an important—and ultimately successful—role in the campaign to repeal the Gun Free School Zones Act.

Supreme Court ruled it constitutional in 1976. Prisoners are executed by electrocution, lethal injection, hanging, gassing, and shooting. The 1994 Crime Bill extended the death penalty to cover over fifty federal crimes. Executions are increasing yearly, and over three thousand people are on America's death rows.

Ten states allow the execution of pregnant women; twenty-seven states permit the execution of the mentally retarded, and twenty-four states permit the execution of those who committed a crime while a juvenile. With respect to the execution of juveniles, the countries besides the United States permitting this practice are Bangladesh, Iran, Iraq, Nigeria, Pakistan, Saudi Arabia, and Yemen, according to Amnesty International.

Both the race of the victim and the race of the convicted criminal play an enormous role in determining whether a death sentence will be handed down. Although African-Americans make up only twelve percent of the general population, forty percent of those on death row are black. Eighty-three percent of those executed have been convicted of crimes against whites. Only thirteen percent of those executed were sentenced for committing a crime against a black person, according to the NAACP Legal Defense and Education Fund, despite the fact that just under fifty percent of murder victims are black. In 1989, Amnesty International's *When the State Kills* report singled out the United States and South Africa as embodying racism in the application of their death penalties.[25]

The overwhelming majority of those sentenced to death are impoverished and near-illiterate, and generally represented during their trials by court-appointed, ill-paid public attorneys who are often grossly unqualified to argue a capital case. Yet, the House of Representatives has voted to eliminate the federally funded Post-Conviction Defender Organization, a group of non-profit law centers that handle the appeals of those sentenced to die. Congress also voted to curtail habeas corpus motions for those on death row, effectively limiting many appeals to a one-year time period.

Restrictions on death penalty appeals, which are supported by many right-wing figures, would allow capital punishment to be used more frequently, while at the same time cutting costs. Indeed, a comprehensive study at Duke University in 1993 found that the death penalty costs North Carolina $2 million per execution over the cost of a nondeath penalty murder case with a sentence of imprisonment for life.[26] On a national basis, these figures translate to an extra cost of half a billion dollars between 1976 and 1993 from the death penalty. However, making appeals more difficult is a serious violation of justice and human rights. The appeals process is crucial in these life-and-death cases.

Since 1970, forty-eight people have been released from death row with evidence of their innocence. According to the Death Penalty Information Center in Washington, D.C., researchers have documented the executions of twenty-three confirmably innocent people this century.

POSITIVE ALTERNATIVES

A number of organizations, localities, and states are developing alternatives to increased incarceration and retributive justice.

Vermont, Oregon, and Minnesota have begun using "restitutive" justice for nonviolent offenders, often bringing communities—through a series of community boards—into the process of determining punishment. Offenders can be ordered to pay compensation to the victim or community, either through direct financial restitution or through a form of community service that will, hopefully, bring home to them the effects of their actions. In Vermont, for example, drunk drivers have been required to do community service in the emergency rooms of hospitals; those who destroy a neighbor's fence could be required to work in that neighbor's garden as compensation. In Dakota County, Minnesota, "Crime Repair Crews" have been set up; convicted offenders who enroll get reduced prison time. According to Kay Pranis, the Department of Corrections restorative justice planner, each of these is made up of "a crew of offenders who can go out and repair property damage within twenty-four to forty-eight hours of something happening."

Genesee County, New York, has long had alternatives to incarceration for a number of offenses. These include mandatory drug treatment and counseling for petty drug offenders and community service for nonviolent property offenders. The Drug Treatment Alternative to Prison (DTAP) program, in Brooklyn, New York, targets nonviolent drug offenders, giving pretrial defendants the option of entering residential treatment centers instead of prison.

Twenty-two states, with Massachusetts at the lead, have established Day Reporting Centers (DRCs) for nonviolent criminals. According to a 1995 Justice Department report, 114 of these centers now exist, offering a more rehabilitative, and less costly, alternative to imprisonment. At these centers, convicted offenders are required to undergo drug counseling, family counseling, job training, and basic education.

Another pilot program is Financial Assessment Related to Em-

A Model Prison

McKean, a medium-security federal correctional institution in Bradford, Pennsylvania, has shown that offering educational, training, work, mentor, and recreational programs may be the most effective way to lower prison costs and recidivism rates. Each inmate at McKean costs taxpayers about $15,370 a year, well below the overall federal average of $21,350. And though no recidivism studies have been conducted there, Robert Worth reports in *The Atlantic Monthly* that senior staff members and local parole officers say that McKean parolees return to prison much less often than those from other prisons. On top of this, in the six years McKean has been in operation, there have been but three serious assaults on staff members and six on inmates—practically a clean slate when compared to other facilities.

The secret to McKean's success is a warden named Dennis Luther, who ran the prison like a well-managed business until he retired in 1995. Recreation, for example, is not looked upon as a frill, but good management. Luther says, "On a summer evening you've got three to five hundred men in this rec yard, with three staff. If you had less recreation, you'd need more staff. There's a clear economic advantage. You'd *definitely*

ployability, detailed in the report *Seeking Justice,* put out by the
Edna McConnell Clark Foundation, an alternative sentencing
think tank. This is a system pioneered in Germany whereby offenders are ordered to pay restitution to the victim in proportion to the amount of money they earn each day. The system is
being studied by the Vera Institute, an alternative sentencing
think tank in New York. Judges in Phoenix, Arizona, have begun
handing out sentences based on this program.

have more fights. We do surveys every year, and they
show that as inmates get more involved in the rec program, they get in less trouble. Also, they tend to have
less health trouble, and that saves money."

This practical attitude is also taken with education
programs. A high 47 percent of the inmates participate in classes, and many learn job skills to help them
find jobs when they are released. Princeton University
criminologist John Dilulio is quoted by Worth as saying, "Especially with respect to certain types of prison
educational programs, you save money by hiring fewer
officers in the short run *and* reducing recidivism in
the long run." Numerous studies back up Dilulio's
claim.

Despite McKean's outstanding rating from the
American Correctional Society, it has been attacked as
a "resort" by politicians calling for more retributive
forms of criminal justice. Indeed, the "no frills" strategy is taking hold. Vocational programs have been cut
in at least twenty-five states, and college-aid, GED, and
literacy programs have been slashed. Worth notes that
"the increase in prison violence over the past few years
has coincided with big cuts in educational and vocational programming at all levels."[27]

How This Issue Affects You

High crime and fear of crime have led to the emergence of a multitiered security apparatus. At its base is an overstretched police force, increasingly unable to maintain public safety in major cities. Then there are the private security companies that work for the business districts and large apartment complexes within these cities. And finally, there are the rapidly growing private police forces that protect the gated suburbs within which the middle and upper classes increasingly seek refuge.

With more money being pumped into a punishment complex, less money is then available for other public sector needs. California now spends more on its prison system than on its higher education system. According to a RAND study, by the year 2004, nearly 20 percent of the state budget will be spent on prisons, while higher education spending will have fallen to one percent. The result of budget cuts to California's prestigious state university system is already being seen: Programs have greatly detriorated, and the fees charged have risen drastically. Over 200,000 students have dropped out of the California public higher education system since 1992.

By investing more money into mechanisms of incarceration and control rather than social programs and poverty relief, we are facilitating the emergence of a rigid, hierarchical class system. America locks up one in every two to three hundred of its citizens, with some cities locking up one in seventy. The disproportionate burden borne by African-Americans and the poor has the makings of a cataclysmic racial explosion and societal breakdown.

What You Can Do: Action Sampler

- *Start a Prison Awareness Group on Campus*

Josh MacPhee, a student activist at Oberlin College in Ohio, is working to educate people in the college community on issues involving prisons, criminal justice, and social control. He is part of a prison awareness group, called Oberlin Action Against Prisons, that organizes lectures, discussions, and film screenings on such topics as AIDS in prison, women in prison, and political prisoners.

Oberlin Action Against Prisons works closely with other prison activist groups in Ohio. "Every year we hold an Ohio Prison Activists Conference here in Oberlin. . . . We talk with these groups, strategize, pass around knowledge," says MacPhee. The college group has developed information flyers and packets to publicize the issue, organized students to write letters to local papers, and designed a bumper sticker to give out to people who support criminal justice alternatives.

If you are interested in starting a prison awareness group, contact the Prison Activist Resource Center, a collective volunteer-run project launched in 1994. The center's resources include the *Handbook for Educators and Activists on the Crisis in Prisons*.

Prison Activist Resource Center
P.O. Box 3201
Berkeley, California 94703
(510) 845-8813
fax: (510) 845-8816
e-mail: parcer@igc.apc.org

Promote Innovative Policies in Your Own Community

These can include those discussed in the Positive Alternatives section of this chapter. Develop a coalition made up of several people, preferably including some with a degree of local stature. Then arrange a meeting to discuss alternative sentencing programs with your county commissioner, generally the official who determines local responses to crime. To alter the law on a broader front, pressure state and federal legislators to look at new approaches to punishment. For more information on criminal justice and alternative sentencing programs, contact the following organizations for their publications lists.

Vera Institute of Justice
377 Broadway, 11th Floor
New York, NY 10013
(212) 334-1300

The Vera Institute works to improve the American justice system. Its research and demonstration projects have catalyzed changes throughout the United States, as well as a number of other countries, in policing procedures, court administrations, bail, prosecution and defense services, sentencing, community supervision, employment devices, and addiction treatment.

Sentencing Project
918 F Street, NW, Suite 501
Washington, DC 20004
(202) 628-0871

The Sentencing Project provides training and technical assistance on sentencing alternatives and engages in research and advocacy on criminal justice policy issues.

Listen to the "Voice of the Convict"

Prison Life is the only national magazine by and for prisoners, fighting for prisoners' rights and striving to give convicts and ex-cons the dignity all people deserve. The magazine is a compelling resource for "freeworlders" seeking an inside look into prison life. Subscriptions are $19.95 for 1 year (6 issues). Contact:

Prison Life
1436 West Gray, Suite 531
Houston, Texas 77019-4946
(800) 207-2659
fax: (713) 694-8131

Oppose the Death Penalty

Many activists view the death penalty as a crucial human rights issue. To get more involved in fighting the use of the death penalty, contact Amnesty International, a human rights organization with several hundred local chapters in the United States. Amnesty International defines itself as "a worldwide movement of people working for the release of all prisoners of conscience, for fair and prompt trials for all political prisoners, and an end to torture and the death penalty."

Amnesty International USA
322 Eighth Avenue
New York, NY 10001
(212) 807-8400

Sample Letter

The following is a sample letter written to a local TV station in response to the increase in crime coverage on its news program.

Dear [Name of Station Manager]:

As a longtime viewer of [name of news program], I've noticed that the program has stepped up its coverage of violent crime. While awareness of such incidents are important to viewers, please consider that they also may be contributing to an unnecessary fear of crime in our community.

Murder and violent crime rates per capita have leveled off, and in some circumstances decreased, according to the Bureau of Justice Statistics. Yet the media doesn't reflect this trend—a study conducted by the Center for Media and Public Affairs shows that television coverage of crime more than doubled from 1992 to 1993, with murder coverage tripling!

I encourage your station to balance the segments on crime with more innovative news coverage. Perhaps you could show the flip side of the crime issue by highlighting innovative strategies being used to rehabilitate prisoners. I would appreciate any action you take to address this complaint.

Sincerely,

Armchair Activist

10

Immigration: America's Identity Crisis

D espite the fact that America has always been a land of immigrants—a place Walt Whitman celebrated as "a nation of nations"—each wave of newcomers has been shunned as outsiders. In the mid-nineteenth century, the Native American Party decried "the peril from the rapid and enormous increase of the body of residents of foreign birth, imbued with foreign feelings and of an ignorant and immoral character."[1] During the same period, the anti-Catholic Know-Nothings organized to limit the access of immigrants from Germany and Ireland. In the early twentieth century, southern and eastern Europeans were scorned by the racist Immigration Restriction League. Robert DeCourcey Ward, the driving force behind the League, summed up the immigration debate as "a race question, pure and simple. . . . It is fundamentally a question as to what kind of babies shall be born; it is a question as to what races shall dominate in this country."[2]

Today America is experiencing an influx of immigrants higher than at any time since World War II (although the percentage of the American population who are foreign-born is much lower than it was during the last great peak between 1900 and 1920). Because of national legislation in 1965 that eliminated racially discriminatory immigration quotas, this new wave of immigration consists mostly of people of color, with most new immigrants coming from Latin America, Asia, and the Caribbean. Alarm at the changing skin color of Americans still dominates much of the anti-immigration sentiment currently voiced by the radical right. David Duke wrote in the National Association for the Advancement of White People's newsletter in 1983:

> Immigration . . . along with nonwhite birthrates will make white people a minority totally vulnerable to the political, social, and economic will of blacks, Mexicans, Puerto Ricans, and Orientals. A social upheaval is now beginning to occur that will be the funeral dirge of the America we love.[3]

Like the anti-immigration voices from earlier decades of the century, Duke rationalizes his racial fears by warning that immigrants of color are a fount of all social ills: "I shudder to contemplate the future under nonwhite occupation: rapes, murders, robberies multiplied a hundredfold, illiteracy such as in Haiti, medicine such as in Mexico, and tyranny such as in Togoland."

By stirring up old prejudices and new hatreds, figures such as Duke reinforce the misconceptions and misinformation that cloud the immigration issue. Indeed, as we enter the second half of the 1990s, more and more Americans appear to believe that immigrants are a burden to the country. Concerns about jobs, education, and crime fuel a debate about whether the increasingly multiethnic makeup of this nation is an opportunity or a threat.

Though anti-immigrationist arguments are often communicated in seemingly race-neutral language, a rigid, exclusive definition of what it means to be American comes through loud and clear. Peter Brimelow, a senior editor of *Forbes* magazine and himself an immigrant from England, questions in his 1995 book *Alien Nation: Common Sense About America's Immigration Disaster,* "Why does America have to be transformed?"[4] He worries what it will be like for his little son, Alexander, a "white male with blue eyes and blond hair," to grow up in a multiethnic nation.

Obviously, part of what makes a country cohere is some sense of a unifying culture. Extreme community identification and nationalist politics within a state generally serve to weaken the political structure and undermine civic peace. But the pride and assertiveness of ethnic subgroups can also enrich the society as a whole. As *New York Times* columnist Thomas L. Friedman writes: "Unless we give people of diverse ethnic backgrounds a sense of belonging, unless we give them a sense that their identity and heritage are valued threads in the tapestry of American society, real community is impossible."[5] Moreover, attempting to impose the culture of a single dominant group frequently leads to a massive backlash, sparking the very ultranationalist forces so feared in the first place.

The deep ethnic rifts which have opened in our urban areas contribute to anxiety over whether too much diversity will weaken the country. But right-wing efforts to stamp out diversity do nothing to address these complex problems. Throughout America's history, interaction among its different racial and ethnic groups has defined the culture, generating creativity and innovation. The same holds true today. The strength of this country depends on the willingness of newcomers and established residents alike to overcome the forces that divide and inflame them. To shrink from this challenge will, in the words of writer Cornel West, "produce a cold-hearted and mean-spirited America no longer worth fighting for or living in."[6]

OPPONENTS OF IMMIGRATION

• **The Federation for American Immigration Reform (FAIR).** Founded in 1979 by John Tanton, today FAIR has a budget of $3.5 million and claims a membership of seventy thousand. FAIR receives significant funding from the controversial Pioneer Fund, a foundation dedicated to "race betterment" through eugenics. Dan Stein, FAIR's executive director, has appeared unopposed on the *Today* show, *60 Minutes,* and CNN, and has testified before Congress in support of laws restricting immigration. He has said about Asian and Latino birthrates, "It's almost like they're getting into competitive breeding."[7]

• **U.S. English.** Also founded by Tanton, U.S. English has campaigned since 1983 to have English declared the official language of the United States, lobbying extensively at both state and federal levels. Today, it has a membership of 620,000 and includes such high-profile figures on its board of advisors as former U.S. Senator Barry Goldwater. When supporters were asked what had prompted them to support U.S. English, 42 percent endorsed the statement "I wanted America to stand strong and not cave in to Hispanics who shouldn't be here."[8]

• **Cordelia Scaife May.** An heiress to the Mellon family fortune, May has poured millions of dollars into U.S. English, FAIR, and other Tanton-led groups. Her Laurel Foundation has also provided funding for the U.S. distribution of an obscure French novel by Raspail, *The Camp of Saints,* which portrays Third World immigrants invading Europe and destroying its civilization. The author warns readers: "We need only glance at the awesome population figures predicted for the year 2000 . . . seven billion people, only nine hundred million of whom will be white."[9] *The Camp of Saints* is currently being distributed in the United States by National Vanguard Books, run by neo-Nazi William Pierce.

• **English First.** This English-only advocacy organization is headed by Larry Pratt, executive director of the extremist group Gun Owners of America. Pratt is also a former officer on the Council on Inter-American Security (CIS), a right-wing group that actively undermined democratic movements in Latin America throughout the 1980s. According to Michael Novick, in the book *White Lies/White Power,* one CIS paper discussed the supposed link between bilingual education and terrorism, declaring "Bilingual education has national security implications." The paper describes the Indian ancestors of Latinos as "uncivilized barbaric squatters . . . [with a] penchant for grotesque human sacrifices, cannibalism, and kidnapping women."[10]

• **The American Immigration Control Foundation (AICF).** This advocacy group publishes *Border Watch,* a monthly publication popular in anti-immigrant circles, with a reported circulation of 200,000. Americans for Immigration Control, the lobbying arm of AICF, claims to be the nation's largest grassroots lobby for immigration reform.

DISTORTIONS ABOUT IMMIGRATION

"America's changing ethnic blend rips at the social fabric."

The Immigration Act of 1924, lobbied for by the Ku Klux Klan, eugenicists, and isolationists, set a low yearly ceiling on immigration to the United States and introduced a quota system based on national origin which clearly favored the British and northern Europeans. A headline in the *Los Angeles Times* hailed this as a "Nordic Victory."[11]

The 1965 Immigration and Nationality Act Amendments sparked a revolutionary change in immigration patterns by abolishing the national origin quotas. The growing civil rights movement contributed to the passage of the 1965 law, which allowed people from any nation to come to the United States, no longer distinguishing on the basis of the immigrants' race but focusing instead on family relationships and job skills. The law allowed people from third world countries to immigrate to America on a large scale. Today, over 80 percent of recent immigrants are people of color.[12]

Anti-immigrationists fear that the United States is moving toward becoming a fully multiethnic nation. In *Alien Nation,* Peter Brimelow writes, "It is simply common sense that Americans have a legitimate interest in their country's racial balance. It is common sense that they have a right to insist that their government stop shifting it."[13] He also comments that "the American nation has always had a specific ethnic core. And that core has been white."[14] John Vinson, president of the American Immigration Control Foundation, says, "I'm afraid that if we keep letting them come here, then we will lose our distinctness, and become as they are."[15]

In fact, America has always flourished because of its diversity, its sometimes chaotic blend of distinct cultures. The recent influx of immigrants is a source of vitality rather than a harbinger of disaster. Opponents of immigration forget that the real strength of America is in its pluralism, that its very democratic heritage is based on the acceptance into its midst of the world's seekers and dreamers.

"Immigrants in the past were more easily assimilated than the immigrants coming today."

John Vinson, president of AICF, argues that "in the past, most of the immigrants were Christian, and now a much larger percentage are Muslim, and they're having a harder time assimilating."[16] Despite this common misconception, there is no evidence that past immigrants adapted more easily to American culture. In fact, a century ago, when New York City had newspapers written in English, Spanish, Russian, Yiddish, Chinese, Italian, Hungarian, German, and a host of other languages, the *New York Times* made a similar claim to Vinson's: "There is a limit to our powers of assimilation, and when it is exceeded, the country suffers from something very much like indigestion."[17]

America has always had a tension between its English-speaking heartland and the multitude of cultures and languages represented in the cities. Yet generations of immigrants and their children have survived these tensions and flourished. By adapting to American culture while at the same time holding on to their native traditions, immigrants not only became "Americanized," but simultaneously added to the definition of what it means to be American. So it is with today's immigrants. Acceptance and equal opportunity will only make this assimilation process easier.

"Immigrants steal jobs and drive down wages."

A number of economists have concluded that the overall effect of recent immigration has been, on balance, neutral for the U.S. economy. Still, economic competition from immigrants can be felt by native-born Americans in certain areas of the country (especially in the urban areas of the five states with the largest numbers of migrants—California, Florida, Illinois, New York, and Texas) and in certain industries. This is a subject, however, that ties into broader issues of worker protection and the balance of power within the economic system, and it must be understood in that context.

The exploitative working conditions of immigrants have been used to undermine trade unions and the higher wages for which they have struggled. As immigrants enter the country, a pool of unprotected, vulnerable, and often desperate workers emerges—often taking jobs native-born Americans would not take. In some cases, competition for scarce jobs occurs with those already insecure in the low-wage economy: working-class whites, inner-city African-Americans, the children and grandchildren of previous immigrants. Los Angeles's General Accounting Office, for example, reports that the janitorial firms serving downtown have almost entirely replaced their black unionized workforce with nonunionized (and thus lower paid) immigrants.[18]

In both New York and California, garment industry sweat-shops have reemerged, with similar working conditions (sixteen-hour days, no benefits, extraordinarily low wages) to those existing before World War I. Not surprisingly, this has occurred at the same time as the weakening of garment industry trade unions, such as the International Ladies Garment Workers' Union, an organization that grew up to fight the atrocious conditions of the earlier sweatshops. In Los Angeles alone, 55,000 native (often unionized, and frequently African-American) garment workers were displaced by immigrant workers in the 1970s.

Yet, when immigrants are not available to be used as pawns to lower wages, many companies now simply export their jobs to low-wage countries such as those in eastern Europe, Asia, and Latin America. In 1995, Boeing attempted to lower the benefits and wages of its highly skilled workforce, and to replace a number of American jobs (and workers) with low-paying jobs overseas. The plan was successfully resisted by a well-organized and powerful trade union. This example shows that immigrants are not the biggest foe of workers, and that even in their absence, wages and jobs are not secure.

Doug Brugge, writing in *The Public Eye,* sums up how working people disenchanted with the system have been manipulated:

> Displaced workers, along with others who fear for their liveli-hood, are fertile ground in which to sow anti-immigrant senti-ment, since angry and frustrated people often seek some target on which to blame their problems. The right wing has orga-nized and manipulated such anger and resentment and turned it away from corporations and directed it against the govern-ment, decrying high taxes and the inability of the State to solve problems such as social deterioration, homelessness, crime and violence. . . . Immigrants make a convenient scapegoat and a very tangible target for people's anger.[19]

And while many cast blame on immigrants for economic prob-lems, ignored is the salient fact that immigrants start many new businesses and that they revitalize urban areas. Maria En-chautegui, an economist at the Urban Institute, studied the four hundred largest U.S. counties and found that for every one hun-dred adult immigrants arriving in an area, forty-six new jobs were generated—compared to only twenty-five after a migration of one hundred native-born Americans.[20] In a downtrodden, immigrant section of Los Angeles, for example, some three hundred wholesalers sell over $1 billion worth of low-tech toys each year. Most of the merchants were born in Hong Kong, Vietnam, and Taiwan, and arrived in the United States almost penniless. Today two thousand people are employed in Toy Town.

"Immigrants take advantage of welfare."

The debate about immigration is also a debate about poverty. Bob Goldsbrough, president of Americans for Immigration Control, objects that "the legal ones [immigrants] are breaking the law too—they're taking welfare, which they have no legal right to."[21] Many of the attacks against immigrants on public assistance are the same as those launched against the native-born poor.

In 1990 over 9 percent of immigrant households, compared to 7 percent of native households, were on public assistance. Local governments in areas such as Los Angeles, where many immigrants live, are severely overburdened. But Urban Institute researcher Michael Fix emphasizes that use of welfare by immigrants is concentrated among refugees (individuals unwilling or unable to return to their countries because of a well-founded fear of persecution) and elderly immigrants. Fix writes, "Working-age immigrants are less likely to use benefits than working-age natives."[22] An Urban Institute study estimated that about 74 percent of adult male immigrants hold jobs, verses 72 percent of the general male population.

History suggests that immigrant communities generally work their way out of poverty fairly rapidly, and begin putting more back into the system than they take out. Providing immigrants with welfare ought to be viewed as a social investment in the future, not as a social drain.

RIGHT-WING PROPOSALS

Favor Would-be Immigrants with Skills over those Related to U.S. Residents

Anti-immigrationists, including Peter Brimelow and FAIR, support reforms that would change priorities so that immigration preferences are given to people with job skills more than to people with relatives already in the country.

Current legislation in the Senate and House of Representatives would drastically scale back the number of immigrants allowed in to unite families. The proposed legislation would enact the most restrictive immigration laws in 30 years and the first cuts since the 1920's in the number of foreigners entering the country legally. Antonia Hernandez, president and general counsel of the Mexican American Legal Defense and Education Fund, points out that restrictions like these go against the "pro–nuclear family" values that the right supposedly wants to bolster in America.

Deny Public Services to Undocumented Immigrants

In November 1994, 59 percent of California's voters passed Proposition 187, an initiative that declares the state's undocumented immigrants ineligible for most public services, including education and nonemergency health care. The initiative requires public education, health, social services, and law enforcement agencies to deny services to—and report—an individual if he or she is "suspected" of being an illegal immigrant. The courts immediately suspended the enforcement of the law pending an examination of its constitutionality.

Proposition 187 was championed by an organization called Save Our State (SOS), a coalition of conservative groups and individuals. SOS promoted the proposition as a cure-all that would alleviate many social and economic problems facing California. The ostensible goals of denying benefits to those lacking residency rights are to save tax money, halt the immigrant influx into California (an influx that was actively promoted by Governor Pete Wilson and others at a time when the large farmers

needed to import cheap labor quickly), and effectively force employers to pay a minimum wage to legal workers.

Many people dedicated to public service are uneasy about
their new role, as outlined in Proposition 187. One family practice physician at the Venice Family Clinic was quoted in the *Los
Angeles Times* as saying, "I will continue to carry out the mission
of the clinic, which is to provide care to people with no access
to health care. A patient's immigration status is completely
irrelevant to my relationship with them, to managing the medical problem. This initiative violates a doctor's ethic of confi-
dentiality." [23]

Critics of Proposition 187 argue that identifying "suspected"
individuals as illegal immigrants encourages discrimination—all
people of color or those who speak with accents are suspect. Although most of the proposition has never been implemented
since it was enjoined by both federal and state courts, immigrant
rights groups reported many complaints of civil rights abuses
after the legislation passed. Those aggrieved ranged from a car
accident victim who was denied emergency treatment when he
couldn't prove his legal status, to the Hispanic mayor of
Pomona, who was stopped by the INS and told to prove his citizenship.[24] According to the Los Angeles County Commission on
Human Relations, hate crimes against Latinos in Los Angeles increased 23.4 percent in 1994, and the Commission attributes the
rise to the passage of Proposition 187.

Deny Citizenship to Children Born in the United States to Undocumented Immigrants

Figures such as Pat Buchanan and California Governor Pete Wilson have suggested that children of undocumented immigrants
be denied citizenship. Such a measure would clearly violate the
U.S. Constitution. And its proponents would be unlikely to
gather enough support to amend the Constitution, as those who
speak out in favor of it are well aware. Like the English-only
movement, what the proposal does is to provide politicians with
a great rhetorical device, allowing them to sound tough on illegal immigration while not requiring them to deal with the issue
seriously.

Deny Benefits to Legal Immigrants

"The Personal Responsibility Act" detailed in the Republican Congress members' *Contract with America* proposes to create fiscal savings by eliminating social welfare programs not only for illegal immigrants, but for legal ones as well. The legislation would deny virtually all of the social safety net to immigrants. Noncitizens would be excluded from some sixty programs—including Medicaid, food stamps, welfare, children's school meals, children's immunizations, housing loans, job training, higher education assistance, and child care. They would be left only with emergency medical assistance.

The chair of the House Ways and Means Subcommittee, Representative E. Clay Shaw, Jr., (R-FL) claims that "our welfare benefits are an attraction to people to come to this country, and they should be cut off. We should take care of our own with the resources we have."[25] However, holding back essential services from a group of people who have the potential to be great successes in this country would be tremendously shortsighted, creating a subculture of destitute individuals with nowhere to turn and little prospect of emerging from poverty.

The proposal has historical precedent. In the early twentieth century, immigrants who became a "public charge" were deported; those thought likely to become so were not allowed in. Throughout the latter half of the twentieth century, however, the courts have viewed immigrants as future citizens, entitled to the same protections under the law as citizens.

Make English the Official Language of the United States

Establishing English as the country's official language is one solution offered to remedy perceived disunity in America. The English-only movement is sweeping the states: twenty-two have enacted legislation making English their official language, and several more are considering similar legislation.

More than a third of the members of Congress, including House Speaker Gingrich and Senate Majority Leader Dole, support English-only legislation. Gingrich argues that "English has to be our common language; otherwise we're not going to have a civilization."[26]

Such measures are almost entirely symbolic; 97 percent of Americans, including most immigrants, already speak English well or very well, according to the U.S. Census Bureau.[27] And immigrants with poor English language skills are lining up for adult ESL (English as a second language) classes: San Francisco City College, for example, teaches English to twenty thousand adults every semester, and the waiting list is long. Rather than passing English-only legislation, a Congress serious about this issue would allocate more public money to ESL classes instead of slashing such programs.

Meanwhile, one out of every seven Americans speaks a language other than English at home, the most common being Spanish. English-only proponents target the "wasteful" accommodations government has made for bi-lingual speakers. Representative Roth (R-WI), chair of the House's English-language Task Force, says "[I]n LA, you can vote in seven different ballots. We're saying, no. . . . When you work with the government, it should be done in English language forms."[28] Yet according to a General Accounting Office survey, of the 400,000 publications put out by the federal government, only 265 documents are given in more than one language other than English—that's fewer than one tenth of one percent of total government printing jobs!

State and local English-only laws have led to language-discrimination complaints with the U.S. Equal Employment Opportunity Commission. According to the ACLU, some clients have been denied credit and insurance because they don't speak English. In Amarillo, Texas, a judge told a mother in a child custody case that she was committing "child abuse" by speaking Spanish to her child at home. A drunk driver in Texas was denied probation because he couldn't benefit from an all-English Alcoholics Anonymous program.

James Crawford writes in *Hold Your Tongue: Bilingualism and the Politics of "English Only"* that to Hispanics, " 'the legal protection of English' sounds a lot like 'equal rights for whites'; a demand inspired by the paranoia of the dominant group, a backlash against Hispanic advances in civil rights, education, and political empowerment. In a word, racism."[29] Crawford believes that "elevating English as an icon has an appeal for the insecure and the resentful. It provides a clear answer to the question: Who belongs?"[30]

Positive Alternatives

Easing the assimilation process for immigrants is perhaps the best way to ensure that these newcomers achieve their potential in this country. Organizations such as the Center for Immigrant Rights (CIR) in New York run confidential hotlines to answer the questions of those facing a new culture, new language, and new laws. A hotline can be invaluable to immigrants who must wait in line for hours at the Immigration and Naturalization Service to get answers to simple questions—in San Jose, for example, immigrants often arrive the night before to secure a place in line for the information counter. CIR's hotline operators, who speak English, Spanish, Cantonese and Mandarin, receive inquiries about workplace rights, eligibility for benefits, and resources for political asylum. They advise battered women whose only claim to citizenship is through abusive husbands, and explain changes in immigration policy. The Northern California Coalition for Immigration Rights (NCCIR) in San Francisco received 5,000 calls to its hotline in 1994.

Californians for Justice (CFJ) is a new grassroots political action committee created to garner popular support against an anti-affirmative action initiative and a follow-up to Prop 187 (known as SOS II), which will appear on California's ballot in the fall of 1996. CFJ aims to motivate politically inactive immigrants, minorities, and youths to stand up for their rights, through their Million Voices for Justice campaign. The campaign is working to gather one million signatures of people stating their opposition to these initiatives, and to use the names to build a statewide activist database, which will then be used to conduct voter registration and identification efforts, precinct-level organizing, and get-out-the-vote drives.

Voter registration efforts enable immigrants rights groups to remind new citizens that their voice in government is one of the most important parts of citizenship. In San Francisco, over three thousand immigrants become citizens each month. NCCIR's new strategy is to send volunteers to INS citizenship ceremonies in San Francisco; after immigrants are sworn-in, NCCIR registers them as voters.

One ambitious experiment in accommodating soaring numbers of students from widely diverse educational and cultural backgrounds is the Newcomer School in Long Island City, New York. This high school for immigrants, which opened its doors in the fall of 1995, is one of but a few of its kind in the country. The Newcomer School, with twenty-seven teachers who speak a total of nineteen foreign languages and dialects, configures class schedules to fit students' language and learning needs. For example, a Latino student in an English-language math class will be transferred to a class taught in Spanish if language difficulties are impeding his progress. Combining English instruction with academic classes in a multitude of languages, the school aims to transfer immigrant students to regular high schools after a year.

How This Issue Affects You

The United States is a country built in part by hardworking immigrants who came here to achieve a better life for themselves and their families. Whether we just arrived or we can trace our family tree back to the Revolutionary War, most of our families are or once were newcomers. This is an important link to keep in mind when confronted by xenophobic political debate.

Sharpening the distinctions between immigrants and citizens (and further between naturalized and native-born citizens) makes for second-class membership in our culture, which the Center for Immigrant Rights views as "the road to divisiveness, exploitation, and an abridgement of fundamental constitutional and human rights." Immigration "reform" that locks immigrants (legal and illegal) out of the most basic public services would widen this distinction tremendously, excluding certain members of our society from the most basic government services.

Across the country, advocacy organizations are reaffirming the need for all people to defend immigrants' rights. Fostering a successful life for immigrants in the United States and developing humane and equitable immigration policies begins with increasing public awareness of the rights and contributions of immigrants. It is in this area that Armchair Activists can make a big difference on the issue.

WHAT YOU CAN DO: ACTION SAMPLER

Take a Stand

Insist on human and civil rights protections for all immigrants, including strict and uniform enforcement of labor, health, and safety laws so that the exploitation of immigrants ceases to be feasible and profitable. Oppose the scapegoating of immigrants for current economic and social problems in the United States.

Keep the Lines of Communication Open

If you are a native-born American, get to know newcomers who are neighbors or colleagues and make them feel welcome. Consider learning a new language and practicing it with immigrants who are native speakers.

Bring up the topic of immigration in conversation—at church, at work, or in a community center. A group discussion on the issue is a good way to illuminate, and perhaps alter, any assumptions individuals may have about America's changing ethnicity.

Keep Updated on Immigration Reform

Immigration rights groups are the best source to keep you on top of the immigration debate. Many publish newsletters and send out action alerts to immigration rights activists with timely policy updates:

National Immigration Forum
220 I Street, NE, Suite 220
Washington, DC 20002
(202) 544-0004

Californians for Justice
1611 Telegraph Avenue, Ste. 206
Oakland,CA 94612
(510) 452-2728

Center for Immigrants Rights
48 St. Marks Place
New York, NY 10003
(212) 505-6890

National Council of La Raza
1111 19th Street, NW, Suite 1000
Washington, DC 20036
(202) 785-1670

National Network for Immigrant and Refugee Rights
310 8th Street, Suite 307
Oakland, CA 94607
(510) 465-1984

Northern California Coalition for Immigrant Rights
995 Market Street, 11th floor
San Francisco, CA 94103
(415) 243-8215

The Environment: The Planting
of an Astroturf Movement

Sam Hamilton's troubles started when the Interior Department proposed a plan to protect a songbird called the golden-cheeked warbler. Local landowners were outraged that the plan might restrict development of their property. Hamilton, who was the Texas state administrator for the U.S. Fish and Wildlife Service, was shouted down at public meetings, and death threats were directed at him and his family. He started bringing a bodyguard along to meetings, had Fish and Wildlife insignia removed from official vehicles, and told his staff not to wear their uniforms to work. Finally, when a new job opened up out of state, Hamilton took it.

During the past decade, many communities have experienced an escalating campaign of terror intended to prevent government employees from enforcing environmental laws and to intimidate environmental activists—including bombings, arson, beatings, pet killings, and possibly, murder. This militant anti-green extremism has burgeoned alongside the more conventional organizing efforts of anti-environmental activists on the political right. Like the other progressive movements that grew out of the social changes of the 1960s, environmentalism has provoked a reaction, in the form of a well-financed alliance of diverse interests committed to reversing all the environmental gains of the last thirty years.

Polls consistently show that a great majority of Americans want to keep our planet clean, green and healthy. Yet anti-enviros, who misleadingly give their organizations green-sounding names and their activities green disguises, have reaped influence beyond all proportion to their small numbers. In Congress and in state legislatures around the country, bills which could throw the nation into an ecological dark age have come frighteningly close to passage.

WHAT IS THE ANTI-ENVIRONMENTAL MOVEMENT?

The anti-environmental movement is a loose coalition ranging from large corporate funders like DuPont and Exxon to loggers fearing for their jobs, from ranchers who graze their cattle on federal land to dirt bikers who race across it. Stitching together this patchwork are the professional eco-destruction organizers, of whom Alan Gottlieb, Ron Arnold, and Chuck Cushman are the most notorious, as well as opportunistic fellow travelers in the worlds of politics, journalism, and inevitably, talk radio.

Though the anti-environmental movement is best known west of the Mississippi, where it is called "Wise Use," it is also active in the East, where it is known as the "property rights" movement. In the West, controversy tends to revolve around exploitation privileges on government-owned lands; in the East, where most land is privately owned, anti-environmentalists assert the absolute right of owners to do what they will with their land, with no attendant responsibilities to their neighbors or the public at large.

Hundreds of legal and research foundations, such as the Mountain States Legal Foundation, the Heritage Foundation, and the Cato Institute, give theoretical grounding to the movement, provide connections with the political establishment, and funnel in money from major corporations. In addition, the American Legislative Exchange Council (ALEC) develops model anti-environmental legislation to be introduced at the state level.

The Sagebrush Rebellion

The so-called Sagebrush Rebellion flared up in the Western states during the late 1970s in response to the environmental movement. It was particularly strong in Nevada and Utah, where the federal government owns most of the land and had traditionally managed it for the benefit of industry. Ranchers and mining and logging companies had grown dependent on cheap access to federal land, granted by laws such as the 1872 mining law, which allows companies to buy public land for only $2.50 to $5.00 per acre. This law, still on the books, is fiercely defended by right-wing groups even though it blatantly conflicts with the free market philosophy they profess.

When people began questioning why a small fraction of the population was being allowed to exploit public land, those who had built their livelihoods on the old system were enraged. They started to agitate for control of federal lands to be given to the states, and the Sagebrush Rebellion was born. But before it could come to a crisis, Ronald Reagan, a Westerner with a cowboy image, was elected president. He appointed James Watt, one of the Sagebrush leaders, as his Secretary of the Interior, and there seemed to be nobody to rebel against anymore.

When George Bush declared his intention to become the "environmental president," however, the stage was set for renewed agitation. Enter Ron Arnold and Alan Gottlieb, partners in the Center for the Defense of Free Enterprise (CDFE), the most influential of the anti-environmental organizations. Arnold was a former volunteer for the environmentalist Sierra Club who had switched sides and gone to work for the timber industry, later becoming a protégé of New Right strategist Paul Weyrich; Gott-lieb was a direct mail fund-raiser for right-wing causes, who had spent seven months in prison for cheating on his taxes, according to the Greenpeace Guide to Anti-Environmental Organizations. They held a conference in 1988—financed by the American Freedom Coalition, itself funded by for the Reverend Sun Myung Moon of the Unification Church—and published a manifesto, The Wise Use Agenda. Explaining his choice of the vague term "Wise Use," Arnold has said, "Symbols register most powerfully in the subconscious when they are not perfectly clear."[1]

Connections with the Far Right

Though the Wise Use and militia movements developed separately, they have an overlapping constituency and leadership. Both are sympathetic to county supremacist theories, which hold that the federal government is a usurper with no valid claim on public lands, and that the county sheriff's decisions override those of the federal government. All over the West, these doctrines have been invoked to justify resistance, sometimes armed, to the enforcement of federal laws.

On July 4, 1994, Dick Carver, a commissioner of Nye County, Nevada, became a hero to the county supremacy movement when he bulldozed open a road in the Toiyabe National Forest that the Forest Service had closed, as two Forest Service agents and two hundred county movement supporters watched. Carver later bragged that if one of the feds had drawn a weapon, "fifty people with sidearms would have drilled him."² He parlayed the incident into a barnstorming speaking career, appearing at events sponsored by the white supremacist Christian Identity newspaper *Jubilee*. In 1995, the U.S. government sued Nye County as a test case to reaffirm federal control over federal land; in early 1996, a federal district court ruled that the county's claims had no validity.

Support in Congress

The 1994 elections, which put the Republican party in charge of both houses of Congress, elevated anti-environmentalists to unaccustomed power. Veteran Western Republicans cozy with the anti-green resource industries suddenly found themselves in committee chairmanships, and industry lobbyists were given carte blanche to suggest revisions to hated environmental laws. Lobbyists such as timber industry man Mark Rey even began doubling as congressional staff members—Rey landed a position with Senator Larry Craig, chair of the Subcommittee on Public Lands, National Parks and Forests.

Since legislators were still frightened of being branded as anti-environmental to an eco-aware electorate, they usually didn't try to repeal environmental laws outright. Most of the measures were buried in complex appropriations and budget bills, or were designed to cripple environmental laws instead of killing them. The Clean Water Act, credited for returning many American rivers to wholesomeness, was so weakened by a proposed revision that environmentalists scorned the new measure as the "Dirty Water Bill."

The Sierra Club reported in October 1995 that the House Republican Conference had distributed an internal memo warning

GOP lawmakers that the party's "common sense reforms" to the Endangered Species Act and the Clean Water Act might draw fire from "the environmental lobby and their extremist friends in the eco-terrorist underworld." "To build credibility," the memo suggested members start engaging in activities such as tree plantings, highway cleanups, passing out tree saplings, creating public service announcements about battery disposal, touring a recycling plant, or issuing pro–Earth Day statements. They were nudged to perform these green stunts soon, before opponents could "label [such] efforts [as] 'craven, election-year gimmicks.'"[3]

Rep. Helen Chenoweth of Idaho is leading the posse of militant anti-environmentalists in Congress. She was sent to Congress in 1994 with the support of the whole spectrum of the radical right. Her allies include militiamen, Christian rightists, John Birchers, county rulers, home schoolers, and hate radio jocks. But she is closest to the Wise Use movement, having put in years as a traveling organizer for the movement, sometimes in tandem with Chuck Cushman.

Congressional support for defiant wise users can be seen in the case of Kit Laney, a Catron County rancher. In April 1995, the Forest Service told Laney to reduce his herd of cattle on public land, saying that they had degraded the range. Laney's response was "If you come out and try to move my cattle off, there will be a hundred people out there with guns to meet you."[4] The federal government backed down after intervention from Senator Pete Domenici of New Mexico, and Laney's cattle stayed put.

TACTICS OF THE ANTI-ENVIRONMENTALISTS

Planting Phony Grassroots

The anti-environmental movement is an Astroturf movement with expensive simulated grassroots organizations, most of which are nothing but innocuously named corporate fronts. Ron Arnold once advised a timber company: "Give them the money. You stop defending yourselves, let them do it, and you get the hell out of the way. Because citizens' groups have credibility and industries don't."[5]

Test Your Eco-awareness!

Can you guess which industry founded and funded each of these organizations?

1. People for the West!
2. Environmental Conservation Organization
3. Alliance for Environment and Resource
4. Blue Ribbon Coalition
5. Sea Lion Defense Fund
6. Council for Solid Waste Solution
7. Alliance for Responsible Chlorofluorocarbon Policy
8. Colorado River Resources Coalition
9. Keep America Beautiful, Inc.

ANSWERS
1. mining 2. construction 3. timber 4. off-road vehicles 5. fishing
6. chemical 7. refrigeration 8. energy 9. chemical/metal

The broadest-based Wise Use coalition, Alliance for America, tries to appear salt of the earth. Before a Washington lobbying event, the Alliance issued a dress code to its members: "Wear work clothes, with special attention to gloves, boots, hard hats, bandannas."[6] The group claims "millions" of members, but the circulation of its newsletter is only 2,500. AFA is funded by the Moon-backed American Freedom Coalition, as well as the American Farm Bureau Federation, the Cattlemen's Association, the Petroleum Institute, the Chemical Manufacturers Association, and the American Mining Congress.

Wise Users know that the American archetype of the rugged "real man" individualist fighting the big bad government has great popular appeal. Witness *Time* magazine's cover photo of a cowboy-hatted Dick Carver in October 1995, eerily resembling the Marlboro ad on the back. A photo of a Gucci-shod lobbyist in a congressman's office rewriting the Endangered Species Act would have been just as accurate a portrait of Wise Use, albeit a less colorful one.

Spreading Fear and Anger

In many communities across the nation, Wise Users have developed a deliberately misleading and manipulative politics of polarization to accomplish their aims, labeling environmental activists as "anti-Christian," "anti-family," and "anti-American." A common fear, writes journalist James Ridgeway, is that environmentalists plan "a socialist experiment to depopulate the rural West, ultimately turning it into an eco-theme park for the pleasure of Easterners on vacation."[7] Tourism, in fact, is replacing resource extraction as the mainstay of rural economies—and displaced workers are looking for someone to blame. Wise Use leaders hope to transform the West's anger and anxiety at economic shifts into a forceful right-wing movement. Many of the movement's foot soldiers are unaware of the real forces pulling their strings, or of these forces' true agenda.

Paul de Armond of Whatcom County in Washington State tells the story of the arrival of the movement in his area. Local businessmen created a property rights group called the Coalition for Land Use Education (CLUE). "CLUE's first act was to bring [Wise Use organizer] Chuck Cushman to town to disrupt critical planning meetings. . . . Almost immediately, we had elected officials getting death threats, vandalism, intimidation," says de Armond.[8]

Cushman, who goes by the nickname "Rent-a-Riot" and charges hundreds of dollars a day for his services, claims that he doesn't call for violent tactics: "Personally, we've always advocated nonviolence, like Martin Luther King or that guy from India—what's his name?"[9]

Terror and Intimidation

> "Try telling a logger who's lost his job and house
> and whose neighbor is molesting his daughter be-
> cause he has nothing else to do that he should re-
> main non-violent, that we'd rather see him work
> within the system."

—Ron Arnold[10]

There are several hundred documented cases of serious violence directed against environmental activists. These crimes, mostly unsolved, have occurred across the West, in the Deep South, and in the Northeast.

A bomb exploded in the office of U.S. Forest Service ranger Guy Pence in Carson City, Nevada, on March 30, 1995. On August 4, 1995, another bomb exploded under his van, which was parked outside his home. Luckily, no one was hurt in either incident. Pence, a twenty-five-year veteran of the Forest Service, has been a vocal opponent of county supremacy in Nevada. He helped design the Tonopah Forest management plan, which was the basis for decisions to restrict grazing in Nye County.

Jim Nelson, Pence's boss, commented on the changing role of the Forest Service, to which the bombings may have been a response: "We aren't in the business of producing range for cattle. . . . We're managing an ecosystem. Grazing is not the primary thing we do anymore."[11] The Toiyabe and Humboldt National Forests have been damaged due to over-grazing, says Nelson. "Riparian areas in this forest are devastated. I can show you five-hundred- and thousand-acre meadows that are now nothing but sagebrush and gullies."

So far, the federal government has not aggressively backed up its besieged employees. "There's a mistaken impression by the White House that if you take [the extremists] seriously, you lose votes," says Jim Baca, former director of the federal Bureau of Land Management. "It's a policy of appeasement. The more they get away with it, the more likely threats are to be delivered."[19]

Activists Under Attack

The nationwide pattern of crimes against environmental activists is not labeled as terrorism, and is thus given low priority. As a result, the terror continues with impunity. Rick Sieman, a leader of the Southern California anti-enviro biker group the Sahara Club (whose name parodies the pro-enviro Sierra Club), has conducted dozens of dirty tricks workshops across the country, promoting tactics similar to those used by antiabortion activists.

Some examples of attacks on activists who have spoken out on environmental dangers posed by industry:

- **Leroy Jackson,** a Native American environmentalist, was found dead in suspicious circumstances in 1991, several days before he was scheduled to travel to Washington, D.C., to testify against logging on the Navajo reservation. He had received death threats and had been hanged in effigy at a pro-logging rally.
- **Pat Costner,** director of toxics research for Greenpeace, watched her Arkansas home burn to the ground in a 1991 arson attack.
- **Stephanie McGuire,** who had protested dioxin pollution in Florida's Fenholloway River by a Procter & Gamble pulp mill, was raped and tortured by three men in 1991. "After they cut my throat," she recalled, "they poured water in it from the river and said, 'Now you'll have something to sue about.' "
- **Judi Bari,** a leader of the radical environmental group Earth First!, was permanently disabled by a car bomb in Oakland, California, in 1990. The case was handled in an anomalous manner by government investigators—the FBI tried to pin the crime on Bari herself, never considering any suspects other than members of Earth First!. The crime remains unsolved.[13]

According to David Helvarg, author of *The War Against the Greens,* the Sahara Club lists "the names, addresses, phone numbers and license-plate numbers of environmentalists in its newsletter and on its computer bulletin board. These listings have often been followed by 'Dear Faggot' letters, death threats and harassment of identified activists."[14] The "Sahara Club Agenda" published in July 1994 included instructions for using pepper spray on "obnoxious and violent eco-freaks."

Legal Terrorism

In a legal equivalent of terrorism, anti-environmentalists have increasingly turned to SLAPPs—Strategic Lawsuits Against Public Participation. These lawsuits are not meant to be won, but are launched solely with the intention of tying up environmentalists' time and financial resources, making it too costly for them to pursue their campaigns. They are a profoundly undemocratic attempt to censor opposing voices. In Squaw County, California, an environmentalist was, in Helvarg's words, "slapped with a $75 million lawsuit for speaking out and writing letters to the editor against a planned development." In Florida, 15 percent of growth management advocates have been hit with SLAPPs.[15]

Greenwashing

Greenwashing is a form of corporate public relations that gives polluting companies a quick coat of green, without burdening them with the responsibilities of actually being green. The following are typical greenwashing campaigns, as listed by Greenpeace:

- A giant oil company professes to take a "precautionary approach" to global warming.
- A major agrochemical manufacturer sells a pesticide so hazardous it has been banned in many countries, while suggesting the company is helping to feed the hungry.
- A company cuts timber from natural rain forest, replaces it with plantations of a single exotic species, and calls the project "sustainable forest development."[16]

In his 1994 book, *Going Green: How to Communicate Your Company's Environmental Commitment,* E. Bruce Harrison (who made his name back in the 1960s when he was hired by the chemical industry to smear Rachel Carson's ecological best-seller *Silent Spring*) advises businesses on "what to do when you're attacked by an activist group": "Offer to meet with them. . . . Your task is to try and deflate their balloon and to get direct information about what's motivating them, how serious they are, who they are, what they will consider 'success.' . . . Politely put off giving more direct information."[17] Harrison goes on to suggest hiring a private detective to spy on environmentalists—taking precautions, of course, not to get caught.

Scapegoating of Environmentalists

It is easy to understand why opposition to the green movement would come naturally to corporations whose profits are threatened by environmental regulations. Less obvious, perhaps, are the reasons for the demonization of environmentalists by right-wing ideologues. The fact is that the radical right has long depended on scapegoating tactics to build anger and cohesion in its ranks. During the period from the end of World War II to the breakup of the Soviet Union, the right had a ready-made enemy in communism. But in our post–Cold War era, it has been difficult to identify an external adversary which seemed sufficiently foreboding. Hence, the right has turned its attention to the enemy within. It may seem ludicrous to cast the Audubon Society in the villainous role once played by the KGB, but the smearing of the environmental movement has been remarkably successful among some political enthusiasts, if not the American people as a whole.

Demonization of environmentalists is made easier by appealing to the fears of workers whose livelihoods are tied to resource industries. Anti-enviros label greens as elitist and out of touch with ordinary people. They try to wedge apart environmentalists and blue-collar workers who have potential common interests in opposing corporate power.

DISTORTIONS ABOUT ENVIRONMENTALISM

"Environmentalism is ungodly."

The anti-environmentalists on the religious right, as epitomized by President Reagan's secretary of the interior, James G. Watt, espouse "dominion theology," holding that God gave Man stewardship over the earth for a finite time, which will end with the Second Coming and Armageddon. To oppose human exploitation of natural resources is considered pagan and idolatrous.

Ron Arnold has declared a "holy war against the new pagans who worship trees and sacrifice people,"[18] while Watt opposed long-term conservation policies because, he said, "I do not know how many future generations we can count on before the Lord returns."

Nevertheless, more than 80 percent of Americans, most of whom are religious believers, consider themselves environmentalists.

"Government environmental regulations are unfair to property owners."

Property rights activists talk about what the government is taking away, while ignoring what the government has given to them. A study by the Environmental Working Group shows that the value of U.S. farmland has been increased by government commodity subsidies far more than it has been diminished by regulations. Taxpayer dollars have added 15 to 20 percent to farm values— $85 to $110 billion in all. In addition, much of the settled part of the West would have fared poorly without the federal provision of water, rangeland, infrastructure, and fire control.

"Environmental problems aren't worth being concerned about."

Anti-green organizers have a habit of spreading questionable information to further their causes. "Facts don't matter," says Ron Arnold. "In politics, perception is reality."[19]

Anti-environmental science (examples of which are given on p. 182) is scorned by real scientists, that is those who are respected by their colleagues and who submit their work to peer-reviewed scientific journals. Yet, even after bogus claims have been fully debunked, they have a way of bouncing around for years. Meanwhile, if necessary environmental action has been stalled, they've served their purpose.

Pseudoscience is regularly featured by Rush Limbaugh, who is especially fond of the argument that volcanoes are to blame for the hole in the ozone layer.[20] The June 1993 issue of *Science* magazine traced the volcano squiblet to a surprisingly unsavory source: Limbaugh lifted it from *Trashing the Planet*, the popular anti-green tract by former Washington governor Dixy Lee Ray. In turn, Ray, who did no original research, got her disinforma-

Distortion: There's no hole in the ozone layer, and if there is, it was caused by volcanoes.

Correction: According to Dr. Sherwood Rowland, an atmospheric chemist at the University of California at Irvine and an officer of the National Academy of Sciences, "Ozone depletion is real, as certain as Neil Armstrong's landing on the moon. Natural causes of ozone depletion are not significant." In 1995, the ozone hole was more than twice the size of Europe.[21]

Distortion: Most scientists don't believe in global warming.

Correction: The scientific consensus is that humankind has raised global temperatures by burning fossil fuels. According to the Environmental Working Group, "if left unchecked, global climate change could develop deserts where croplands now flourish, dramatic sea-level changes would flood low-lying areas, and shifting rainfall patterns would affect crops and fisheries."[22]

Distortion: Since extinction is part of the natural process of evolution, there's no need to protect endangered species.

Correction: While extinction *is* a part of evolution, human activities have drastically accelerated it. According to Harvard entomologist Edward O. Wilson, "The rate of extinction is now about 400 times that recorded through recent geological time and is accelerating rapidly. If we continue on this path, the reduction of diversity seems destined to approach that of the great natural catastrophes at the end of the Paleozoic and Mesozoic eras—in other words, the most extreme in 65 million years."

tion from a book by Rogelio Maduro called *Holes in the Ozone Scare,* which was described in the *Science* article as "a good job of collecting all the bad articles [in the field] in one place." Maduro is a follower of right-wing cult leader and anti-environmentalist Lyndon LaRouche and the former editor of a LaRouchite magazine, *21st Century Science and Technology.* He is a fixture at Wise Use events, and many of his fictions have become common currency via Ray and Limbaugh.

"Environmentalists are plotting to take away our rights."

Like other radical rightists, anti-environmentalists back up their positions with conspiracy theories.

Followers of LaRouche, for example, have traced an alleged environmentalist plot to ruin the economy back to George Bernard Shaw, Aristotle, and the Babylonian matriarchy. In 1993, Maduro suggested that there was a scheme afoot by environmentalists to murder billions of people through deliberately creating mass starvation.

A current focus of Wise Use paranoia is a proposal for an international park straddling Washington State and British Columbia. The Snohomish County Property Rights Alliance believes the park will be used to stage a United Nations invasion of the United States.

RIGHT-WING PROPOSALS

Commercialize the National Parks

National Parks, such as Yellowstone and the Grand Canyon, were established to preserve America's unique natural areas for all citizens to enjoy. But the *Wise Use Agenda* calls for opening them to mining and oil drilling, as well as allowing commercial development and motorized recreation in over 30 million acres of federal wilderness. It also advocates bringing in companies "with expertise in people-moving such as Walt Disney" to run the parks.

Such ideas have support in Congress. Representative James Hansen, (R-UT), chairman of the National Parks, Forests, and Lands Subcommittee, sponsored legislation that would set up a commission to decide which national parks should be closed down. Hansen has also opposed the designation of 5.7 million acres of Southern Utah's red rock country as wilderness, against the wishes of a majority of his constituents. Huge cuts in the National Park Service's budget are planned, and in 1995 a House subcommittee allocated only one dollar to manage the new 1.4-million-acre Mojave National Preserve.

Compensate Owners for "Takings" of Private Property by Environmental Regulations

Property rights advocates have made an issue of a peculiar interpretation of the Fifth Amendment to the Constitution, which reads: "nor shall private property be taken for public use, without just compensation." Property rightists stretch this clause to the breaking point, demanding payment out of the public purse for every conceivable impact on their property from a law or regulation. So far, no court has accepted a constitutionally based "takings" argument. But property rights activists have proposed takings laws which, legal experts warn, could bankrupt public treasuries, clog court systems, and bring government activity to a standstill. Nevertheless, Senate Majority Leader Bob Dole has introduced a takings bill which would require reimbursement to property owners whenever any federal action dimished the value of their property.

Strengthening property owners' "rights" in this way would lead to interesting legal results: A gun dealer in California demanded compensation for lost sales of assault weapons after Congress banned them; a Georgia motel operator who claims the value of his property was reduced by federal civil rights laws that forced him to rent rooms to blacks as well as whites wants to be reimbursed; a tavern owner in Arkansas sued the government for business lost due to sobreity checkpoints. Under stringent takings laws, all of these actual court cases could be winnable.[23]

Get Rid of the Endangered Species Act

The *Wise Use Agenda* advocates excluding "non-adaptive species such as the California Condor" from protection under the Endangered Species Act, as well as any species whose survival hinders resource exploration.

Representative Don Young of Alaska, whose Capitol Hill office is festooned with hunting trophies, is championing a crippled version of the Endangered Species Act that would make it legal to destroy a species' habitat as long as one didn't kill the animal outright. Young, who calls environmentalists a "waffle-stomping, Harvard-graduating, intellectual bunch of idiots," chairs the House Resources Committee (its name was changed from the Natural Resources Committee, which apparently sounded too green).[24]

In Wyoming and Arizona, legislators have proposed measures that would place a bounty on wolves—a federally protected endangered species. In Wyoming, the measure, which was vetoed by the governor, would have created a defense fund to protect individuals prosecuted under the Endangered Species Act.

Cut Down Old-growth Forest

Old-growth forest is becoming scarce due to logging. Environmental groups have launched intensive campaigns to save what is left of these ancient trees, especially in the Pacific Northwest. The *Wise Use Agenda,* on the other hand, actually suggests that the trees are using too much oxygen, and calls for cutting them down and replacing them with young "oxygen-producing carbon dioxide–absorbing trees to help ameliorate the rate of global warming."

Defund the Environmental Protection Agency

The Environmental Protection Agency is essential for ensuring public health and safety. However, the EPA funding bill considered by Congress in 1995 included seventeen provisions restricting the agency's operations in areas such as issuing standards to protect the public from arsenic, radon, and cryptosporidium in tap water; protecting wetlands; and listing new hazardous waste sites for cleanup. In addition, the bill proposed cutting funding to the agency by 33 percent in the House bill and 23 percent in the Senate bill. Representative Chenoweth has advocated the abolishment of the EPA.

POSITIVE ALTERNATIVES

It must be recognized that the anti-environmental movement has managed to take root among certain elements of the American people. Wise Use organizers have played on the fears of those who feel they are being left behind by social and economic changes, especially workers whose traditional livelihoods depend on the use of natural resources. They've created a stereotype of the high-handed environmentalist who cares more about owls than people—and unfortunately environmentalists have sometimes allowed themselves to be seen that way.

Savvy activists are now realizing that they must reach out to all kinds of people to transcend the owls vs. people paradigm and find environmental solutions that will benefit everybody. Steve Thompson and Lill Erickson, both environmentalists in Montana, are pursuing promising new approaches to activism.

Thompson, of the Montana Wilderness Association, in Kalispell, Montana, says: "I'm working with small, progressive loggers. Environmentalists tend to see the timber industry as a monolithic thing, and it's not. There are very good people who are loggers. They have chafed against what they have been forced to do by the big corporations and even by the Forest Service.

"The loggers I'm working with are interested in long-term sustainability. I met with one of them, and he showed me a job that he'd done. He said, 'What I try to do out here is try to leave the best of the forest intact, and just take some of the worst stuff. Leave the best and take the rest. Because I hate clear-cutting—the corporations are just taking the big trees and leaving the junk.'

"I said, 'Well, I can agree with that, if you can agree to leave those areas alone that have never been roaded, that are still wilderness.'

"He said, 'Oh yeah! We don't need to be going into there. We've got lots of areas where we can do fixing, where we've screwed everything up for the last hundred years. We don't need to be building more roads into roadless areas.'

"I said, 'Hey, I think we can work together!' So we started a local group called the Flathead Forestry Project."

The Flathead Forestry Project has since drafted groundbreaking legislation, which holds great promise for small logging firms, small mill owners, and environmentalists concerned about the future of the national forests. The Forest Ecosystem Stewardship Demonstration Act, introduced in Congress by Representative Pat Williams, (D-MT), would change the way the Forest Service conducts business. Currently, timber is sold to the highest-bidding mill owner, who in turn hires the lowest-bidding logger to cut it as cheaply as possible. The bill proposes that the Forest Service instead offer stewardship contracts for particular stands of trees, with predetermined management goals for timber, wildlife, and recreation concerns. Loggers, not mill owners, would bid on these contracts, and would be chosen for their ability not only to cut trees, but also to protect the land. Loggers would be paid a per-acre price for their work by the government; the government would in turn sell the logs to the mills.

Says Thompson: "We want to change the incentive system so the logger isn't working for a timber company on public lands, but is actually working for the public and doing the right thing. I get calls from both loggers *and* environmentalists from probably every state in the West now who say, 'That makes so much sense! How can we help out, how can we get involved, how can we support this legislation in Congress?'"

Lill Erickson, of the Corporation for the Northern Rockies in Livingston, Montana, discusses her innovative approach to environmentalism: "We support sustainable development projects in Montana, Wyoming, and Idaho. We're working with one right now called Predator Friendly, Inc. It was initiated by environmentalists and sheep ranchers in the area north of Yellowstone National Park. Typically, sheep producers have called for killing predators [such as coyotes, wolves, and bobcats] because sheep are vulnerable animals. Predators definitely have an impact on flocks of sheep. But a lot of sheep ranchers have started using guard animals—dogs, donkeys, llamas—to protect their flocks. Environmentalists decided that they could help these ranchers by opening a green market for their wool.

"The ranchers market the wool for a premium price. It's made into products that have a hang-tag and a trademarked name. They're finding manufacturers that are willing to pay double the ordinary price for the wool. Which doesn't cost the manufacturer all that much, because raw wool makes up such a small percentage of the manufacturing cost of a product, but it makes a huge difference to the rancher.

"You couldn't find two more different kinds of people than a predator advocate and a sheep producer. And yet they've found common ground, they're working together really well, and they're learning a lot about each other. The environmentalist will come out to a sheep ranch and help 'em shear, and then conversely, the sheep rancher goes into Yellowstone Park and talks with the biologists and the environmentalists about animal behavior.

"Whether it's a newcomer or an old-timer or an environmentalist or a sheep rancher, people who are here in the West are committed to staying. Somehow we have to figure out how to live together."

How This Issue Affects You

Since the modern environmental movement got under way in the 1960s, it has piled success on success. A crucial series of laws has been enacted in Congress, slowing and in some cases reversing the degradation of the American environment by human activity. These laws include the Wilderness Act, the Clean Air Act, the Clean Water Act, the Endangered Species Act, and the Safe Drinking Water Act. The production of such dangerous substances as DDT, dioxin, lead paint, leaded gasoline, chlorofluorocarbons, and asbestos has been severely restricted or banned outright.

The Clean Water Act is an example of environmental legislation whose benefits are sparklingly evident. In 1969, Ohio's Cuyahoga River, which flows through Cleveland into Lake Erie, was so saturated with noxious chemicals that it caught fire. Biologists declared Lake Erie a dead lake, unable to support fish. The plight of the Cuyahoga galvanized support for the Clean Water Act. Now the mouth of the river has become a magnet for fun-seekers, creating thousands of jobs, and the lake boasts some of America's best fishing. The good news from Ohio is echoed in other parts of the country: In 1972, when the Clean Water Act passed, only 36 percent of our waters were considered safe for swimming and fishing; by 1995, the figure had increased to 66 percent.[25]

Along with the tangible effects of environmentalism have

come changes in public attitudes. Through successful educational campaigns, such as Earth Days, the American people as a whole have become eco-aware. In opinion poll after opinion poll, the public states that it wants more environmental protections, not less. Most people today understand that problems like global warming and the depletion of the ozone layer must be addressed if life as we know it is to continue.

As the radical right has gained momentum, however, it has become easier for anti-environmentalists to hijack the debate about the environment and its effect on jobs and public health. Corporate institutions, which are the biggest winners when environmental legislation is weakened, have managed to instigate regulation rollbacks. Pushing for "free-market environmentalism"—the abolition of existing environmental laws and the deregulation of industry—they promote policies that serve the interests of the few rather than those that benefit the whole world.

Most of the recent attempts to cripple environmental legislation have been beaten back, at least for the time being. Still, it's important for those who care about the environment to remain vigilant. In today's political climate, an important part of our strategy must be to continue the environmental progress we've begun. If you consider yourself an environmentalist, the following proposals can offer a way to get involved.

WHAT YOU CAN DO: ACTION SAMPLER

Learn About and Enjoy the Environment

The first step toward helping the environment is to get out into it. Many people spend more time watching nature programs on TV than actually experiencing nature—don't be one of them! Visit the natural areas near your home. Note the changes of the seasons—bring a camera, a sketch pad, or a notebook. Get a field guide, and learn to identify birds, rocks, flowers, or whatever appeals to you. Take advantage of educational programs offered by the parks near you. And in your wanderings, be alert for signs of despoilation caused by humanity.

Take Concrete Actions to Help the Environment

An attempt to put your environmental convictions into practice is sure to give a richer texture to your life. The best activities to get involved in are those that will bring you into contact with other green activists in your area. A recycling center or a natural food co-op will often be a focus for local environmentalists, and may have a bulletin board with useful information. Parks, highways, and beaches often announce clean-up days, when nature lovers volunteer to pick up accumulated litter. These events are more fun than they may sound, and are a great way to meet environmentally concerned people.

Pick up one of the many books on how to live a greener life (one is *50 Simple Things You Can Do to Save the Earth* by the Earth-Works Group, published by EarthWorks Press in Berkeley, California) and try out a few of the suggestions.

Join an Environmental Organization

You can multiply the power of your green activism by joining an organization. Two venerable groups, each with a network of chapters blanketing the country, are the Sierra Club and the National Audubon Society. Both of them fight for the environment on both local and national levels, as well as offering their members educational programs and outings. Both also publish environmental information in various forms, including magazines *(Sierra* and *Audubon,* respectively) that offer news about political struggles over the environment, among other subjects.

Sierra Club
730 Polk Street
San Francisco, CA 94109
(415) 776-2211
fax: (415) 776-0369
WWW: http://www.sierraclub.org

National Audubon Society
700 Broadway
New York, NY 10003
(212) 979-3000
WWW: http://www.audubon.org/audubon

It's often local grassroots groups that have taken the lead in defending the environment against its attackers. Usually, if you can find one local environmentalist, he or she will be able to tell you who else is active in your area.

Subscribe to Newsletters That Track the Anti-Environmental Movement

A CLEAR View, an electronic newsletter published by the Environmental Working Group, covers the national scene from Washington, D.C.; *New Voices,* published by the Wilderness Society's Denver office, focuses on the West.

A CLEAR View
Environmental Working Group
1718 Connecticut Avenue, NW, Suite 600
Washington, D.C. 20009
(202) 667-6982
fax: (202) 232-2592
e-mail: clear-view@ewg3.ewg.org
WWW: http://www.ewg.org

New Voices
The Wilderness Society
7475 Dakin Street, Suite 410
Denver, CO 80221
(303) 650-5818
e-mail: newvoices@tws.org

Sample Letter

The following letter is intended to influence a vote in the House of Representatives on a crucial piece of environmental legislation.

Dear Ms. [your Representative's name]:

I urge you to support the Utah Redrocks Protection Act, H.R. 1500, and to oppose the Utah delegation's wilderness bill, H.R. 1745.

The Utah Redrocks Protection Act would preserve 5.7 million acres of southern Utah, some of our country's most beautiful unspoiled landscape, for Americans to enjoy forever. By contrast, H.R. 1745 would set aside only 1.9 million acres as wilderness. It would allow some development even in this smaller area, undermining the purpose of the 1964 Wilderness Act. Furthermore, the areas not preserved could not be managed as wilderness by the Bureau of Land Management, and could never again be considered for wilderness designation.

Every poll has shown that Americans, including Utahns, overwhelmingly support the more inclusive wilderness bill. The Utah delegation is going against the wishes of its own constituents in order to help foreign mining interests. Please vote no on H.R. 1745 and yes on H.R. 1500.

Sincerely,

Armchair Activist

PART III
Approaches to Activism

12

In-Your-Armchair Activism

The momentum of the radical right poses a challenge and an opportunity for the rest of us. Your participation in the democratic process will awaken your own power to change the world. It can also be a source of joy and meaning to your life. Once you get involved, you may be astonished how many people you'll find who are just as concerned as you and who also want to make an impact. And together, we can.

When surveying the political landscape these days, a reaction that's all too common is a shrug of the shoulders and the sigh, "Oh well, what can you do?" Well, as the Christian Coalition and other right-wingers have proved, when you're well organized and motivated, you can do quite a bit. Citizen activism is the antidote to political apathy. When conducted honestly and inclusively, it brings to life the meaning of the word "democracy": *rule of the people.*

Today, democracy is under seige. Those of us who have seen our communities torn apart by the radical right's polarizing tactics, or who have had right-wing violence directed at ourselves, our families, or our friends, know all too well that it's time to take action. To others, the danger may seem more remote—yet signs of it are all around, and it's only a matter of time until your life feels the impact. The decisions made in Washington, D.C., and in state capitals by politicians who are beholden to the extremist right will affect us all.

The radical right's secret is that it still represents only a small minority of Americans. But the sleeping majority is waking up, and its voice will be heard. Remember, though, that the individual people who have been mobilized by right-wing leaders to support their repressive brand of politics are not our enemies, they are our neighbors—and potentially our allies. They, too, are searching for answers to complex societal problems. If we expose the anti-democratic right's agenda, we can curb its appeal and bring people together to work for positive change.

An Activist's Schedule

Some people have dedicated their lives to social activism; others can barely find the time to make it to the voting booth on election day. The excuses we give for not being politically active are the same ones we give for not starting an exercise routine: "I'm too busy," "I'm too shy," "I haven't done it in so long." But anything can fit into your life if you make it part of your routine. Just like exercise, activism can become an integral part of your life, increasing in intensity as time goes on. Our advice: Start slow, and keep to your own pace.

The activism suggestions in this part are listed in order of difficulty. The tips are divided into two chapters: things you can do "in your armchair" and things you can do "out of your armchair." The way you choose to fight the radical right is up to you—the trick is to create a schedule for your activism so that you keep on fighting.

Level 1. Beginners should strive to undertake at least one action a month. Mark a day on your calendar. You can devote as little as fifteen minutes at first and gradually work yourself up to a half hour or more. Think through which issues you'd like to take on—what are your goals and capabilities? Use this time to educate yourself and others about the radical right by subscribing to newsletters that track right-wing politics. Perhaps the most enjoyable way to embark on your path to social activism is to enlist a friend or two to join you in your efforts.

Level 2. Aim for at least one action every week, building on activities you've already tried. Set aside a half hour every Monday night, for example, to write a legislator about something in the news that struck you that week. Begin to break out of your "armchair" by scheduling a visit with a local policy maker.

Level 3. Keep to a weekly schedule, but broaden your audience and contacts. Write an op-ed piece for a local paper, or join an organization working for social change. You may want to start organizing your community—begin by inviting a few friends and neighbors over for a letter-writing party. Keep up a steady pace, but most importantly, have fun. The rewards of working to make a difference, whether on your own or with other people, are surprisingly rich.

KEEPING AN EYE ON THE RADICAL RIGHT

For all activists, the first task is to stay informed. Right-wing groups, knowing that most people will not support their more extreme ideas, consistently use stealth tactics. But secrecy is their Achilles heel—once people see what they're really up to, their effectiveness is crippled. So dig deep, Armchair Activists, and share your discoveries with the world.

Besides researching the radical right, you'll be learning the skills it takes to navigate the American political system. Much of this knowledge is best acquired by firsthand participation—but the next best thing is to ask someone who's been there. If this is your first attempt to get politically involved, reach out to other activists who can show you the ropes. A mother in a town thousands of miles away who helped take back her school system; a civil-rights lobbyist in the state capital or Washington, D.C.; a neighbor of yours who's long been involved in community affairs—any of these people may be thrilled to share with you their hard-won expertise. If you're lucky, you may even find yourself a mentor. And before long, you'll have your own information worth sharing. You'll become part of the informal nationwide network of fight-the-right activists.

Your research will be much more useful if you put a little thought into organizing it. Facts on paper are worth more than vague mental impressions, especially if they're filed in some rational way. When you observe rightists at a public event, concentrate on gathering factual data: How many people are in attendance? Who are they? What groups do they belong to? When it comes time to share information with other activists, your systematic research will be invaluable.

Tracking the Right in Your Community

What is the right up to in your area? Here are some ways to find out:

• *Check the newspaper.* Keep a look out for signs of radical right activity—articles, letters, notices of events, even classified ads.

• *Visit religious bookstores.* They exist almost everywhere, and they often are important religious right propaganda nodes. You can look them up in the yellow pages under Book Dealers (Religious) or Religious Goods. Go and scan their bulletin boards.

• *Go to a fundamentalist or evangelical church.* Though many conservative churches are not active politically, the ones that are form the organizing backbone of the religious right. Find out where they are located in your area. It may be illuminating to attend a service. Look for a bulletin board in the foyer.

• *Attend school board meetings.* School board meetings are a common venue for religious right activists. Look in your local newspaper for meeting announcements, or call the school superintendent's office for information. PTA meetings are also worth attending.

• *Hit the gun shows.* The far right often proselytizes quite openly at gun shows, survivalist events, "preparedness expos," and the like. If you're not a "gun person," these events can be real eye-openers.

• *Be attentive.* See that smudgy sign on a lamppost, using radical right buzzwords to advertise a meeting? It may be worth checking out. How about the loud conversation concerning the "one-world government" you overhear from the next booth at a café? Prick up your ears!

• *Attend right-wing events.* If you do hear about a radical right event that will be held in a public place, or a meeting to which the public is invited, try to attend without drawing attention to yourself. Collect as much information, printed or otherwise, as you can.

Tracking the Right Nationally

Effective activism requires you to keep an eye on both the local and national scenes. It's good to find out about radical right organizations and ideas before they arrive where you live.

If a local radical right group seems to have an unusual amount of money or expertise, you may suspect that it's getting help from a national organization. If you can establish that it is, you can then ask it questions like the following: Why wasn't the local group forthcoming about its connections? What business does the national group have coming into your community? Does the local group support the more extreme elements of the national group's program? Does it want to put them into place in your community?

Subscribe to newsletters. A number of research groups have sprung up to track the radical right from a critical perspective. Their newsletters are by far the most convenient source of information about the right. You'll be fascinated by the behind-the-scenes details that never make it into the mainstream media. These newsletters are reasonably priced, and your money is going to fight the good fight. (See Appendix I for information on how to contact the following organizations.)

- *Activist Alert,* National Gay and Lesbian Task Force.
- *Church and State,* Americans United for Separation of Church and State.
- *Culture Watch,* DataCenter.
- *Freedom Writer,* Institute for First Amendment Studies. Covers the religious right.
- *Public Eye,* Political Research Associates. Covers the spectrum of the American right.
- *c.c. watch.* Covers the Christian Coalition.

There are a number of other excellent organizations, most of them with a regional focus, that monitor the far right and hate groups. All of their newsletters are worthwhile:

- *The Right Unmasked,* Center for Democratic Renewal. Atlanta, Georgia. Covers hate groups nationally.
- *Dignity Report,* Coalition for Human Dignity. Portland, Oregon.
- *Klanwatch Intelligence Report,* Southern Poverty Law Center. Montgomery, Alabama.
- *Network News,* Montana Human Rights Network. Helena, Montana.

- *Northwest Beacon,* Northwest Coalition Against Malicious Harassment. Seattle, Washington.
- *Turning the Tide,* People Against Racist Terror. Burbank, California.

Tune in to radical right media. For an update on the right's latest exploits and political targets, stay tuned to its media propaganda, including:

- Pat Robertson's cable TV networks (Family Channel and Christian Broadcasting Network), especially the news segment of the "700 Club."
- Religious radio stations. *Focus on the Family* is the most influential show.
- Secular right-wing radio and TV talk shows like Rush Limbaugh's.
- Right-wing hangouts in cyberspace. Search for them using buzzwords like "pro-family." See the section about on-line activism, p. 218.
- Shortwave radio. Discover what American right-wingers are beaming around the world—stuff that's too far out for commercial radio. (Plus a lot of interesting programs from other countries!)
- Right-wing literature. Magazines and books can give you new insight into the right's ideology. If you order something by mail, you'll likely receive fund-raising letters, where the most extreme rhetoric can often be found.

Tracking the Right in the Media

One reason that we felt there was a need for this book is that the media's coverage of the radical right has been, at best, spotty. Once in a while, as in the aftermath of the Oklahoma City bombing, a feeding frenzy occurs—but in between such episodes, the media offer a thin diet to those hungry for information about the right. Considering the power wielded by groups like the Christian Coalition—who were instrumental in the Republican takeover of Congress in the 1994 elections, besides putting thousands of their supporters in state and local offices—they have been given remarkably cursory attention by news organizations.

At the same time, opinion makers regularly promote right-wing ideology in the media without any balancing voice. On talk radio in particular, the right dominates in both airtime and stridency.

According to Chip Berlet of Political Research Associates, the right has been building its network of think tanks since the sixties. "Today, the vast majority of 'experts' featured on television and radio talk shows, and many syndicated print columnists, have been groomed by the right-wing infrastructure, and some of these figures were first recruited and trained while they were still in college."[1]

The lesson for Armchair Activists is that we can't rely on the mainstream news media to keep us informed about trouble from the right. Often, the problem is not that their information is incorrect, but that they've omitted essential parts of it. When the media let statements by radical right leaders go unchallenged, or otherwise don't do their job, it's up to us to call them on it. Stealth is a key element of the right's strategy; let's get the media's klieg lights shining on its shenanigans.

Types of media. As the media universe continues to expand, it's difficult to keep track of it all. Most people have a favorite magazine or radio station with which they feel comfortable. But as an activist, it's good to keep aware of the whole range of media. Here are some suggestions:

- *Newspapers:* national, local, neighborhood, college, alternative
- *Television:* national networks, local stations, cable channels, public access
- *Radio:* nationally syndicated and local; commercial, public and college
- *Magazines* of all stripes, especially those read by groups that are under attack from the right, such as women, African-Americans, gays and lesbians
- *Religious media*

Don't forget the alternative media. Alternative weekly newspapers have often been leaders in exposing the radical right. Once the alternative paper has taken the risk, the mainstream media, loath to be scooped, often jump in. The same goes for alternative radio and TV stations. If you contact them about local radical right activities, you may interest them in covering the story themselves. Good alternative coverage of politics can also be found in such magazines as *The Nation, The Progressive, Mother Jones, CovertAction Quarterly,* and *Z* magazine.

Pacifica. Pacifica, a listener-supported radio network, is an excellent resource for activists. There are five Pacifica stations (in Berkeley, Calif.; Los Angeles; New York; Houston; and Washington, D.C.), along with fifty-seven affiliates across the country. Though the Pacifica stations in the past have had a reputation for a kind of doctrinaire leftism, they actually feature a surprisingly diverse array of perspectives. Unafraid to sail uncharted waters, they have been more than generous in their coverage of the radical right. If your local public station doesn't carry Pacifica programming, ask them to do so.

Pacifica
2390 Champlain St., NW
Washington, D.C., 20009
(202) 588-0988
fax: (202) 588-0896
WWW: http://www.pacifica.org

FAIR. Providing an essential corrective to the mass media's blurry view of the anti-democratic right is an organization called FAIR (Fairness & Accuracy In Reporting—not to be confused with the anti-immigration group with the same acronymn). FAIR keeps a close watch on the media's omissions and distortions. Its incisive findings are presented in an easy-to-take style. FAIR's offerings include *EXTRA!,* a bimonthly magazine; *Counterspin,* a weekly syndicated radio show; and its Media Activism Kit, which is loaded with tips on how you can influence the media. It also published the definitive deconstruction of Rush Limbaugh, *The Way Things Aren't: Rush Limbaugh's Reign of Error.* Your news diet isn't complete unless it's supplemented by FAIR.

FAIR
130 West 25th Street
New York, NY 10001
(212) 633-6700
fax: (212) 727-7668
WWW: http://www.igc.org/fair
• *EXTRA!* magazine, $19/year
• FAIR's Media Activism Kit, $5

- *The Way Things Aren't: Rush Limbaugh's Reign of Error,* $6.95 (also available in bookstores)

GETTING THE SCOOP ON YOUR ELECTED OFFICIALS

Who Are My Legislators, and How Do I Contact Them?

Many people are deterred from participating in our political system by a simple lack of knowledge. They may not know who their elected representatives are, how to get in touch with them, or which one to ask for help. Not to worry—the answers to these questions are close at hand.

The League of Women Voters. The League of Women Voters is an often overlooked and underappreciated group that performs services that are vital to our democracy. Voter education (for both women and men) is the League's number one mission.

The LWV is organized at the national, state, and local levels, mimicking the structure of the government. It publishes scads of information about government and the democratic process, in the form of cheap, handy, and easy-to-use booklets.

The League's flagship publication at the national level is called *Tell It to Washington.* Revised yearly, it's a guide for citizens who want to influence government. It contains addresses, phone and fax numbers for all members of Congress. Similarly helpful guides are issued by state and local Leagues.

If you have a question about the workings of government, give the League a call, and a member will be happy to point you in the right direction. Look up your nearest League of Women Voters chapter in the white pages of the phone book, or ask the national office to help you locate it.

League of Women Voters
1730 M Street, NW
Washington, DC 20036
(202) 429-1965
fax: (202) 429-0854
- *Tell It to Washington,* $3.75

Government sources. What if you have no idea who's representing you in government? Even if you're armed with a direc-

Buzzwords of the Religious Right

The following list of words and phrases can help identify religious right literature, programming, and candidates. Though the use of these buzzwords does not prove a candidate or organization advocates theocracy, it should raise a red flag for Armchair Activists.

- anti-Christian bigotry, anti-religious, anti-God, anti-Bible
- anti-family bigotry, anti-parent
- back to basics in education
- Bible reading in school
- biblical law, biblical principles
- creationism, creation science
- choice in education
- Christian nation, Christian values
- condom-based
- excellence in education
- family values
- gay (or homosexual) agenda
- Godless humanism, Godless education system
- Judeo-Christian values or principles

tory from the League of Women Voters or another source, you will still need to know which districts include your home to find out who your legislators are. It's a bit of a tricky question—redistricting being the political art form that it is, district lines can bisect the smallest communities.

Finding the answer, however, is simple enough. At each level of government, there's an office or official in charge of elections. At the local level, it could be the board of elections, voter registrar, or municipal clerk. Ask your local League of Women Voters, or simply look in the blue (government) pages of the phone book. Call the proper office, and someone will be able to tell you which legislative districts you're in, and who's currently

- Kinsey-based
- media elite
- moral absolutes, moral decency, moral rebirth
- morals and ethics in school
- natural law
- new age
- new world order, globalism, one-world government
- outcome-based education (OBE), Goals 2000
- paganism, pantheism
- parental control or rights
- pro-family
- pro-life
- protect unborn children
- psychotherapy, psychological testing
- put prayer back in school
- right to life
- secular humanism
- satanism, witchcraft, the occult
- values clarification
- volunteer prayer

occupying the seats. They may even know the office phone numbers of your representatives. And, if you haven't registered to vote, they'll be able to tell you how to do it.

Where Do Your Elected Officials Stand on the Issues?

One thing that keeps many potential voters away from the voting booth is a lack of information. Even those who keep an eye on media coverage of politics may find themselves, come election day, with only a sketchy idea of candidates' positions on the issues.

Project Vote Smart. Now there's a great resource you can use to educate yourself about politics. It's called Project Vote Smart. Hundreds of volunteers and student interns at two universities are hard at work compiling an incredibly complete compendium of political data and making it available to the public for free—by telephone, in print, and on-line.

Project Vote Smart was started in 1992. By 1994, its database covered the presidency, the U.S. Congress, and governorships. In 1996 it includes state legislatures, covering nearly twenty thousand positions. The project administers the National Political Awareness Test to candidates. The NPAT is designed to be a "no-wiggle-room test," enabling voters to find out where politicians really stand and hold them to their positions.

Here's some of what you can find out from Project Vote Smart:

- Biographies of elected officials and candidates for office
- Their voting records and positions on the issues
- Evaluations of them by special interest groups, from conservative to liberal (including the Christian Coalition)
- Who has financed their campaigns
- Texts of their speeches
- Briefings on important issues
- Sources for further information
- Postal and e-mail addresses and phone and fax numbers for members of Congress

A call to PVS's toll-free Voter's Research Hotline will connect you to a live human being, who will be happy to tell you, for example, how your congressperson has voted on recent environmental bills. For a more comprehensive view of what's going on in government, ask them to send you the *U.S. Government Owner's Manual,* or in election years, the more campaign-oriented *Voter's Self-Defense Manual.* And if you're on the Internet, don't miss the PVS web site: They've put much of their database on-line in an easy-to-use format, plus a well-chosen set of links to information about issues and civic affairs.

Project Vote Smart is scrupulously nonpartisan, with even-handed information about Democratic, Republican, and other candidates. Offering facts, not opinions, it takes no position on any candidate or issue. It accepts no funding from corporations or special interest groups. Because the project is relatively new and has had little money for publicity, it's not yet well known. But if information is power, Project Vote Smart is just what we need to empower us.

Project Vote Smart
129 NW 4th Street, Suite 204
Corvallis, OR 97330
(800) 622-SMART (622-7627)
e-mail: comments@vote-smart.org
WWW: http://www.vote-smart.org
- *U.S. Government Owner's Manual,* free
- *Voter's Self-Defense Manual,* free

The public library. A trip to the local library is also a great way to find out what your representatives are up to. Your reference librarian will be of invaluable help in pointing you to sources you probably didn't even know existed. New on-line indexes make it easy to find information in magazines, journals, newspapers, and government periodicals. Minutes of government meetings, legislative proposals, and state and municipal codes may also be available. You'll also find books that can give you a refresher course on how government works—essential knowledge for an activist.

Though your local branch library is full of good resources, main libraries will have more detailed information. Ask your local librarian where the government depository library is in your area. That's where you'll find official publications like *The Congressional Record* and *The Federal Register.* These are slow going, but essential for in-depth research on what's happening in government. *The Federal Register* is where an activist discovered a proposed regulation that would have counted ketchup as a vegetable in school lunch programs. After that fact had been publicized, the Reagan administration was forced to withdraw the regulation in embarrassment.

Other Sources of Information About Government

- Official guidebooks. Many government bodies have one— call the clerk of that body, or your representative.
- Your representatives and their staffs.

- Advocacy groups working on issues that concern you. Their lobbyists will be very knowledgeable.
- Local Democratic and Republican clubs.
- The United States Government Printing Office. Offers a staggering array of publications. Particularly useful to activists is the *United States Government Manual,* which is published annually. To order documents from the GOP, contact:

Superintendent of Documents
United States Government Printing Office
Washington, DC 20401
(202) 512-1800

WRITING LETTERS TO ELECTED OFFICIALS, THE MEDIA AND CORPORATIONS

Communicating your views in written form can be done three ways: the traditional letter, fax, or e-mail. Politicians, decision makers, and people in the media pay attention to their mail no matter how they receive it. Even handwritten letters, if readable, are fine. Fax and e-mail are ideal for expressing your views on time-sensitive material, such as an upcoming vote on a piece of legislation. (For e-mail addresses and fax numbers of legislators, see sections on League of Women Voters, p.203, and Project Vote Smart, p.205.)

Writing to Elected Officials

There are millions of Americans who feel strongly about political matters. They're mumbling their opinions at the TV set, grumbling them to their families, calling them in to talk radio, arguing them in beauty salons and barbershops, in cafés and bars, in schools and churches around the country. But very few of them ever take the logical step of speaking their minds to those who are paid to listen—their elected officials.

You'll find the offices of your legislators to be among the most user-friendly provinces of government. Many have staff just waiting to answer your mail or register your opinions. Don't worry that your letter will go unnoticed—each letter is read and answered. Thoughtful letters presenting clear and forceful arguments carry the most weight, and are the ones most often passed from the staff to the official. But remember, any letter, even a postcard, is better than no letter at all.

• *Do your research.* You'll want to know the pros and cons of your issue and the courses of action that have been proposed. In addition, it helps to know whether the official to whom you're writing has already taken a stand. An hour at the public library looking up your issue in recent newspapers will pay off.

• *Be concise.* Don't include massive documentation. Keep your letter to one page, two at the most. Discuss only one issue in each letter.

• *State your purpose.* In the first paragraph, state the issue that concerns you and what you think should be done about it. If your letter is about a specific bill, cite it by name (or number) if you can, and say whether you support or oppose it and why. Show your familiarity with the official's past action on an issue.

• *Identify yourself.* Tell the official where you live. If the issue affects you, your family, or your business personally, explain how.

• *Make your case logically.* It's your job to present public officials with a convincing rationale that they can incorporate into their own argument. Build your case point by point, appealing to reason, not emotion. Speak to them in the language of policy.

• *Show them how they can take credit.* All politicians are in the credit-taking business. They will be much more inclined to do what you want if you can convince them that it will put them in a favorable light before a large number of people. Enlist others to sign your letter.

• *Ask for a commitment to a specific action.* A common mistake is to sound off in vague terms about the state of the world. This may make the letter writer feel better, but it lets the recipient off the hook, giving him or her the chance to match generalities with generalities. Instead, let the official know exactly what you want done.

• *Praise is as important as criticism.* When your representative does make a brave stand against the radical right, get in touch to express your thanks. Our representatives need to know we're backing them up when they do the right thing. When you disagree with your representative, do it politely, and try to find something praiseworthy about him or her. Sweeten the bitter pill, and you and your cause may get better treatment in the future, if not right away.

• *Expect a reply.* Most elected officials have a policy of replying to all constituent mail. To avoid getting a form letter in response, be specific in your comments and questions.

• *Forms of address, salutation, and closing.* Letters to the President are closed with "Very respectfully yours," others with "Sincerely yours."

President
The President
The White House
Washington, DC 20500

Dear Mr. President:

Vice-President
The Vice-President
The White House
Washington, DC 20500

Dear Mr. Vice-President:

Senator
The Honorable _____
United States Senate
Washington, DC 20510

Dear Senator _____:

Representative
The Honorable _____
United States House of Representatives
Washington, DC 20515

Dear Mr./Ms. _____:

Writing to the Media

Letters to the news media are an essential weapon in the Armchair Activist's arsenal. Editors, like politicians, see it as part of their job to keep a finger on the public pulse. Local newspapers generally publish about half of the letters they receive. Even if your letter isn't published, it will help convince the paper's staff that your issue is worth taking seriously. For every letter they receive on a subject, they assume that there are many readers who feel the same way but didn't bother to put pen to paper.

Readers, likewise, are fascinated by the opinions of their neighbors and fellow citizens. Surveys have found that the letters page is one of the most widely read parts of the paper—many readers turn to it first. And with good reason. Letters to the editor express diverse points of view that are often too controversial to appear in the rest of the paper, where the editors must be concerned with giving an impression of balance, as well as with not scaring away advertisers. Politicians keep an eye on the letters column as well.

For the addresses and fax and phone numbers of national newspapers, magazines, and television programs/networks, see Appendix II. Here are some guidelines to follow when writing to the media:

• *Be professional.* Type or word process your letter—but be sure to sign it by hand. It should be double-spaced, neat-looking, and free of grammatical and spelling errors. Include your address and daytime phone number—the editor may call to verify authorship.

• *Read before you write.* Get a feeling for the style of the letters that have been printed by your target newspaper. If your letter is too far out of the ballpark, it won't run.

• *Keep it short.* Again, look in the newspaper for a model—some papers like to print letters of only one sentence! A letter that's too long and unfocused may run in a bizarrely edited form or not at all.

• *Get to the point.* State your topic clearly at the beginning of your letter. Deal with only one issue per letter.

• *Be relevant.* Your letter should be related to breaking news. It's best to jump off from an article or editorial that has recently appeared. The quicker your response, the better.

• *Be factual.* Use truth to combat the radical right's distortions. Make sure you can back up any statistics or quotes you include.

• *Use their words against them.* Radical rightists are fond of mak-

Consider an Op-ed

Op-eds are longer than letters to the editor, and there is more competition for space. You will want to call the paper for length requirements (usually 600–800 words).

• *Try to write on a controversial issue being covered currently.* If you can use a professional title that suggests authority, do so. If you work for an organization, get permission to sign the op-ed as a representative of that organization. Feel free to send it to papers far from where you live, but avoid sending it to two papers in the same market (e.g., the *San Francisco Examiner* and the *San Jose Mercury News*).

• *Assure the op-ed editor in your cover note that the piece has not been submitted to any other paper remotely near their market.* Often larger papers like to print op-eds from far away because it implies nationwide readership. Except for national dailies such as the *New York Times, Los Angeles Times, Washington Post, Christian Science Monitor,* and *USA Today,* you can submit the same piece to five

ing patently outrageous statements. You can use their own (carefully documented) words to expose them.

• *Keep your cool.* Angry ranting is a turnoff, both to editors and readers. Far better to let the facts speak calmly for themselves.

• *Use humor.* Wit comes off much better in print than anger. If you can make the opposition look silly, you've won half the battle.

• *Go ahead and do it.* Not every communication to the media has to be a masterpiece. If you're not up to composing a letter that's polished enough for publication, go ahead and write anyway. Sometimes a one-line, handwritten note is enough to set an editor or journalist on the right track.

or ten dailies in different regions. If, on the other hand, you send it to one paper only (or one at a time), let that paper know you are offering an exclusive.

• *Most op-eds are written or signed by "experts."* You might consider approaching a local person with name recognition to write or sign the op-ed.

• *Avoid excessive rhetoric.* State the subject under controversy clearly. You are trying to persuade middle-of-the- road readership. If you rely on facts not commonly found in mainstream media, cite your sources—as respectable as possible.

• *Try to think of a catchy title.* If you don't, the paper will be more likely to run its own headline, which may not emphasize your central message.

• *Be prepared to shorten and resubmit your article* as a letter to the editor in case it does not get accepted as an op-ed.

SOURCE: *FAIR's Media Activism Kit*, a publication of Fairness & Accuracy In Reporting, New York.

• *Get friends to write, too.* If a paper receives several letters on an issue, the editors will understand that many individuals in the community are concerned. They will be more likely to publish a letter on the issue, even if it isn't yours.

• *Send it to several publications.* Send your letter to various local papers in your area, as well as the national dailies. School or community newsletters are also a great forum for your opinions. You can also forward your letter to your alumni magazine, or your college paper.

Writing to Corporations

Another audience for your letters is the heads of major corporations, who are extremely sensitive to their consumers and to their reputation as socially conscious enterprises. Sponsors of right-wing organizations, either through donations or advertising in right-wing publications or on right-wing programs, should be the target of your letters. Address your letter to the CEO (Chief Executive Officer) of the corporation. The addresses of major corporations, and the names of their executives, are listed in the following reference books, which can be found in most libraries.

• *Standard and Poor's Register of Corporations, Directors and Executives* (New York: Standard and Poor's, 1996).

• *Hoover's Handbook of American Business 1996*, Spain, Patrick J. and Talbot, James R. (Austin, TX: The Reference Press, 1995).

PICKING UP THE TELEPHONE

The telephone is a quick and easy way to reach people with your ideas. It's especially appropriate for responding to fast-breaking news. Many politicians and media outlets keep a count of phone calls pro and con on hot issues as a rough gauge of public sentiment.

It's a good idea to keep a log of your activist phone calls. As soon as you get off the phone, jot down the date, what you said, and the response. This is especially important when trying to get commitments from politicians.

Calling TV and Radio Stations

Phone the media to give them instant feedback on the news and how they've covered it. Some broadcasters—for example, the National Public Radio news shows—will actually record your comments and play them on the air.

Calling Right-Wing Talk Radio Programs

One way Armchair Activists can use the telephone is to puncture the hot-air balloons on right-wing talk radio. Periodically, a caller manages to score a point at Rush Limbaugh's expense during his own show. Calling the radio station is a way to reach thousands of people, some of whom just might be influenced by hearing a new point of view.

Jean Zimmerman is the author of *Tailspin: Women at War in the Wake of Tailhook*. She has appeared on many right-wing radio shows to discuss the contentious topic of the role of women in the military. We asked Jean for pointers for talk-show callers:

• *Organize your thoughts in advance.* Three minutes is about as long as you're going to have on the radio. It helps if you jot down on a note card the three points you want to make. If some other brilliant, incisive thought occurs to you, then you can say that, too. But at least you've got those things that you want to say, and you're not going to be tongue-tied.

• *Lead with your main point.* You want to get your main point across in the first sound bite. Lead with that, and back it up afterward. Then at least you've made your point.

• *Don't fill empty spaces.* If you don't have something to say just that minute, then don't say anything. You don't have to fill the space. Just be silent—it's better than saying, "Mmmmm, well . . ." Think about what you're going to say, and then say it.

• *Don't be fazed by name-calling.* They want you to identify yourself as something they can run into the ground. In my case they're always going to talk about "feminazis." They all use that word, they all think it's hysterical, and they'll shout it at you— they use it like a club. Just let those things roll over you and maintain your own level. Don't get caught up in it.

• *Look for common ground.* They will listen to you more if they can't pigeonhole you. Don't lose your point of view, but say, "Well, I understand that a lot of people have strong feelings about that," or "I can see why that's difficult to understand." If the subject is welfare, say, "Nobody wants to see somebody get something for nothing." Establish the common ground and then say why you disagree with them.

• *Be polite, up to a point.* Some of these people are ravers. They'll shout at you, they'll shout over you. They'll talk really loudly and really fast. It's their way of establishing themselves with their audience.

You have to be willing to just shout back. It's good to be polite, but you've got to know when to cut your losses and stop being polite. If you're too meek, you can't make the point.

• *See them as people, not monsters.* Don't be disappointed when you get off the phone and you hear the talk show host making some creepy comment about you afterward. A lot of times, they sound like monsters because they're in the entertainment business, and they think they know what is going to sell. They're patterning themselves after Rush. If you had the chance to talk to them off the air, you would find out that some of them are quite nice. Remember that they're human beings and you can talk reason to them.

• *Pretend you're speaking one-on-one.* The most important thing to realize is that calling up one of these shows is like having a conversation. You have to try to forget that there's a zillion people listening. Assume that they want to know what you have to say and you want to know what they have to say. Then it's a conversation of equals.

It's worth it. Some people worry that these talk shows are preaching to the converted and they don't have a chance to change someone's opinions. But there's a huge radio audience

---

Government Phone Numbers

The Federal Level
To leave a message for the President: (202) 456-1414

To be connected with the office of any member of Congress, a committee, or a subcommittee: (202) 224-3121

To find out the status of legislation and dates of hearings: (202) 225-1772

The State Level
For state capital switchboard numbers, see Appendix III. These numbers will connect you to all branches of the state government, including the governor or any of the state legislators.

out there, and there have got to be some people who would see a different side.

Calling Your Government Officials

Normally, the best time to telephone government officials is when you want them to take immediate action, as on an upcoming vote, and there isn't time enough for a letter or a visit. Phone calls should be concise—don't expect to get into an in-depth discussion. Talk about only one issue per call. Often, when a vote is imminent, all that's necessary is to mention the number and/or name of the bill and how you want the legislator to act. You may want to add one or two pithy points to support your position.

If you're calling an official with a large staff, such as a member of Congress, ask to speak to the assistant who handles your particular issue. Give your name, address, and phone number. That way, the official will know that you are a constituent, and will be able to get back to you with more information.

At the end of the call, be sure to ask for a commitment to a course of action. Sometimes, the official or staff member will not be able to give you an immediate yes or no. In that case, ask when you can expect an answer.

Remember always to be cordial with government officials and their staff. Though they may not share your position on a particular issue, when you contact them you're building a relationship which may be fruitful in the future.

Sample Phone Call to Congress

"Congressman Swayable's office."

"Hello. May I speak to the legislative assistant who deals with the issue of separation of church and state?"

"Just a moment."

. . .

"This is Gary Greeter."

"Hello. My name is Anne Activist, and I live in Anytown, in Congressman Swayable's district."

"How may I help you?"

"I'd like to urge the congressman to oppose the Dominion over America Bill, H.R. 1234. Specifically, the provision that calls for adulterers to be stoned to death. Though it may have been acceptable in Old Testament times, it has no place in modern society."

"All right, I'll let him know how you feel."

"Has he indicated how he plans to vote?"

"I don't believe he's announced his position yet. Can I get back to you on this?"

"Surely. My address is 99 Elm Street, Anytown, and the zip code is 99999. My phone number is 555-6789, area code 999."

"Got it."

"Thanks very much for your help."

THE ON-LINE ACTIVIST: CREATING A VIRTUAL COALITION

At a time in our history when there is growing concern about the lack of participation by ordinary citizens in our democracy, the Internet has arrived, heralding a revolutionary promise. Suddenly there's a new way to exchange information—a way that's easy, convenient, inexpensive, and almost instantaneous. Best of all, the Internet is owned by no one. Unimpeded by the dictates of the marketplace, you can now reach out to any number of strangers around the world who share your interests. All you need is a personal computer and a telephone line.

The freewheeling culture of the Net attracts people with passionate beliefs who are unsatisfied by conventional forms of media. Among these enthusiasts are political activists of every stripe. In researching this book, we unearthed on the Net everyone from unregenerate Nazis to their most ardent opponents. Much of what we learned has found its way onto these pages.

The Net gives organizations an unprecedented ability to stay in touch with their members and recruit new prospects. Advocacy organizations have often suffered from poor communication between their staff and their membership. The staff may be preoccupied by the arcane details of day-to-day governmental activity, while members, whose only participation is to send in their dues and read an occasional newsletter, feel alienated. Now, using the Internet, the staff can post up-to-the-minute news and action alerts, and get instant feedback from members.

What does this mean to the Armchair Activist? The Internet is like a huge political toy store. Just a few keystrokes give you news and views from thousands of sources. Political groups put their best information on-line to entice you—you don't have to become a member, send in a contribution, or even put a postcard in the mail or pick up the phone. Of course, if you find a group with whom you're in sympathy, you can fire them off an e-mail message asking how to join. Or you can merely take the information they provide and act on it yourself. You can also create your own informal e-mail list of activists and friends who keep one another posted.

The Internet, the Commercial Services, and IGC

While our crystal ball is as cloudy as anyone's when it comes to the future of telecommunications, it's plain that the nonpropri- etary computer network called the Internet, especially the part of it known as the World Wide Web, is currently experiencing a supernova-like explosion. Though commercial on-line services such as CompuServe and America Online still have much to offer, the action seems to be migrating to the free and untram- meled precincts of the Internet. Therefore, we're emphasizing the Internet in this brief guide.

However, any discussion of on-line activism would be incom- plete without a mention of the Institute for Global Communica- tions. IGC was born in 1986, back in the prehistory of computer networking. It has grown into an alliance of hundreds of pro- gressive organizations, organized into five networks: PeaceNet, EcoNet, ConflictNet, LaborNet, and WomensNet. Through the Association for Progressive Communications, they're connected to activists in 133 countries.

Much of IGC's incredible smorgasbord of information, which includes a feast of alternative journalism, is available free to any- one with access to the World Wide Web. To get the full benefit of IGC, though, it's necessary to join one of its networks, which can be done for as little as $12.50 per month. Members are able to access IGC conferences, where activists exchange news and views among themselves. It's stirring to see the progressive com- munity, which often seems fragmented in the real world, united in cyberspace on the IGC networks.

Institute for Global Communications
P.O. Box 29904
San Francisco, CA 94129
(415) 442-0220
fax: (415) 561-6101
e-mail: outreach@igc.org
WWW: http://www.igc.apc.org

Finding Comrades in Cyberspace

More people every day are getting on-line and discovering the convenience of e-mail. Just dash off a couple of paragraphs, and with a click of the mouse your message is instantly on its way. It's so much simpler than writing a letter—and it arrives instantaneously! With e-mail, activists can keep in touch with colleagues around the nation and around the globe. They can steadily expand their electronic universe by meeting fellow activists in on-line conferences, forums, and newsgroups.

Because it's so easy to send the same message to many people at once, the electronic mailing list has become an important tool. There are mailing lists too numerous to mention, dealing with all the issues discussed in this book. Some are open to the public, others are by invitation only. E-mail lists are a perfect way for activists to receive action alerts from national organizations. When you're on-line, keep an eye out for interesting lists—you don't have anything to lose by joining one for a while and seeing if it offers anything of interest.

And now the government and the media are making their e-mail addresses public, offering Armchair Activists a new way to sound off. That's especially handy when you've just received an on-line action alert calling for an immediate response. But where to find the addresses you need? Among the sites on our Hot List below, Institute for First Amendment Studies, Project Vote Smart, and Voters Telecommunications Watch all offer Congressional e-mail addresses, while the IFAS and FAIR sites list those of the media.

The Shadow of Censorship

The new possibilities for free expression opened up by the Internet seem almost too good to be true—and indeed, they will not last long if some right-wingers have their way. While the libertarian wing of the right has welcomed the Internet, those with more authoritarian views are hugely uncomfortable with it. Self-appointed family values crusaders like Lou Sheldon of the Traditional Values Coalition, smelling a divisive issue, have jumped into the debate. They've frightened parents with lurid depictions of the Internet as a hotbed of perversion, which have been picked up and amplified by the media and politicians.

Under heavy pressure from the right, Congress included provisions in the Telecommunications Act of 1996 which may hobble free expression on-line. The measures have been challenged in court by a broad coalition of civil liberties groups and Net-based businesses. If the law is found constitutional, anyone who posts an electronic message which is deemed, under ill-defined standards, to be "indecent" could go to prison. The legal situation is further complicated by the Net's global nature. Restrictions imposed by the United States, even if only on sexual content, will encourage other governments to issue their own bans, which may target overtly political material.

Fortunately, both the technology and the culture of the Internet are highly resistant to repressive political interference. It's been said that "the Internet interprets censorship as damage and routes around it." Owned by no one, spilling amorphously across national borders, designed to survive even nuclear attack, the Internet will be a hard beast to tame.

For the latest dispatches from the front lines of the Battle of the Internet, check out the World Wide Web site of Voters Telecommunications Watch (see below).

The Armchair Activist Hot List: Mighty Sites to Fight the Right

Following are some of our favorite jumping off spots on the World Wide Web. For the uninitiated, the Web is a part of the Internet where individuals or organizations publish their own "sites" or "pages," containing text, graphics, sound, and even video. Each site can be linked with an arbitrary number of others, at the discretion of the site owner. The unpredictability of these links can make cruising the Web an exhilarating adventure.

Since the Web is always growing and changing, it's impossible to give a definitive list of activist sites. We've concentrated on ones that seem stable, and that have many links to useful material. Most of them have been put up by activists who are fighting the radical right. We've listed only a few right-wing sites: however, the anti-right sites provide links to many more of them (it's interesting that the reverse is rarely true). A tip for finding radical right material on the Net: Make use of the right's reliance on buzzwords. If you run any of the buzzwords found in this book through a search tool such as Lycos (http://www.lycos.com), you may hit the jackpot.

The Radical Religious Right
http://www.tcp.com/qrd/www/RRR/rrrpage.html
The most complete list of links to the religious right and its adversaries. Includes full text of the *Fight the Right Handbook* published by the National Gay and Lesbian Task Force, based on its successful battles against antigay initiatives. Brought to you by the Queer Resources Directory.

How to Win: A Practical Guide to Defeating the Radical Right
http://gopher.well.sf.ca.us:70/1s/Politics/activist.tools/
how.to.win
A compendium of trenchant articles on combating the religious right over a variety of issues, by activists who have been there. Compiled by the National Jewish Democratic Council.

Institute for First Amendment Studies
http://www.berkshire.net/~ifas
The generous web site of the preeminent research group tracking the religious right. Includes IFAS's excellent newsletter, *The Freedom Writer;* an e-mail directory of Congress, state legislatures, and the media; and a well-chosen catalog of books about the right.

Fairness & Accuracy In Reporting (FAIR)
http://www.igc.org/fair
The media watch group features selections from its *EXTRA!* magazine, *CounterSpin* radio show, and "Media Beat" syndicated column on-line.

Coalition for Human Dignity
http://www.halcyon.com/burghardt/chd.html
In-depth research on the radical right from the Oregon-based human rights group.

The Left Side of the Web
http://paul.spu.edu/~sinnfein/progressive.html
A large collection of progressive links, including much material on militias and the far right.

Institute for Global Communications
http://www.igc.apc.org/
The mother of all progressive web sites, with an inexhaustible roster of organizations.

AlterNet
http://www.igc.apc.org/an
The Institute for Alternative Journalism brings you a wide range of reports about the radical right, from many sources. Includes the Democratic Values Project, Militias in America, and *MediaCulture Review.*

Progressive Publications and News Services
http://www.igc.apc.org/igc/www.news.html
Alternative journalism goes electronic.

Economic Democracy Information Network (EDIN)
http://garnet.berkeley.edu:3333
A directory of information on the issues from progressive sources. Also, extensive lists of progressive links, including magazines, news services, nonprofit organizations, and e-mail lists.

The Sierra Club
http://www.sierraclub.org
Contains archives and subscription information for SC Action, a bulletin sent out every weekday which details the latest environmental battles inside the Washington beltway. Much more is at this site, including electronic editions of the magazines *Sierra* and *The Planet.*

Women Leaders Online
http://worcester.lm.com/women/women.html
This group was organized in 1995 to mobilize women using the Internet. Its comprehensive newsletter, *Political Women Hotline,* featuring a section on the religious right, appears on line every two weeks.

The Interfaith Alliance
http://www.intr.net/tialliance
  A promising site for faith-based activism.

Center for Campus Organizing
http://envirolink.org/orgs/cco
  A great starting place for student activists. Includes a Campus Organizing Guide and issue briefs.

Voters Telecommunications Watch
http://www.vtw.org
  VTW keeps the public informed about attempts to restrict on-line civil liberties. Its site also boasts an excellent Citizen's Guide to the Net.

Vote Smart Web
http://www.vote-smart.org
  Project Vote Smart has put together the single most useful site we've found concerning U.S. politics. Find out where officehold-ers and candidates really stand on the issues, plus biographical, campaign finance, and contact information. Covers the federal and state levels. The site also includes many links to other gov-ernment information.

THOMAS: Legislative Information on the Internet
http://thomas.loc.gov
  Congress's official web site. Search the full text of proposed legislation or the *Congressional Record*. Get schedules for Con-gress or C-SPAN.

Town Hall
http://www.townhall.com
  A site shared by a number of right-wing groups, including the American Conservative Union, the Family Research Council, and the Heritage Foundation.

Stormfront White Nationalist Resource Page
http://stormfront.wat.com/stormfront
  Far right links you'll need a strong stomach to follow.

13

Out-of-Your-Armchair Activism

"The lesson that emerges from history is that [far right] groups are hindered more by the attitudes of the community than they are by laws. Fear and silence allow hate groups to flourish. People coming together, organizing and speaking out—saying 'Not in my town!'—make the extremists' tasks that much more difficult."[1]

—KEN TOOLE, director of the
Montana Human Rights
Network

SPEAKING UP IN PERSON

The most crucial point to remember when raising your voice against the radical right, whether it be to neighbors in conversation or your legislators, is to keep the truth on your side. Stick to the facts, and if you don't know the answer to a question, admit it. You'll be respected for it.

Educating Friends, Neighbors, Relatives

Don't miss the opportunity when the occasion arises to educate those closest to you about right-wing organizations. If you're in conversation with a neighbor who slips in a stereotype or two about people on welfare, that's your cue. Don't be didactic, just set the record straight in a casual, matter-of-fact way: "Well, actually the average mom on welfare has only two kids. And you know, I've heard some of those same stories about welfare fraud. But from what I've been reading, it's not the norm. In fact you'd be shocked to hear how little a mother of two has to live on for a month." Once you've straightened out any misconceptions your neighbor had about the issue, and you sense that his or her interest is piqued, offer some more information about the right's agenda. Who knows, you may have a budding activist on your hands.

Visiting Your Representatives

Meeting with public officials in person is one of the most important steps you can take to increase the power of your activism. For your representatives and their staff, keeping track of the activists in their district is part of their job. When they put your name together with a face, your concerns really begin to register. From then on, you'll be a real person to them, not just a voice from the void. So go ahead and get yourself on their VIP list.

The federal officials who depend on your vote are the president and vice president, two senators, and one congressperson. Of these, your congressperson will normally be most available to you. In addition to their Washington offices, congresspersons typically have at least one office in their district, where they keep regular hours for their constituents. Many congresspersons try to be in their districts every weekend while Congress is in session, and even more often at other times.

It should be easy enough to set up a meeting with your congressperson in his or her district office. But if you happen to be in Washington, D.C., as a tourist or for any other reason, don't miss the chance to visit your congressperson's office on Capitol Hill, where you can see the lawmaking process up close.

You'll find your state legislature to be a much lower-key affair than the U.S. Congress. Most state legislatures only meet for part of the year, usually from January till sometime in the spring. State legislators usually don't have individual staffs, so you will probably find them to be quite approachable. Often they don't have nearly enough time to research all the issues that come before them and will be grateful for any information you can provide.

The following are some tips to keep in mind when meeting with your representatives.
- *Be businesslike.* Make an appointment in advance. If it's a

member of Congress with whom you want to meet, you'll be dealing with his or her scheduler or appointment secretary. Be specific about your reason for wanting to visit with the official. On the morning of your meeting, call to confirm it. Look presentable—business attire is best.

- *Be on time, but be prepared to wait.* Elected officials have busy schedules that are subject to interruption. If you end up only speaking with a staff member, don't be disappointed. Elected officials rely heavily on their staff for information, so treat the staffer with courtesy and respect. If you get him or her to see your point of view, you'll have been successful.

- *Introduce yourself.* Make sure the official knows that you're a constituent. Mention any organizational affiliations you may have.

- *Be direct and concise.* Fifteen minutes is an adequate amount of time to discuss your views on a particular vote or issue. Prioritize the points you want to make, and lead with the most important. Bring along written material to drive your points home. Don't take it personally if your meeting is cut short.

- *Remember that they're human.* No matter how unapproachable your representatives may seem, try to relate to them on a human level. Be friendly but respectful.

- *Know something about them.* Before you visit your elected officials, look them up in the reference section of the library. Try to find out where they stand on questions that concern you. Check back issues of the local paper to see what they've been up to. Identify common ground between their interests and yours.

- *Don't threaten them.* Don't imply that they'll lose your vote unless they do what you want. Appeal to reason, making your points in a logical way. The rest can be left unsaid.

- *Speak for your community.* If you speak for a large group of voters, or can otherwise show that your views have widespread support, by all means do so. Let the official know that you plan to communicate with this group of people about your visit.

- *Bring friends along.* Your visit will have far greater impact if you recruit a few allies to accompany you. The official, impressed by this show of strength, will find it more difficult to deny your requests. It's especially helpful if one of your group has experience dealing with government.

- *Ask your member to lobby others.* In Congress and state legislatures, most bills must be approved by a committee before they can come to a vote. Committee members have disproportionate influence over legislation in their domain. But what if you're concerned about a bill, and your own representative isn't on the committee that is considering it? In that case, it's protocol to ask him or her to talk to committee members on your behalf. They will be more easily swayed by one of their colleagues than by a citizen who isn't a constituent.

• *Watch out for smokescreens.* Politicians are skilled at getting themselves off the hook by making small talk, changing the subject, retreating into generalities, passing the buck, making excuses, etc. Don't let these techniques throw you—they're all in the game. Stick resolutely to your topic, and ask for commitments to specific actions.

• *Make yourself available as a resource.* If you can provide good, factual information, you may become a valuable source to your officials and their staff. Suggest that they call you if they have further questions.

• *Follow up with a thank-you note.* Besides being good manners, a thank-you note increases the likelihood that you'll be remembered in the future. Use it to summarize the meeting and reemphasize your main points.

Speaking Out in Public

We hope that after that you've read this book and followed some of our suggestions for further research, your curiosity will only have been whetted. You may want to see the democratic system in action with your own eyes. You may even find that you're bursting with newfound knowledge that you want to share with the world. If so—then congratulations! You're ready to bring your activism into the public arena.

Most American citizens, even those interested in public life, never take the step of attending a local government meeting. We guarantee that if you become one of those who do go and speak out, you'll experience a new feeling of empowerment. You'll begin to see for yourself that the average person really can make a difference.

The religious right has become a force in American politics by taking ordinary citizens, motivating them, and giving them the skills necessary to become winners in the political system. Some of those citizens are sitting in Congress today.

Local government and school board meetings. It's at this humble level that government is at its most accessible. Here's where the decisions are as small, and as important to your life, as whether to put a new traffic light on your street. The participants are your friends and neighbors. When you go, you'll realize that there's nothing intimidating about politics; and that you have as much right as anyone to offer your input to government.

Notices for these meetings will be published in the local newspaper and posted at the local government center. Just go and observe a few meetings to get a feeling for the procedures and personalities involved. Maybe you'll see a neighbor there who can give you the inside scoop. You'll probably have the opportunity before or after the meeting to meet your local officials and tell them what's on your mind.

Town hall meetings and candidates' nights. At these meetings, local and not-so-local politicians prove their accountability to their constituents. Candidate nights are held in the heat of election campaigns, giving voters a chance to winnow the candidates. A town hall meeting is convened by one official to hear questions and comments from the voters. If one is announced in your community, don't pass it up—and bring your friends along, too. Few better opportunities exist to make personal contact with your representative and his or her staff.

Public hearings. Often, legislators will take their show on the road, convening hearings in the field to get popular input. This is another golden opportunity for you to make yourself heard. Of course, if you live near Washington, D.C., or a state capital, you will have many opportunities to attend legislative and regulatory hearings. Even if you happen to be visiting a capital city, it's worth finding out whether anything interesting is going on. Look it up in government publications or ask your legislator's office.

Making statements at public meetings. While many government meetings nowadays are run informally, some follow a set of rules known as parliamentary procedure. If you don't understand what's going on at first, there's no reason to be intimidated—you'll catch on soon enough. An inexpensive edition of *Robert's Rules of Order* will help you get oriented.

A resource that can be found right in your own living room is the C-SPAN cable TV network, broadcasting sessions of the U.S. House of Representatives, as well as other government meetings. C-SPAN is giving a new generation of activists an education in the rules of the political game.

Public Speaking Tips

Many people are paralyzed by the thought of speaking in public. They're certain that they're congenitally incapable of getting up before a crowd without falling utterly flat. However, public speaking is a skill that can be learned like any other. It's actually more difficult to speak to five friends than to fifty strangers. The friends all bring their own conflicting expectations of you to bear on what you're saying, while with the strangers, to whom you're a blank slate, you can strive for any effect you wish.

There are many good books that can teach you the rudiments of public speaking. We'll just offer a few general principles:

Know what you want to say; write down select points.
Create a mood.
Tell a story.
Don't go on too long.
Speak to each audience member individually.
Don't worry if you're nervous—it makes you speak *better*!
Practice . . .

TAKING PART IN ELECTORAL POLITICS

Know the Power of Your Vote

The religious right's goal is not to get the majority of Americans to agree with them, but to get the minority that does out to the polls. Guy Rodgers, former national field coordinator of the Christian Coalition, told an audience of supporters:

> In any good voter-turnout election . . . only 15 percent of the eligible voters determine the outcome. . . . How could that be? Of all adults 18 and over who are eligible, only about 50 to 65 percent are registered. And of those registered, only 50 per-cent actually vote. . . . Is this sinking in? We don't have to worry about convincing a majority of Americans to agree with us . . . They're not involved, they're not voting, so who cares?[2]

One of the most powerful tools Armchair Activists have is their vote, so use it! Remember, every election is important—be it for the local school board or the presidency.

Volunteering in a Campaign

An exciting way to get into the thick of political action is to work for an election campaign. If you hear about a candidate who's making a stand against the radical right, by all means get in there and help him or her out. Volunteer your time, or, if you can afford it, make a financial contribution. Now more than ever, "good guys" need our support—without a doubt, the foot soldiers of the right will be busy working for their opposition.

In an election campaign, you'll get a ground-level view of how American politics really works. At first you'll probably be asked to do small tasks. But if you show you can handle important jobs and cope with the stress of a fast-paced campaign, you may be given more responsibilities. Many people who hold positions of power in our political system first proved their mettle in election campaigns.

Once you're bitten by the political bug, you may want to jump into party politics, and possibly even run for office yourself. Sociologists say that Americans have steadily become less engaged with civic life. It's difficult to find candidates to run for local government positions, and many Democratic and Republican party posts are going begging. That's one reason that the radical right has swept into power in so many places. Getting involved in local party politics is one way activists can make a big difference.

JOINING AN ORGANIZATION

So far, we've outlined some of the ways you can fight the right as an individual. Joining an advocacy group can be a shortcut to becoming an activist. Plus, working with others can have an impressive impact; organizing has always been at the heart of social activism.

Suddenly, as a new member, you have the benefit of all the experience of strategists who have been working on the issues for years. You have many new sets of eyes and ears telling you what the radical right's been up to, what right-fighters have been doing to thwart them, and how it's all playing out in the halls of government. Best of all, you have new friends to help make activism stimulating.

America is a country of organizations. There are many thousands of them, ranging from tiny local ones to national ones with millions of members. They are involved in politics from every point of view, employing every tactic that's been invented. And now that the radical right is intruding into so many spheres of American life, there are many groups that have gotten involved in fighting the right. It's up to you to choose one or more that do it your way.

Throughout this book are references to excellent organizations that you can join. Part II offers selected groups working on specific issues. The section about newsletters (p. 199) has a list of some of the most informative research groups. The internet section (p. 218) gives you addresses of organizations you can access on-line. The list of potential allies on p. 242 tells you types of organizations that often get involved in fighting the radical right, although that's not their primary purpose. Possibly you're already a member of one of these groups and are in a position to influence its policy from the inside. Finally, in Appendix I, "Further Resources," we list still more useful organizations. We en-

The Activist's Almanac

For those activists who want to see the big picture, there's a book called *The Activist's Almanac: The Concerned Citizen's Guide to the Leading Advocacy Organizations in America* by David Walls (New York: Simon & Schuster, 1993). It's a thorough reference to advocacy groups in America that's also fascinating to read. Walls covers the major organizations involved in a whole spectrum of issues, concentrating on progressive groups but with some information on conservative ones as well. An activist himself, as well as a scholar, he provides a sympathetic history which helps put today's movements in context. In this book, we've noted many organizations that are directly involved in countering the radical right. But if you'd like to know what else is on the activist landscape, *The Activist's Almanac* is an excellent starting point.

courage you to get materials from any of the groups referenced in this book, and see whether they arouse your sympathies. All of them are worthy of your support.

Though these listings necessarily concentrate on national organizations, don't overlook the work of local grassroots advocacy groups. Many of them are doing innovative work that runs rings around their larger counterparts. Your public library or local government may compile a list of advocacy groups in your area. Otherwise, the best way to find them is through word of mouth—ask a local activist to tell you what's going on.

FAITH-BASED ACTION

There are people of faith by the millions who oppose everything the religious right stands for and who are outraged when groups like the Christian Coalition claim to represent them. Among them are activists who have been pillars of the social justice

movements in America. In the last few years, religious leaders
and laypeople alike have realized that the time has come to
stand up in support of a diverse and tolerant society.

Though churches have formed the backbone of the religious
right, religious groups can also be hives of organizing *against* the
right. Religious people who don't accept the right's political
dogma are among those most threatened by its narrow vision of
a Christian America, and Armchair Activists should find ready allies among them. If you belong to a church or other religious organization, it may be the most natural arena for your
right-fighting activities.

It's crucial for people of faith who don't accept the right's narrow brand of religion to speak up. Clergy can be among our
strongest allies—encourage them to use religious language to
denounce the religious right's exclusionary worldview.

The Interfaith Alliance. One organization for people of faith
who want to fight the right is the Interfaith Alliance. The Alliance was founded in July 1994 as a faith-based response to the
Christian Coalition and similar groups. As of November 1995, its
membership had grown to twenty thousand, and it was adding
two thousand members a month. The Alliance has filled a vacuum, says executive director Jill Hanauer: "People started sending money in and started local chapters without even telling us."
Determinedly ecumenical, the Alliance spans the ideological
and theological spectrum. Its board of directors includes leaders
from most of the major Protestant denominations, as well as
Roman Catholicism and Judaism.

The Interfaith Alliance doesn't take positions on issues, focusing instead on the religious right's tactics. It shines a light on
stealth candidates, speaks out against those who use religion as a
weapon, and works to establish civility and tolerance in the public debate. The Alliance has distributed voter guides to counter
the Christian Coalition's slanted ones. It has smoked out local
candidates who tried to hide their religious right affiliations, and
spoken out against demonizing rhetoric used by such figures as
Oliver North.

If a local Alliance already exists in your area, you can join it; if
not, you can help set one up. An initial meeting can be sponsored by six people, representing at least three denominations

and including two members of the clergy. Or, simply join the national organization as an individual member.

Contact the Interfaith Alliance at:

The Interfaith Alliance
1511 K Street, NW, Suite 738
Washington, DC 20005
(202) 639-6370
e-mail: tialliance@intr.net
WWW: http://www.intr.net/tialliance

More Religious Alternatives to the Right

There are many religious people who feel called to bring their faith to the political arena, but who find the mean-spirited views of a Pat Robertson abhorrent. The religious right's recent success has provoked considerable soul-searching in some of them. Now two groups have been independently formed by people who want to transcend old left-right divisions with a renewed spirituality. One, the Call to Renewal, is associated with the evangelical Christian *Sojourners* magazine; the other, started by *Tikkun,* a Jewish magazine, is called the Foundation for Ethics and Meaning. Both have provocative ideas; if you're interested, pick up a copy of either magazine on the newsstand, or contact them for more information:

The Call to Renewal
2401 15th Street, NW
Washington, DC 20009
(202) 328-8842
fax: (202) 328-8757
e-mail: call-to-renewal@convene.com

The Foundation for Ethics and Meaning
251 West 100th Street, 5th Floor
New York, NY 10025
(212) 665-1597
fax: (212)864-4137
e-mail: foundation@tikkun.org
WWW: http://www.panix.com/~fem

STAY STRONG!

Here are a few of the inspirational tips for people of faith fighting the religious right offered by Rev. Meg Riley, director of the Office for Social Justice Advocacy at the Unitarian Universalist Association in Washington, DC:

- This is a long haul; we need to congratulate ourselves on small successes. Celebrate small steps along the way.
- In the words of long-time activist Barbara Majors: It isn't going to be easy, so we'd better make it fun!
- Spiritual discipline—prayer, meditation, holy housecleaning—can give strength for the journey.
- A trusted group of colleagues in this work is essential. Invite other activists to do fun things with you, as well as working on the issues together!
- Creativity is essential for good organizing. When you feel trapped, burned out, reactive, and reptilian, take a day off, go to the beach, hang out with a three-year-old, fingerpaint, watch a silly movie.
- If the news is making you crazy, avoid it for a while. Pray while you read it. Turn it over to the wind.
- Cultivate hope as a discipline. When you hear yourself thinking negatively, remind yourself about the power that we have to make change.

COUNTERING HATE GROUPS

To people who live in communities where hate groups like the Nazi skinheads and the KKK have made their presence known, the threat of violence is all too real—it's something they live with every day. The problem of how to deal with these groups deserves a book of its own, and fortunately an excellent one is available. It's called *When Hate Groups Come to Town,* and it's published by the Center for Democratic Renewal, an organization that has been fighting hate groups for many years. Such vital topics as "Security Tips for Activists" and "What to Do If You're the Victim of a Hate Crime" are well covered. If you find yourself on the front lines against hate groups, this book should be on your shelf. (If you or someone you know has been the victim of a hate crime, contact the Center for Democratic Renewal. They can give you information on how to respond or a referral to a group in your area.)

For communities which are being faced specifically with militias, there's a newly published booklet called *What to Do When the Militia Comes to Town*. Written by Ken Toole, who has confronted militias up close as director of the Montana Human Rights Network, and published by the American Jewish Committee, the booklet is concise, yet full of good advice. It will be useful for people who want to organize opposition not only to militias, but to any right-wing force in their community.

When Hate Groups Come to Town, $18.95
Center for Democratic Renewal
P.O. Box 50469
Atlanta, GA 30302
(404) 221-0025
fax: (404) 221-0045

What to Do When the Militia Comes to Town, $2.50
American Jewish Committee
165 East 56th Street
New York, NY 10022
(212) 751-4000

ORGANIZING YOUR NEIGHBORS

Most of political organizing is nothing more than getting together with people, on the phone or in person, and talking to them. Especially now, when so many Americans feel disconnected from their communities, the experience of working with your neighbors on a cause can be unexpectedly rewarding. You'll find that some of the nicest and most interesting people are the ones who get involved in fighting the radical right. And you'll discover a sense of mission and belonging that may be new in your life.

Action Alerts

The action alert is a basic tool for getting people involved in your cause. It consists of a short notice that informs people about an urgent problem and tells them what they can do to help. An action alert can be in the form of a flyer, a fax, or an e-mail message. It can be used to keep members of an existing group posted, to organize a new group, or simply to alert neighbors about an issue.

Let's say that an upcoming school board meeting is scheduled to discuss accusations of witchcraft in the schools, and you've learned that a religious right group plans to raise tensions by bringing in busloads of outsiders. Type out a succinct and snappy flyer, one page at most, explaining the situation and urging people who value diversity and tolerance to attend the meeting. Make a stack of copies.

Now, how to distribute them? The simplest way is to go door to door, leaving them at the entrances to your neighbors' houses and apartment buildings, and underneath windshield wipers of parked cars. (Don't put them in mailboxes—that's a federal offense.) You can also distribute the flyers at shopping areas—sympathetic shopkeepers may let you leave them on a counter or display one in a window. Don't forget about bulletin boards in places like supermarkets, libraries, and coffeehouses. And, of course, mail them out to anyone you know who might be interested, with a personal note attached.

You may be tempted to issue your action alert anonymously, but it's far better to include your name and phone number at the bottom, so that people whom you've roused have a chance to contact you. Then you can start building a list of supporters, which will be good as gold if you engage in any further community activism. Of course, you may get some nasty calls from the opposition as well—that, unfortunately, comes with the territory.

Phone, fax, and e-mail trees

To a large extent, modern communications technology is what makes Armchair Activism possible. A case in point is the tree technique. Basically, it's just a way to get word out to a large number of people quickly. The radical right has used it very effectively, but there's no reason right-fighters can't use it as well.

A tree normally consists of fifteen people. One participant serves as the "trunk." When the trunk receives an action alert, he or she contacts two people, each of whom contacts two more people, each of whom in turn contacts two more people. Then the people at the farthest branches of the tree contact the trunk to confirm that they've gotten the message. Each participant can then serve as the trunk of a new tree.

The tree technique works with phone calls, but now that fax and e-mail have come into common use, it's gotten even faster and easier. One action alert issued by a Washington insider can mobilize thousands of people to blitz Congress with instantaneous pressure. Trees are equally useful for mustering activists on the local level.

Show a Video

One way of drumming up people's interest in fighting the radical right is to ask them to view a video. You can build a fun, informal evening around a video showing that will also be highly educational and motivating. Several organizations offer videos geared to giving viewers a crash course on the religious right. Simply invite family members, friends, neighbors, and coworkers to your house, and pass the popcorn while they take in tales of the radical right. Afterward, host a discussion, and try to get your guests involved in some of the activities listed here—letter writing, for example. Have photocopied materials available for your guests to take home.

Here are some sources for anti-right videos (see Appendix I for contact information):

Institute for First Amendment Studies

- *Onward Christian Soldiers* (1996) 50 minutes, $24.95

People for the American Way

- *The Religious Right: In Their Own Words* (1993) 8 minutes, $25.00
- *Vista: a Battle for Public Education* (1995) 11 minutes, $29.95

- *Redondo Beach: A Stand Against Censorship* (1990) 14 minutes, $20
- *Censorship in Our Schools: Hawkins County, TN* (1987) 19 minutes, $20

Host a Letter-writing Party

Another fun way to bring people together is to have a party at which individuals write letters on a particular issue. An informal gathering of a few concerned friends is a good way to start. But if the issue affects your local area, you may want to invite your whole block or apartment building. The point of the party is to make it easy for others to write letters to their legislators that they otherwise wouldn't get around to writing. Provide information on the issue and sample letters for your guests.

STARTING YOUR OWN GROUP

As a committed activist, you may reach a limit of what you can do on your own. If there's no local or national organization already dealing with the issue that concerns you—and especially if the radical right is mobilizing in your community, and people are looking for a way to stop them—it may be time to form your own group. Getting an organization off the ground is a difficult but exciting job. We'll offer here just a hint of what you can expect, together with pointers toward more detailed guidance.

What's Involved

Most community groups start with a dedicated core of just two or three people. There's no magic to building an organization—the key is simply talking to people. On the phone and in person, to friends and to strangers—there's simply no substitute for personal contact.

The first thing the initial organizers must do is to plan a meeting with a somewhat larger group. Along with reaching out to friends, family, neighbors, and colleagues, try to recruit people from as many segments of the community as possible. There are many different kinds of people who have a natural interest in opposing the radical right. Some of them are listed below under "Potential Allies" (p. 242). Make contact with people who are already involved with community organizations—they may join and bring their friends with them. Experienced activists are particularly valuable.

If the initial meeting is very small, it can take place in someone's living room; otherwise, arrange to use a public space such as a school, library, or church. The key to building a strong organization is to make sure that each member has a sense of ownership toward it and feels that his or her contributions are valued. Focus on giving each member something concrete to do, and on achieving a positive goal as quickly as possible. Often, the goal will be to organize a forum or speaking event to which the general public will be invited. If all goes well, the event will launch your organization with a bang.

Things Your Group Can Do

There is a far wider sphere of activities available to a group than to an individual activist. We list some of them briefly here; for more detailed information, consult the sources in "Recommended Reading for Serious Organizers" below.

- Collect information systematically.
- Publish a newsletter.
- Establish a presence on-line.
- Activate a phone, fax, or e-mail tree.
- Get the press to cover the fight against the radical right.
- Question candidates on their right-wing views and affiliations.
- Distribute scorecards detailing what you've learned about candidates.
- Organize public forums and speaking events.
- Circulate petitions and present them to government officials.
- Organize rallies and demonstrations.

Coalition Building

Sometimes, when there is widespread concern about the radical right in a community, and a quick response is necessary, the best course of action is to form a coalition. A coalition is an organization of organizations, convened for a specific purpose. Each group within the coalition typically contributes one member as a liaison. The brunt of the work falls on a small coordinating committee.

The coalition organizers should contact all community organizations that are not aligned with the radical right. Diversity is important to the coalition's credibility—it should be interfaith and multiethnic, if at all possible. By working together against the radical right's divisive tactics, many communities have gained a new sense of unity.

Potential Allies

The following is a list of potential allies among whom organizers might look for recruits:

- Mainstream, liberal and nontraditional religious groups
- Civil rights groups
- Lesbian and gay groups
- The Jewish community
- Pro-choice groups
- Labor unions
- Teachers' and school administrators' associations
- The university community
- Librarians and library associations
- Booksellers
- Artists and arts groups
- Democrats and moderate Republicans
- Environmentalists

Recommended Reading for Serious Organizers

If you want to take the initiative and organize your community, the following sources are a good place to begin (to order, see contact information in Appendix I):

- Toole, Ken. *What to Do When the Militia Comes to Town* (The American Jewish Committee, 1995), $2.50.
- *How to Win: A Practical Guide for Defeating the Radical Right in Your Community* (National Jewish Democratic Council, 1994), $25.00.
- Pick, Maritza. *How to Save Your Neighborhood, City, or Town: The Sierra Club Guide to Community Organizing* (San Francisco: Sierra Club Books, 1993), $12.00. Available in bookstores.
- *The San Diego Model: A Community Battles the Religious Right* (People for the American Way, 1993), $6.95.

FIGHTING THE RIGHT: THE NEXT GENERATION

Students Against the Right

The right has made on-campus recruiting a priority. Bill Bright's Campus Crusade for Christ mobilizes students behind right-wing evangelical causes, as does the InterVarsity Christian Fellowship-USA. Collegians Activated to Liberate Life (CALL) works against legalized abortion. Many far-right groups specialize in infiltrating local Young Republican groups. Some right-wing groups and newspapers, such as the *Dartmouth Review* (which sprang to notoriety in the 1980s with stunts such as outing gay students to their parents), receive funds and training from a right-wing coordinating body known as the Intercollegiate Students Institute (ISI).

If you are a concerned student, how can you counter the right on your turf?

- *Find issues that are of importance to fellow students.* It is easier to organize around student-related issues than to try to convince people to care about something they haven't thought about before. If you are challenging a broad agenda, such as the *Contract with America,* draw people in by spotlighting areas of direct concern to students, such as cuts in health care funding and the elimination of many government-subsidized student loan programs.
- *If you think an organization such as ISI is funding right-wing groups, challenge these groups.* If they deny outside funding but seem still to be spending large amounts, you can request the 990

tax forms they filed in the previous years. These are public information, and show (in general terms) how much money the group receives, and how much it has available to pay its officers and dole out for expenses. Additionally, you can try to pass a motion in the student government mandating that all groups who receive campus grants reveal all outside funding they receive. This is known as a disclosure law. If a group refuses to reveal its funding, you can then push for student funds to be withheld. If the group continues to operate, it should be clear that outside money is supporting it.

• *Get help from the experts.* Overarching campus organizations such as the Student Environmental Action Coalition (SEAC) and the Center for Campus Organizing link high school, college, and university activists across the fifty states.

SEAC, a group that coordinates actions among different organizations, affiliates over two thousand groups. Nearly half its members come from high schools, which have become increasingly political in recent years. During the debate over Proposition 187 in 1994, high school students in California led the protests against the anti-immigration measure.

The Center for Campus Organizing has a subgroup called the University Conversion Project, which monitors how much money organizations such as Accuracy in Academia and the Intercollegiate Studies Institute pump into the right-wing campus machine. Currently, says coordinator Rick Cowan, the right on campus has at its disposal a total of approximately $24 million per year. The CCO can help you track right-wing funding at your school.

SEAC and CCO both publish literature on how to beat the right on campus, and provide training sessions and material. For more information, contact:

Student Environmental Action Coalition
PO Box 1168
Chapel Hill, NC 27514-1168
(919) 967-4600
e–mail: seac@igc.apc.org

Center for Campus Organizing
Box 748
Cambridge, MA 02142
(617) 354-9363

e–mail: cco@igc.apc.org
WWW: http://envirolink.org/orgs/cco

Kids in Action

The children of today will determine the future of American democracy. They can start getting involved in changing the world as early as grade school. An excellent resource for children is a book called *The Kid's Guide to Social Action: How to Solve the Social Problems You Choose—and Turn Creative Thinking into Positive Action* by Barbara A. Lewis (Minneapolis: Free Spirit Publishing, 1991). It's packed with tips and real-life examples of kids making a difference—even adults will learn a lot from it. When kids work for change in their communities, they not only have lots of fun while learning, they gain a sense of achievement that will last them a lifetime.

Afterword
By Felice N. Schwartz

E ver since I was an undergraduate, with the exception of
eight years I spent at home with my children, I have been a
full-time social activist. Throughout my life I have chosen to
work within the system to bring about social change—first in
heading up the National Scholarship Service and Fund for
Negro Students (NSSFNS), which bombarded colleges and universities with highly qualified applicants, and, in its second year
(1946), placed 750 black students in institutions that had few or
none in the past. Then I founded Catalyst in 1962, where we
worked to open doors for women, as opposed to knocking those
doors down. When, after thirty-two years, I retired from Catalyst,
it had become the premier organization working with business
and the professions to effect change for women. The board con-
sisted of CEOs from top corporations and women at the highest
levels of accomplishment—individuals who would not have
joined the board of a typical advocacy organizations.

I've loved my professional life, not just the goals I was striving
to achieve but the everyday process and all it entailed. Upon re-
tirement at age seventy, I nonetheless felt liberated. Freed from
the need to direct an organization and to raise funds, I was able
to spread my wings and to do whatever I chose in any manner I
chose. A year later I was immersed in research that I hoped
would culminate in a series of articles and speeches designed to
stimulate a fresh discussion of women's role in society. Quite
suddenly it occured to me that—unconnected to my current en-
deavors—there was at this time a confluence of three factors that
seemed to cry out for expression in a book such as this.

The first was the growing threat of the radical right. The outreach and organization of these groups had become increasingly
and frighteningly effective. I believed that the momentum of

right-wing extremism would transform our country from a democracy to an autocracy if it continued uncountered.

The second factor was the inertia of the vast majority of people in the face of this threat. My agent sent the proposal for this book to sixteen publishers. The initial reaction was largely positive—in fact, unusual interest was expressed. But, one by one, the houses withdrew, until only Riverhead was left. The reason for retreat expressed by several of the publishers was that the era of activism was over—that today most people were largely focused on their careers and their families and did not find the time for involvement in social issues, that nobody would buy the book.

The final factor was the serendipitous meeting with Suzanne K. Levine, a young woman with fire in the belly, who felt that the factions of the radical right were exerting an inordinate influence on mainstream public policy. She reminded me of myself fifty years ago, and in her short career she had demonstrated what I felt were exceptional research and writing skills. Excitedly we settled on a partnership, hired three experienced researchers, and started work.

Putting this book together was a thrilling experience for all of us. As we moved from chapter to chapter we recognized the complexity and interconnection of right-wing movements, and the impact these movements could have on almost every aspect of our lives. We hoped that the book would serve as a call to action: that readers would be drawn permanently into the ranks of social activism, with an active concern for the rights of all people.

Today, as we submit our manuscript, there is a front page story in the *New York Times* about the Christian conservatives who are promoting a "Parental Rights Amendment" in state legislatures across the nation. The *Times* article suggests that the amendment could give small groups of parents veto power over the curricula of public schools, promote suits against school boards and social service agencies, and hinder child abuse investigations. The radical right marches on. It's up to you, the Armchair Activist, to use the tools in this book to defeat it.

January 15, 1996

Felice N. Schwartz fought hard for her ideals throughout her life. She died on February 8, 1996, aged 71, at her home in New York City.

Appendix I
Further Resources

Books on the Radical Right

- *Armed and Dangerous: The Rise of the Survivalist Right,* by James Coates (New York: Hill and Wang, 1987).
- *Blood in the Face: The Ku Klux Klan, Aryan Nations, Nazi Skinheads, and the Rise of a New White Culture,* by James Ridgeway (New York: Thunder's Mouth Press, 1991).
- *The Coors Connection: How Coors Family Philanthropy Undermines Democratic Pluralism,* by Russ Bellant (Boston: South End Press, 1991).
- *Eyes Right!: Challenging the Right Wing Backlash,* edited by Chip Berlet (Boston: South End Press, 1995).
- *The Force Upon the Plain,* by Kenneth Stern (New York: Simon & Schuster, 1996).
- *Old Nazis, the New Right, and the Republican Party,* by Russ Bellant (Boston: South End Press, 1991).
- *Roads to Dominion: Right-wing Movements and Political Power in the United States,* by Sara Diamond (New York: The Guilford Press, 1995).
- *Rush Limbaugh is a Big Fat Idiot and Other Observations,* by Al Franken (New York: Delacorte, 1996)
- *Spiritual Warfare: The Politics of the Christian Right,* by Sara Diamond (Boston: South End Press, 1989).
- *Thunder on the Right,* by Alan Crawford (New York: Pantheon, 1980).
- *The War Against the Greens: The "Wise Use" Movement, The New Right, and Anti-Environmental Violence,* by David Helvarg (San Francisco: Sierra Club Books, 1994).
- *The Way Things Aren't: Rush Limbaugh's Reign of Error,* by Steven Rendall, Jim Naureckas, and Jeff Cohen (New York: The New Press, 1995).

- *White Lies, White Power: The Fight Against White Supremacy and Reactionary Violence,* by Michael Novick (Monroe, Maine: Common Courage Press, 1995).

Organizations Fighting the Radical Right

American Jewish Committee
165 East 56th St.
New York, NY 10022
(212) 751-4000
- *What to Do When the Militia Comes to Town,* by Ken Toole, 1995, $2.50

Americans United for Separation of Church and State
1816 Jefferson Place, NW
Washington, DC 20036
(202) 466-3234
e-mail: amerunited@aol.com
WWW: http://www.netplexgroup/americansunited
- *Church and State,* $25/year

Anti-Defamation League of B'nai B'rith
823 United Nations Plaza
New York, NY 10017
(212) 490-2525
- *The Religious Right: The Assault on Tolerance and Pluralism in America,* 1994, $7.50
- *Beyond the Bombing: The Militia Menace Grows,* 1995, $2.50

Center for Campus Organizing
P.O. Box 748
Cambridge, MA 02142
(617) 354-9363
e-mail: cco@igc.apc.org
WWW: http://envirolink.org/orgs/cco
- *Study War No More: UCP's Guide to Uncovering the Right on Campus,* 1994, $5.95

Center for Democratic Renewal
P.O. Box 50469
Atlanta, GA 30302
(404) 221-0025
fax: (404) 221-0045
e-mail: CDR@igc.apc.org
* *The Right Unmasked,* $25/year
* *When Hate Groups Come to Town: A Handbook of Effective Community Responses,* 1992, $18.95

c.c. watch
3741 NE 163rd Street, Suite #311
Sunny Isles, FL 33160
(305) 751-5001
fax: (305) 759-7193
e-mail: Watch97@aol.com
* *c.c. watch,* $29.95/year

Coalition for Human Dignity
PO Box 40344
Portland , OR 97240
(503) 281-5823
WWW: http://www.halycon.com/burghardt/chd.html
* *Dignity Report,* $25/year

DataCenter
464 19th Street
Oakland, CA 94612
(510) 835-4692
fax: (510) 835-3017
e-mail: datactr@tmn.com
* *CultureWatch,* $35/year

Fairness & Accuracy In Reporting (FAIR)
130 West 25th Street
New York, NY 10001
(212) 633-6700
fax: (212) 727-7668
WWW: http://www.igc.org/fair
* *EXTRA!* magazine, $19/year
* FAIR's Media Activism Kit, $5

Institute for First Amendment Studies
P.O. Box 589
Great Barrington, MA 01230
(413) 528-3800
WWW: http://www.berkshire.net/~ifas
* *Freedom Writer,* $25/year
* *Onward Christian Soldiers,* (video), 1996, $24.95
* *The Field Manual of the Free Militia,* 1996, $10

The Interfaith Alliance
1511 K Street, NW, Suite 738
Washington, DC 20005
(202) 639-6370
e-mail: tialliance@intr.net
WWW: http://www.intr.net/tialliance
* *The Christian Coalition's "Road to Victory": A Report on the Political and Policy Agendas of the Christian Coalition,* 1995

Montana Human Rights Network
P.O. Box 1222
Helena, Montana 59624
(406) 442-5506
e-mail: mhrn@aol.com
* *Network News,* $15/year

National Gay & Lesbian Task Force
2320 17th St., NW
Washington, DC 20009
(202) 332-6483
fax: (202) 332-0207
e-mail: ngltf@ngltf.org
WWW: http://www.ngltf.org/ngltf
* *Fight the Right Action Kit,* 1993, $10
* *Activist Alert,* monthly news sheet free with membership ($35/year)

National Jewish Democratic Council
711 Second Street, NW
Washington, D.C. 20002
(202) 544-7636
* *How to Win: A Practical Guide for Defeating the Radical Right in Your Community,* 1994, $25.00

Northwest Coalition Against Malicious Harassment
P.O. Box 16776
Seattle, WA 98116
(206) 233-9136
* *Northwest Beacon,* $25/year

People Against Racist Terror
P.O. Box 1990
Burbank, CA 91507
(310) 288-5003
* *Turning the Tide,* $15/year

People for the American Way
2000 M Street, NW, Suite 400
Washington, DC 20036
(202) 467-4999
e-mail: pfaw@pfaw.org
WWW: http://www.pfaw.org
* *A Turn to the Right: A Guide to Religious Right Influence in the 103rd/104th Congress,* 1995, $9.95
* *An Activist Guide to Protecting the Freedom to Learn,* 1994, $13.95
* *The San Diego Model: A Community Battles the Religious Right,* 1993, $6.95
* *The Religious Right: In Their Own Words,* (video), 1993, $25

Political Research Associates
120 Beacon Street, Suite 300
Somerville, MA 02143
(617) 661-9313
fax: (617) 661-0059
e-mail: publiceye@igc.apc.org
* *The Public Eye,* $29/year
(contact P.R.A. for an extensive list of publications about the radical right)

ProChoice Resource Center
174 East Boston Post Road
Mamaroneck, NY 10543
(914) 381-3792
fax: (914) 381-3876
* *The Opposition Primer,* 1996, $15

Southern Poverty Law Center
400 Washington Avenue
Montgomery, AL 36104
(334) 264-0286
- *Klanwatch Intelligence Report* and *Teaching Tolerance,* $15/year

Appendix II:
National Media Contact List

National Newspapers

Los Angeles Times
Times-Mirror Square
Los Angeles, CA 90053
Phone: (800) 528-4637
Fax: (213) 237-4712

New York Times
229 West 43rd Street
New York, NY 10036
Phone: (212) 556-1234
Fax: (212) 556-3690
Phone (D.C. Bureau): (202) 862-0300

USA Today
1000 Wilson Boulevard
Arlington, VA 22229
Phone: (800) 828-0909
Fax: (703) 276-5513

Wall Street Journal
200 Liberty Street
New York, NY 10281
Phone: (212) 416-2000
Fax: (212) 416-2658 or 2659

Washington Post
1150 15th Street, NW
Washington, DC 20071
Phone: (202) 334-6000
Fax: (202) 334-5451

Associated Press
50 Rockefeller Plaza
New York, NY 10020
National Desk: (212) 621-1600

Fax (National Desk): (212) 621-7520
Foreign Desk: (212) 621-1663
Fax (Foreign Desk): (212) 621-5449
Phone (D.C. Bureau): (202) 828-6410

Magazines

Newsweek
251 West 57th Street
New York, NY 10019
Phone: (212) 445-4000
Fax: (212) 445-5068

Time
Time Inc.
Time & Life Building
Rockefeller Center
New York, NY 10020
Phone: (212) 522-1212
Fax: (212) 522-0323

U.S. News & World Report
2400 N Street, NW
Washington, DC 20037
Phone: (202) 955-2000
Fax: (202) 955-2049

Network Television

ABC News
47 West 66th Street
New York, NY 10023

Phone: (212) 456-7777
Fax: (212) 456-4968
Phone (D.C. Bureau):
(202) 222-7777

ABC World News Tonight
Phone: (212) 456-4040

Nightline
Phone: (202) 222-7000

Prime Time Live
Phone: (212) 456-1600

20/20
Phone: (212) 456-2020

ABC Good Morning America
147 Columbus Avenue
New York, NY 10023
Phone: (212) 456-5900

CBS News
524 West 57th Street
New York, NY 10019
Phone: (212) 975-4321
Fax: (212) 975-7934
Phone (D.C. Bureau):
(202) 457-4321
E-mail: realitycheck@cbsnews.com

CBS Evening News
Phone: (212) 975-3691

CBS This Morning
Phone: (212) 975-2824

60 Minutes
Phone: (212) 975-2009

CNN
1 CNN Center
Box 105366
Atlanta, GA 30348-5366
Phone: (404) 827-1700
Fax: (404) 827-1593

820 First Street, N.E.
Washington, DC 20002
Phone: (202) 898-7900
Fax: (202) 898-7923

Crossfire
Phone: (202) 898-7655

Larry King Live
Phone: (202) 898-7690

NBC
30 Rockefeller Plaza
New York, NY 10112
Phone: (212) 664-4444
Fax: (212) 664-5705
Phone (DC Bureau):
(202) 885-4200

NBC Nightly News
Phone: (212) 664-4971

Today
Phone: (212) 664-4249

Public Broadcasting

PBS
1320 Braddock Place
Alexandria, VA 22314
Phone: (703) 739-5000
Fax: (703) 739-0775

The NewsHour with Jim Lehrer
356 West 58th Street
New York, NY 10019
Phone: (212) 560-3113/
(703) 998-2844
Fax: (212) 560-3117

National Public Radio
635 Massachusetts Avenue, NW
Washington, DC 20001-3753
Phone: (202) 414-2000
Fax: (202) 414-3329

All Things Considered
Phone: (202) 414-2110

Morning Edition
Phone: (202) 414-2150

SOURCE: FAIR (Fairness & Accuracy In Reporting)

Appendix III:
State Capitol
Telephone Numbers

The following numbers will connect you to all branches of the state government, including the governor or any of the state legislators.

Alabama	(205) 242-8000	New Jersey	(609) 292-2121
Alaska	(907) 465-2111	New Mexico	(505) 986-4300
Arizona	(602) 542-4000	New York	(518) 474-2121
Arkansas	(501) 682-1010	North Carolina	(919) 733-1110
California	(916) 322-9900	North Dakota	(701) 224-2000
Colorado	(303) 866-5000	Ohio	(614) 466-2000
Connecticut	(203) 240-0222	Oklahoma	(405) 521-2011
Delaware	(302) 739-4000	Oregon	No Central
Florida	(904) 488-1234		Switchboard
Georgia	(404) 656-2000	Pennsylvania	(717) 787-2121
Hawaii	(808) 586-2211	Rhode Island	(401) 277-2000
Idaho	(208) 334-2411	South Carolina	(803) 734-1000
Illinois	(217) 782-2000	South Dakota	(605) 773-3011
Indiana	(317) 232-3140	Tennessee	(615) 741-3011
Iowa	(515) 281-5011	Texas	(512) 463-4630
Kansas	(913) 296-0111	Utah	(801) 538-4000
Kentucky	(502) 564-3130	Vermont	(802) 828-1110
Louisiana	(504) 342-6600	Virginia	(804) 786-0000
Maine	(207) 582-9500	Washington	No Central
Maryland	(301) 841-3000		Switchboard
Massachusetts	(617) 727-2121	West Virginia	(304) 348-3456
Michigan	(517) 373-1837	Wisconsin	(608) 226-2211
Minnesota	(612) 296-6013	Wyoming	(307) 777-7220
Mississippi	(601) 359-1000	District of	
Missouri	(314) 751-2151	Columbia	(202) 727-1000
Montana	(406) 444-2511		
Nebraska	(402) 471-2311		
Nevada	(702) 687-5000		
New Hampshire	(603) 271-1110		

SOURCE: *The Book of the States 1994-95* (Lexington, KY: The Council of State Governments, 1994), p.632.

Notes

Introduction

1. David Winkler, "Racism Resurgent Right Here in Arizona," *The Arizona Republic,* July 24, 1995, p. B5.

2. This conversation occurred on January 14, 1995—on the premiere of Grant's nationally syndicated show.

3. Quoted in Chip Berlet,"The Right Rides High," *The Progressive*, October, 1994, p. 22.

Chapter 1: Extremism Goes Mainstream

1. Loretta, J. Ross, "Human Rights and White Supremacy in the 1990s" (Atlanta, Georgia: The Center for Democratic Renewal, October 1994), p. 4.

2. *The News-Sentinel* (Fort Wayne, Ind.), August 16, 1993. Quoted in *The Religious Right: The Assault on Tolerance and Pluralism in America* (New York: The Anti-Defamation League, 1994), p. 4.

3. Philip Weiss, "Outcasts Digging in for the Apocalypse," *Time*, May 1, 1995, p.48.

4. From an August 1992 fundraising letter against the Equal Rights Amendment to the Iowa state constitution.

5. Dick Armey, "Freedom's Choir," *Policy Review*, Winter 1994.

6. Ross, "Human Rights and White Supremacy in the 1990s," p. 7.

7. *Fort Worth Star-Telegram,* September 14, 1993. Quoted in *The Religious Right: The Assault on Tolerance and Pluralism in America,* p. 4.

8. *Extremism in America: A Reader,* edited by Lyman Tower Sargent (New York: New York University Press, 1995), pp. 168–69.

9. *Concerned Women for America News,* March 1991. Quoted in the People for the American Way fact sheet on Concerned Women for America, April 1995.

10. *New York Times,* September 2, 1990. Quoted in the People for the American Way fact sheet on the American Family Association, April 1995.

11. Anti-Defamation League, *The Religious Right,* p. 1.

12. *San Francisco Chronicle,* September 13, 1993. Quoted in *The Religious Right: The Assault on Tolerance and Pluralism in America,* p. 4.

13. The "700 Club," July 11, 1995. Quoted in "The Christian Coalition's 'Road to Victory': A Report on the Political and Policy Agendas of the Christian Coalition," a report by the Interfaith Alliance Foundation and Americans United for Separation of Church and State, September 1995, p. 29.

14. Dale Russakoff, "Fax Network Links Outposts of Anger, Discontented Citizens Find Their Voice," *Washington Post*, August 20, 1995, p. A01.

15. "Beyond the Bombing: The Militia Menace Grows," a report by the Anti-Defamation League, 1995, p. 13.

16. *Aid & Abet Police Newsletter*, #12, Police Against the New World Order.

17. Anti-Defamation League, *The Religious Right*, p. 113.

18. "Paranoia as Patriotism: Far Right Influences on the Militia Movement," a report by the Anti-Defamation League, 1995, p. 33.

Chapter 2: The Religious Right

1. Pat Robertson, speaking at Robert Tilton's Word of Faith World Outreach Church, Dallas, 1984. Quoted in Skipp Porteous, "Contract on the American Family," *Freedom Writer*, June 1995, p. 3.

2. "Christian Coalition: Profile," *Freedom Writer* (the newsletter of the Institute for First Amendment Studies), March 1995, p. 5. Of the candidates receiving a 100% rating by the Christian Coalition's 1994 voter guide, 60% won in the national election.

3. "Religious Conservatives Increase Influence in National Election Data, Pro-Family/Pro-Life Candidates Account for Most of GOP Gains," Christian Coalition Report, November 8, 1994.

4. "National Association of Christian Educators/Citizens for Excellence in Education: Profile," *Freedom Writer*, February 1995, p. 5.

5. R. J. Rushdoony, *Thy Kingdom Come*, 1978. Quoted in *The Religious Right: The Assault on Tolerance and Pluralism in America*, p. 6.

6. According to biographer David Edwin Harrell. Quoted in *The Religious Right*, p. 15.

7. "Christian Coalition: Profile," *Freedom Writer*, March 1995, p. 4.

8. Anti-Defamation League, *The Religious Right*, p. 9.

9. On *Meet the Press*. Quoted in "The Two Faces of the Christian Coalition," a report by People for the American Way, 1994, p. 9.

10. The "700 Club," January 14, 1991.

11. To the *New York Times*. Quoted in "The Two Faces of the Christian Coalition," p. 8.

12. *The State*, November 13, 1993. Quoted in "The Christian Coalition's 'Road to Victory': A Report on the Political and Policy Agendas of the Christian Coalition," p.9.

13. On *Meet the Press*. Quoted in "The Two Faces of the Christian Coalition," p. 14.

14. The "700 Club." Quoted in "The Two Faces of the Christian Coalition," p. 14.

15. Anti-Defamation League, *The Religious Right*, p. 23.

16. Joe Conason, "The Religious Right's Quiet Revival," *The Nation*, April 27, 1992, p. 541.

17. Anti-Defamation League, *The Religious Right*, p. 30.

18. Jonathan Mozzochi, et al, "Stealth: The Christian Coalition Takes San Diego," *Fight the Right Action Kit* (The Gay and Lesbian Task Force, 1993), p. 21.

19. Anti-Defamation League, *The Religious Right*, p. 31.

20. A. J. W. James, "Denominations Unite to Combat Right-wing Force," *Philadelphia Tribune*, April 14, 1995, p. 1.

Chapter 3: The Far Right

1. Ross, "Human Rights and White Supremacy in the 1990s," p. 2.

2. To *The Coeur D'Alene Press*. Quoted in Sidney Blumenthal, "Her Own Private Idaho," *The New Yorker*, July 10, 1995, p. 29.

3. Loretta J. Ross, "The Militia Movement—In Their Own Words and Deeds," Congressional testimony on behalf of the Center for Democratic Renewal, July 11, 1995.

4. James Ridgeway and Leonard Zeskind, "Revolution U.S.A.: The Far Right Militias Prepare for Battle," *The Village Voice*, May 2, 1995, p. 24.

5. Louis Beam, "Leaderless Resistance," *The Seditionist*, February 1992.

6. Anti-Defamation League, "Armed & Dangerous: Militias Take Aim at the Federal Government" (Anti-Defamation League, October 1994).

7. Lewis H. Lapham, "Seen But Not Heard: The Message of the Oklahoma Bombing," *Harper's*, July 1995, p. 31.

8. *Aid or Abet Police Newsletter*, no. 12.

9. Ibid.

10. William T. Vollman, "Almost Heaven," *Spin*, September 1995, p. 128.

11. Dirk Johnson, "Mild-Mannered Engineer Fans Fires of a Movement," *New York Times*, July 6, 1995, p. B9.

12. Dale Russakoff, "Fax Network Links Outposts of Anger; Discontented Citizens Find Their Voice," *Washington Post*, August 20, 1995, p. A01.

Chapter 4: The New Right

1. Sara Diamond, *Spiritual Warfare: The Politics of the Christian Right* (Boston, MA: South End Press, 1989), p. 57.

2. Anti-Defamation League, *The Religious Right*, p. 92.

Chapter 5: Public Education

1. Anti-Defamation League, *The Religious Right,* p. 102.

2. *Federal News Service,* September 11, 1992. Quoted in "The Christian Coalition's 'Road to Victory': A Report on the Political and Policy Agendas of The Christian Coalition," p. 23.

3. Anti-Defamation League, *The Religious Right,* p. 102.

4. David Berliner and Bruce Biddle, *The Manufactured Crisis* (New York: Addison Wesley, 1995), p. 136.

5. Anti-Defamation League, *The Religious Right,* p. 103.

6. Ibid., p. 54.

7. Ibid., p. 12.

8. *Orlando Sentinel,* December 9, 1989, Quoted in "The Christian Coalition's 'Road to Victory': A Report on the Political and Policy Agendas of the Christian Coalition," p. 23.

9. Frank Rich, "Banned from Broadcast," *New York Times,* November 25, 1995, p. 23.

10. Phyllis Schlafly, "What's Wrong with Sex-Education?" *Phyllis Schlafly Report* 14, no. 7 (February 1981). Reprinted in *Extremism in America,* p. 244.

11. Shelley Ross and Leslie Kantor, "Sex Education and Reproductive Rights: Similar Goals, Same Opposition," *ProChoice IDEA* (the newsletter of the Pro-Choice Resource Center, Inc.), Winter 1994/95, p. 12.

12. *Notes on Education Newsline* (National Association of Christian Educators), May/June 1994, p. 2.

Chapter 6: Welfare

1. Committee on Ways and Means, U.S. House of Representatives, *1994 Green Book: Overview of Entitlement Programs* (Washington, D.C.: U.S. Government Printing Office, 1994), table 10–27.

2. Women's Committee of One Hundred, "10 Facts Most Americans Don't Know About Welfare," fact sheet (Washington, D.C.: Women's Committee of One Hundred, August 1995).

3. *1994 Green Book,* table 10–11.

4. Women's Committee of One Hundred, "10 Facts Most Americans Don't Know About Welfare."

5. *1994 Green Book,* table 10–27.

6. Women's Committee of One Hundred, "10 Facts Most Americans Don't Know About Welfare."

7. Ibid.

8. Michael Kramer, "The Myth About Welfare Moms," *Time,* July 3, 1995, p. 21.

9. Denise M. Topolnicki, "No More Pity for the Poor. Special Report on Welfare Reform," *Money*, May 1995, p. 122.

10. Christian Coalition's "Road to Victory" conference, September 8–9, 1995, Washington, D.C.

11. *1994 Green Book*, table 10–1.

12. "Network's Other View on Welfare Reform," *National Catholic Reporter*, April 28, 1995, p. 24.

13. *1994 Green Book*, table 10–1.

14. James Q. Wilson, "A New Approach to Welfare Reform: Humility," *Wall Street Journal*, December 29, 1994, p. A10.

15. Lynn Phillips, "Safety Net Performs Vanishing Act," *On the Issues: The Progressive Woman's Quarterly*, Fall 1994, p. 40.

16. Charlotte Allen, "Welfare Lines," *Washington Monthly*, December 1994, p. 20.

17. "Network's Other View on Welfare Reform."

18. The Republican National Committee, *Contract with America* (New York: Times Books, Random House, 1994), p. 65.

19. Topolnicki, "No More Pity for the Poor: Special Report on Welfare Reform."

20. Congressional Records.

21. The Christian Coalition's "Road to Victory" conference, September 8-9, 1995.

22. *1994 Green Book*, table 10–11.

23. Kramer, "The Myth About Welfare Moms."

24. Ibid.

25. Michael Ebart, "Helping Without Welfare: Innovative Programs Are Changing Lives," *Christian American*, May/June 1995, p. 1.

26. Sara Diamond, *Spiritual Warfare: The Politics of the Christian Right* (Boston: South End Press, 1989), p. 138.

27. Jason DeParle, "Despising Welfare, Pitying Its Young," *New York Times*, December 18, 1994, p. E5.

28. John B. Judis, "Crosses to Bear: The Many Faces of the Religious Right," *The New Republic*, September 12, 1994, p. 21.

29. Judith Gueron, testimony before the Senate Committee on Finance, March 20, 1995.

30. Ibid.

Chapter 7: Abortion

1. Susan Faludi, *Backlash: The Undeclared War Against American Women* (New York: Doubleday, 1991), p. 402.

2. Ibid.

3. Jonathan Hutson, "Operation Rescue Founder Predicts Armed Conflict (Part II)," *Front Lines Research* 1, no. 5 (May 1995), p. 4.

4. Susan Yanow, "How to Increase Abortion Services," *ProChoice IDEA,* Spring/Summer 1994, p. 1.

5. David Frum, "Republican Diversity Over Abortion Rights Is Complex," *Morning Edition,* November 20, 1995.

6. Lowey statement on the Women's Choice and Reproductive Health Protection Act of 1995.

7. NARAL/The NARAL Foundation, *Who Decides? A State-by-State Review of Abortion and Reproductive Rights,* 5th Ed, 1995, p. I.

8. Karen Branan and Frederick Clarkson, "Extremism in Sheep's Clothing: A Special Report on Human Life International," *Front Lines Research,* June 1994, p. 1.

9. Floyd Cochran and Loretta J. Ross, "Procreating White Supremacy: Women and the Far Right," information packet, August 1993, Center for Democratic Renewal, Atlanta.

10. Laura Flanders, "Far Right Militias and Anti-Abortion Violence: When Will Media See the Connection?" *Extra!,* July/August 1995, p. 11–12.

11. Ibid.

12. John Goetz, "Randall Terry and the U.S. Taxpayers Party," *Front Lines Research* 1, no. 2 (August 1994), p. 6.

13. Hutson, "Operation Rescue Founder Predicts Armed Conflict."

14. Sandi DuBowski and John Goetz, "Bushwhacked! The USTP & The Far Right," *Front Lines Research,* November 1994, p.1.

15. National Abortion Federation, "Incidents of Violence and Disruption Against Abortion Providers, 1994" (news release), 1995.

16. Flanders, "Far Right Militias."

17. Stephen J. Hedges, David Bowermaster, and Susan Headden, "Abortion: Who's Behind the Violence?" *U.S. News & World Report,* November 14, 1994, p. 55.

18. NARAL, "The Road to the Back Alley," November 27, 1995, p. 22.

19. S. Polgar and E. S. Fried, "The Bad Old Days: Clandestine Abortions Among the Poor in New York City Before Liberalization of the Abortion Law," *Family Planning Perspectives* (1976), p. 125.

20. The Alan Guttmacher Institute, "Abortion in the United States," 1995.

Chapter 8: Civil Rights or "Special Rights?"

1. Economic Policy Institute report, "Trends in the Low-wage Labor Market and Welfare Reform," February 22, 1994.

2. Herbert Gans, *The Underclass and Antipoverty Policy: The War Against the Poor* (New York: Basic Books, 1995), p. 1.

3. Ibid., p. 7.

4. Ibid., p. 12.

5. Winkler, "Racism Resurgent Right Here in Arizona."

6. Letter by Wilson, May 31, 1995.

7. Michael Novick, *White Lies/White Power: The Fight Against White Supremacy and Reactionary Violence* (Monroe, Maine: Common Courage Press, 1995), p. 19.

8. Elizabeth Kolbert, "Whose Family Values Are They, Anyway?" *New York Times*, August 6, 1995, Sec. 4, p. 1.

9. *When Hate Groups Come to Town: A Handbook of Community Responses* (Atlanta, Georgia: Center for Democratic Renewal, 1992), p. 34.

10. Anti-Defamation League, *The Religious Right*, p. 107.

11. *USA Today*, September 9, 1991. Quoted in the People for the American Way fact sheet on the Eagle Forum, February 1993.

12. Faludi, *Backlash*, p. 34.

13. Skipp Porteous, "OR Founder Calls for a Christian Nation," *Freedom Writer*, September 1995, p. 14.

14. National Committee on Pay Equity report, "Face the Facts About Wage Discrimination and Equal Pay," Winter 1994.

15. Center for Policy Studies 1993 and 1994 Report on the Black Population.

16. Faludi, *Backlash*, p. xiii.

17. Glass Ceiling Commission, "Good for Business: Making Full Use of the Nation's Human Capital" 12, (1995).

18. Steven Rendall, Jim Naureckas, and Jeff Cohen, *The Way Things Aren't: Rush Limbaugh's Reign of Error* (New York: The New Press, 1995), p. 33.

19. Renee Graham, "Talk Radio's Tough Talkers," *Boston Globe*, April 29, 1995, p. 10.

20. Sarah Crary Gregory and Scot Nakagawa, eds., *Fight the Right Action Kit* (Washington, D.C.: National Gay and Lesbian Task Force, 1993), Robin Kane, "Soundbites: Articulate Responses to Homophobic Lies and Rhetoric," p. 75.

21. Stephen Bransford, *Gay Politics Versus Colorado and America: The Inside Story of Amendment 2* (Cascade, Colorado: Sardis Press, 1994), p. 104.

22. Ibid., pp. 62, 73.

23. Susan Goldberg, "Gay Rights Through the Looking Glass: Politics, Morality and the Trial of Colorado's Amendment 2," *Fordham Urban Law Journal*, November 4, 1994.

24. Mab Segrest and Leonard Zeskind, *Quarantines and Death: The Far Right's Homophobic Agenda* (Atlanta, Georgia: Center for Democratic Renewal), pp. 19–20.

Chapter 9: Crime and Punishment

1. Brent Staples, "The Chain Gang Show," *New York Times Magazine,* September 17, 1995, p. 62.

2. Bureau of Justice Statistics, "Prisoners in 1994," 1995. By the end of 1994, 1,053,738 men and women were incarcerated in state and federal prisons, and almost 500,000 were in county jails.

3. Federal Bureau of Investigation, "Uniform Crime Report," 1995.

4. ALEC Foundation Report Card on Crime and Punishment, 1995.

5. Jeff Cohen and Norman Solomon, *Through the Media Looking Glass* (Monroe, Maine: Common Courage Press, 1995), p. 58.

6. James Q. Wilson and Joan Petersilia, eds., *Crime* (San Francisco: Institute for Contemporary Studies, 1995), Travis Hirschi, "The Family."

7. In Wilson and Petersilia. Patricia Brennan, Sarnoff Mednick, Jan Volavka, "Biomedical Factors."

8. The Christian Coalition's "Road to Victory" Conference, September 1995.

9. Author interview with Stratton, December 1995.

10. Mike Davis, "Hell Factories in the Field," *The Nation,* February 20, 1995, p. 230.

11. California Legislative Analyst's Office, "Accommodating Prison Population Growth," January 6, 1995.

12. James Austin, "The Consequences of Escalating the Use of Imprisonment: The Case Study of Florida," National Council on Crime and Delinquency's *FOCUS,* June 1991, pp. 1–7.

13. U.S. Sentencing Commission, *Cocaine and Federal Sentencing Policy,* February 1995.

14. Bureau of Justice Statistics, December 1993.

15. Michael Tonry, *Malign Neglect* (Oxford University Press, 1995), p. 113.

16. Sourcebook of Criminal Justice Statistics, 1991.

17. Bureau of Justice Statistics, "Prisoners in 1994," 1995.

18. Ibid.

19. Ibid.

20. Marc Mauer, "Young Black Men and the Criminal Justice System: A Growing National Problem," The Sentencing Project, February 1990.

21. National Rifle Association Fact Sheet, put out by the NRA's Institute for Legislative Action.

22. The Christian Coalition's "Road to Victory" conference, September 1995.

23. Press release from the State of Arizona executive office, NR 95:65.

24. John Nichols, "Righter Than Thou: In the Republican Presidential Race, Extremism Is the Norm," *The Progressive,* June 1995, p. 30.

25. Amnesty International, *When the State Kills,* 1989.

26. A study conducted at Duke University, May 1993, according to the Death Penalty Information Center, Washington, D.C.

27. Robert Worth, "A Model Prison," *The Atlantic Monthly*, November 1995, pp. 38–40.

Chapter 10: Immigration

1. Nicolas Mills, ed. *Arguing Immigration* (New York: Simon and Schuster, 1994), p. 25.

2. Margaret Quigley, "The Roots of the I.Q. Debate," *The Public Eye* IX, no. 1 (March 1995), p. 8.

3. James Ridgeway, *Blood in the Face* (New York: Thunder's Mouth Press, 1990), p. 148.

4. Peter Brimelow, *Alien Nation: Common Sense About America's Immigration Disaster* (New York: Random House, 1995), p. 119.

5. Thomas Friedman, "My Fellow Immigrants," *New York Times*, September 10, 1995.

6. Cornel West, *Race Matters* (New York: Vintage Books, 1994).

7. Jeff Cohen and Norman Solomon, "Media Help Shut the Door to Immigrants," *Plain Dealer*, August 7, 1993.

8. James Crawford, *Hold Your Tongue: Bilingualism and the Politics of "English Only"* (New York: Addison-Wesley Publishing Co., 1992), p. 163.

9. Ibid., p. 158.

10. Michael Novick, *White Lies/White Power: The Fight Against White Supremacy and Reactionary Violence* (Monroe, Maine: Common Courage Press, 1995), pp. 188–89.

11. Mills, *Arguing Immigration*, p. 15.

12. Ibid., p. 13.

13. Brimelow, *Alien Nation*, p. 264.

14. Ibid., p. 10.

15. Author interview with John Vinson, October 1995.

16. Ibid.

17. Mills, *Arguing Immigration*, pp. 25-26.

18. In Mills, *Arguing Immigration*, Jack Miles, "Blacks vs. Browns," p. 118.

19. Doug Brugge, "The Anti-Immigrant Backlash," *The Public Eye* IX, no. 2 (Summer 1995), p. 8.

20. In Mills, *Arguing Immigration*, Jaclyn Fierman, "Is Immigration Hurting the U.S.?" p. 70.

21. Author interview with Bob Goldsbrough, October 1995.

22. Kenneth Jost, "Cracking Down on Immigration," *CQ Researcher* 5, no. 5 (February 3, 1995), p. 101.

23. "Southern California Vices: A Forum for Community," *Los Angeles Times,* November 14, 1995, p. B5.

24. Brugge, "The Anti-Immigrant Backlash."

25. Jost, "Cracking Down on Immigration," p. 112.

26. "Gingrich Endorses English as 'Common Language,' Gives Boost to Bill to Make English Official," U.S. English press release, June 8, 1995.

27. U.S. Census Bureau, 1990. Cited in "Facts & Figures on Official English," U.S. English Facts and Issues sheet.

28. Susan Rook, *Talk Back Live,* CNN, September 20, 1995.

29. Crawford, *Hold Your Tongue,* p. 149.

30. Susan Headden, "One Nation, One Language?" *U.S. News and World Report,* September 25, 1995.

Chapter 11: The Environment

1. William Kevin Burke, *The Scent of Opportunity: A Survey of the Wise Use/Property Rights Movement in New England* (Cambridge, MA: Political Research Associates, 1992), p. 4.

2. Paul Rauber, "National Yard Sale," *Sierra,* September 1995, p. 30.

3. "Inside the Beltway: GOP Offers Tips to Help Members' Enviro Images," *SC Action #122* (an online newsletter), the Sierra Club, October 24, 1995, p. 1.

4. Vince Bielski, "Armed and Dangerous: The Wise Use Movement Meets the Militias," *Sierra,* September 1995, p. 34.

5. David Helvarg, "Anti-Enviros Are Getting Uglier: The War on Greens," *The Nation,* November 28, 1994, p. 648.

6. Richard M. Stapleton, "Green vs. Green," *National Parks,* November 1992, p.35.

7. James Ridgeway and Jeffrey St. Clair, "Where the Buffalo Roam: The Wise Use Movement Plays on Every Western Fear," *The Village Voice,* July 11, 1995, p. 14.

8. Paul de Armond, "Wise Use Moves into Electoral Politics," 1994.

9. Helvarg, "Anti-Enviros Are Getting Uglier," p. 651.

10. Ibid., p. 648.

11. Jim Robbins, "Target Green: Federal Land Managers Under Attack," *Audubon,* July 1995, p. 84.

12. Ibid., p. 85.

13. David Helvarg, *The War Against the Green: The Wise Use Movement, the New Right and Anti-Environmental Violence* (San Francisco: Sierra Club Books, 1994).

14. Helvarg, "Anti-Enviros," p. 651.

15. Helvarg, *The War Against the Greens.*

16. "Going . . . Going . . . Green!" *PR Watch,* Second Quarter, 1994, p. 3.

17. Ibid., p. 1.

18. Helvarg, "Anti-Enviros," p. 648.

19. 1991 Interview with *Outside,* quoted in William Kevin Burke, "The Wise Use Movement: Right Wing Anti-Environmentalism," *The Public Eye,* June 1993, p. 2

20. Rendall, et al., *The Way Things Aren't,* p. 13.

21. Ibid.

22. "Anti-Environmental Myths Answered," fact sheet, Environmental Working Group.

23. Timothy Egan, "Unlikely Alliances Attack Property Rights Measures," *New York Times,* May 15, 1995, p. 12; "Road to Ruin," *New Voices* (The Wilderness Society) February 1995, p. 1.

24. Richard Lacayo, "This Land Is Whose Land?" *Time,* October 23, 1995, p. 68.

25. Ted Williams, "The Blackstone Now Runs Blue," *Audubon,* December 1995, p. 30.

Chapter 12: In-Your-Armchair Activism

1. Chip Berlet, "The Right Rides High," *The Progressive,* October 1994, p. 27.

Chapter 13: Out-of-Your-Armchair Activism

1. Ken Toole, *What to Do When the Militia Comes to Town* (New York: The American Jewish Committee, 1995), pp. 29–30.

2. Conason, "The Religious Right's Quiet Revival," p. 541.

Index

Limbaugh, Rush, 2, 3, 116, 125, 181, 200, 202, 214
Lind, Michael, *The Next American Nation*, 50
Liotta, Linda, 43
Literacy programs, 91
Lobbies, 21, 27, 207
  Americans for Immigration Control, 157
  environmental, 174
  security industry, 139, 144
  timber industry, 173
Log Cabin Republicans, 27, 124
Loggers. *See* Timber industry, 172
Los Angeles Coalition on Urban Affairs, 78
Lost Tribes of Israel, 37
Lott, Trent, 47
Lowey, Nita, 95, 110
Lowney, Shannon, 99
Luntz, Frank, 20
Luther, Dennis, 148
Lycos (Internet), 222

McAteer, Ed, 45
McCartney, Bill, 122
McDonald's (restaurant), 47
McGuire, Stephanie, 178
McKean prison, 148–49
McLamb, Jack, 16, 40, 41
MacPhee, Josh, 151
Maduro, Rogelio, *Holes in the Ozone Scare*, 181, 183
Magazines, 201, 255. *See also* Media
Magnet schools, 67–69
Magruder, Marion, 47
Maine, 128
Malign Neglect (Tonry), 142
Manpower Research Demonstration Corporation, 89
Mark of the Beast (666), 41
Masonic society, 26
Mast Landing Elementary School (Freeport, Maine), 67
Matriarchy, 183
May, Cordelia Scaife, 157
Mecham, Evan, 43
Media, 29. *See also* specific types
  addresses for, 220, 255–56
  and crime sensationalism, 136
  letters to, 210–13
  tracking the right in, 200–202
  used by far right, 32–33

Media Activism Kit, 202, 251
MediaCulture Review, 223
Media ministries, 23
Medicaid, 78, 83
  abortion funding, 94, 101–2
  federal spending on, 79
Medicare, 78, 102
Mednick, Sarnoff, 138
Meese, Ed, 47
Men
  and affirmative action, 117
  income of, 123
  and social equality, 13
Mentally retarded people, 146
Metzger, Tom, 2, 96
Mexican American Legal Defense and Education Fund, 132, 162
Mica, John, 82
Michigan Militia, 31, 38
Microchips, implantable, 41
Middle class, 50, 64–65, 121
Midwest Sociological Society, 127
Midwives, 107
Migrant health centers and abortion counseling, 103
Military spending. *See* Defense budget
Militias, 1, 9, 31, 35–39, 96, 172, 174, 222, 237
Militias in America, 223
Militias of Montana (MOM), 35, 38, 41
Million Man March, 122
Million Voices for Justice, 166
Mining industry, 172
Minorities, 2, 34. *See also* specific minorities
  organizations for rights, 132–33
  and religious right, 9
  right-wing distortions, 114–16
  right-wing proposals, 116–18
  and social equality, 13
  and welfare, 76–77
Minority rights, 112–34
Misogyny, 119. *See also* Women
Missionaries to the Preborn, 43, 96, 97
Mojave National Preserve, 184
Montana Human Rights Network, 38, 225, 237, 252
Montana Wilderness Association, 186
Monteith, Stanley, 127
Montessori, Elisabeth, 67
Moon, Sun Myung, 47, 62, 172, 175